Resistance and its discontents in South Asian women's fiction

Manchester University Press

Global Textualities

SERIES EDITORS: Amina Yaqin, Peter Morey, Rehana Ahmed, Claire Chambers, Anshuman Mondal and Stephen Morton

The **Global Textualities: Multicultural and Transcultural Narratives** series encourages scholars to engage in interdisciplinary critiques of cultural texts, addressing pressing debates surrounding multiculturalism, cultural pluralism, decolonization, racial difference, secularism, and social conflict. This series examines literary and cultural representations shaped by majority/minority power dynamics and aims to foster new insights into the histories and representations of diasporic and minority communities worldwide. It interrogates how imperial histories continue to influence contemporary identity, power structures, and knowledge formations. These works seek to redefine perspectives on global and local inequalities through interdisciplinary approaches while rethinking cultural politics and representation theory in the modern era.

To buy or to find out more about the books currently available in this series, please go to:
https://manchesteruniversitypress.co.uk/series/global-textualities/

Resistance and its discontents in South Asian women's fiction

Maryam Mirza

MANCHESTER UNIVERSITY PRESS

Copyright © Maryam Mirza 2023

The right of Maryam Mirza to be identified as the author of this work has been asserted in accordance with the Copyright, Designs and Patents Act 1988.

Published by Manchester University Press
Oxford Road, Manchester M13 9PL

www.manchesteruniversitypress.co.uk

British Library Cataloguing-in-Publication Data
A catalogue record for this book is available from the British Library

ISBN 978 1 5261 5061 5 hardback
ISBN 978 1 5261 9116 8 paperback

First published 2023
Paperback published 2025

The publisher has no responsibility for the persistence or accuracy of URLs for any external or third-party internet websites referred to in this book, and does not guarantee that any content on such websites is, or will remain, accurate or appropriate.

EU authorised representative for GPSR:
Easy Access System Europe – Mustamäe tee 50,
10621 Tallinn, Estonia
gpsr.requests@easproject.com

Typeset by
Deanta Global Publishing Services, Chennai, India

This book is dedicated with so much love to my husband, Adrian Pearson, and to my father, Tariq Habib Mirza

Contents

Acknowledgements — *page* viii

Introduction: revisiting resistance (again) — 1

1 Resisting activism: the politics of apathy and disengagement in *Difficult Daughters* and *Broken Verses* — 23

2 Revolutionary love and the romance of resistance: *Broken Verses*, *The Lowland*, *The God of Small Things* and *The Ministry of Utmost Happiness* — 47

3 'Ordinary' defiances and the short story — 87

4 Queering resistance: *A Married Woman*, *Babyji* and *The Ministry of Utmost Happiness* — 118

5 Troubled resistance, troubling resistance: *Homework*, *The Namesake* and *A Disobedient Girl* — 150

6 Writing as resistance? *A Golden Age*, *The Good Muslim* and *The Gypsy Goddess* — 179

Epilogue: resisting idealising resistance — 205

References — 211
Index — 232

Acknowledgements

Spanning over five years, the genesis, research and writing of this book coincided with my moves across three countries as an early and then not-so-early career academic, and with a global pandemic. Without the goodwill of all those mentioned below, this book would quite likely have remained a work-in-progress Word document on my desktop for some years yet.

I would like to offer my heartfelt thanks to:

My friends and colleagues whose support, either directly or indirectly, helped make this a better book than it might have been otherwise: Yael Almog, Claire Chambers, Claire Davison, Marc Delrez, Christel Desjardin, Mandy Green, Daniel Hartley, Ayesha Husain, Zareena Saeed, Barbara Schmidt-Haberkamp, Rachel Schwartz-Narbonne, Mandira Srivastava, Neelam Srivastava, Jenny Terry and Natasha Uzair. I am especially thankful to Claire Chambers and Neelam Srivastava for their faith in this project.

The Department of English Studies, Durham University, which has been my professional home since September 2018.

John Nash, the current Head of the Department of English Studies, Durham University, for his kind support.

The undergraduate students at Durham University who have enrolled in my 'Resistance in South Asian Postcolonial Literature' module during the last three years; this book has benefitted greatly from the exciting discussions that took place during the seminars.

Aidan Bracebridge, who was a hardworking and conscientious research assistant in the weeks leading up to the submission of the manuscript; any and all errors are mine alone.

Acknowledgements

Shehzil Malik for the cover image.

Paul Clarke and Matthew Frost at Manchester University Press for all their help.

Taylor & Francis and the *Journal of Postcolonial Writing* (www.tandfonline.com/journals/rjpw20) for allowing me to reproduce sections of my article 'Serving in the Indian diaspora: The transnational domestic servant in contemporary women's fiction' in Chapter 3 of this book.

And, most of all, my father Tariq Habib Mirza, my brother Vassay Mirza and my husband Adrian Pearson, for their love, support, warmth and patience and for being so very wonderful.

Introduction: revisiting resistance (again)

[F]or she had a fire in her then, born out of some primordial sense of injustice which led her easily into situations where most would fear even lightly to tread.
– Sunetra Gupta, *So Good in Black*, 2009

While certainly not fading away as a scholarly concern within postcolonial studies, the theme of resistance is finding itself subject to increasing interrogation, particularly in the context of how resistance as a socio-historical phenomenon has been addressed in postcolonial scholarship. On the one hand, critical engagement with Dalit-authored texts and other indigenous writings, often in translation, as resistance literature is on the rise; on the other hand, especially in relation to postcolonial theory and postcolonial fiction in English, the prevalent interpretations of the term 'resistance' are being perceived with growing ambivalence, if not suspicion, and their continuing pertinence being questioned and contested. Through the prism of contemporary anglophone writings, *Resistance and Its Discontents in South Asian Women's Fiction* challenges the misgivings about the relevance of resistance as a concept in postcolonial literary studies and complicates existing debates in the field about its possible meanings and manifestations. This book also demonstrates the importance of the notion of resistance when coming to grips with the idea of 'the political' today.

Resistance to resistance

In an essay on Mahmoud Darwish's revolutionary poetry, Patrick Williams evokes what he calls the 'resistance to resistance' strand of thinking within postcolonial studies, which deems that the field 'has for far too long focused on the theme of resistance and that it should move on to other topics with greater contemporary relevance' (2013: 67). Citing Robert Young's remarks made during a 2008 conference, Williams alerts us to the dismissal of the idea of resistance on the grounds that it forms 'part of the triumphalist narrative of postcolonialism' (2013: 67). Using Bill Ashcroft et al.'s *The Empire Writes Back: Theory and Practice in Post-Colonial Literatures* (1989) as a point of departure, Elleke Boehmer has also criticised how history has been understood in postcolonial critical discourse which has often privileged an 'onwards-and-upwards narrative trajectory ... one moving from oppression to freedom, from the draconian pure to the happy impure, from empire to a world without empire' (2013: 310).

Postcolonial literary criticism, perhaps inevitably, has been concerned largely, though not solely, with resistance within the context of colonial domination and anti-colonial nation-building. It has often been preoccupied with literary portrayals of resistance against colonial power and/or has displayed a commitment to interpreting postcolonial literary production itself as resistance, involved in 'a process of questioning and travestying colonial discourses' (McLeod, 2000: 25). Barbara Harlow, the author of the seminal text *Resistance Literature* (1987), has pointed out that her definition of resistance literature deems it 'a very site and history specific literature ... written in the context of organized resistance movements and national liberation struggles' (1998: n.p.). In his essay 'Signs taken for wonders', Homi K. Bhabha argues that resistance

> is not necessarily an oppositional act of political intention, nor is it the simple negation or exclusion of the 'content' of an other culture, as a difference once perceived. It is the effect of an ambivalence produced within the rules of recognition of dominating discourses as they articulate the signs of cultural difference and reimplicate them within the deferential relations of colonial power – hierarchy, normalization, marginalization and so forth. (1985: 153)

Bhabha's discussion sheds valuable light on the ambivalence of both colonial power and anti-colonial resistance, but, as a theoretical framework, it is not adequately attentive to the modes of resistance spawned by hierarchies based on, among other identity markers, class, caste, gender and sexuality, or to the implications of these systems of social stratification straddling (European) colonial and 'postcolonial' periods.[1] For instance, while recognising that communalism in India was 'catalyzed' by colonialism, Ania Loomba reminds us that it 'has other roots as well, and therefore has contemporary manifestations', not all of which can be neatly traced back to British rule in the region (1991: 188). Moreover, with many postcolonial regimes replicating 'the old colonial structures in new terms', it is not surprising that celebratory readings of the practice of anti-colonial contestation and writings that discount the (continuing) challenges faced by the former European colonies have drawn considerable criticism (Said, 1993: 269).[2] In his critique of Frantz Fanon's work, Neil Lazarus has noted that 'moments of (revolutionary) consciousness and (spontaneous) resistance were telescoped together in a prophetic register that made it sound as though the hour of revolution in Africa had already announced itself and needed only to be recognized in order to sweep away all obstacles to its successful realization' (1990: 27). In fact, the criticism of 'resistance' within the field of postcolonial studies extends beyond questions of temporal relevance and jubilant constructions of anti-colonial struggles. In 'The postcolonial aura: Third World criticism in the age of global capitalism' (1994), Arif Dirlik displays a deep scepticism towards postcolonial intellectual work and its resistant potentialities. Dirlik sees postcolonial intellectuals' growing presence in the First World Academy and the increasing importance of the field of postcolonialism as not only a result of the workings of global capitalism which 'can no longer afford the cultural parochialism of an earlier day', but also as a prominent marker of the field's complicity in the transnational capitalist order; by extension, he contests the discipline's ability to 'generate a thoroughgoing criticism of its own ideology and formulate practices of resistance against the system of which it is a product' (1994: 354–6). While offering a more measured appraisal of postcolonial intellectual work than Dirlik, and refusing to collapse it 'to the logic of the market', Graham Huggan in *The Post-Colonial Exotic: Marketing the Margins* (2001) draws our attention to the considerable commercial success enjoyed by many postcolonial novels and to postcolonial literature's entanglement in 'the global processes of commodification', which can complicate the resistant energy of these works. Huggan argues that 'in the overwhelmingly commercial context of late twentieth-century commodity culture, postcolonialism and its rhetoric of resistance have themselves become consumer products' and that 'these ostensibly *anti*-colonial writers/thinkers are all working, some of them conspicuously, within the *neo*colonial context of global commodity culture' (2001: 6–7; emphasis in the original).

The interpretation of women's writing, whether postcolonial or otherwise, as necessarily resistant and subversive has also been challenged in recent decades. More specifically, feminist literary critics have sought to counter the assumption that women's literary production is intrinsically feminist in tenor and to demonstrate that, even when they do challenge the workings of patriarchy, feminist texts do not always contest other societal and literary hierarchies. Gayle Greene has warned us that '[f]eminist fiction is not the same as "women's fiction" or fiction by women: not all women writers are "women's writers", and not all women writers are feminist writers, since to write about "women's issues" is not necessarily to address them from a feminist perspective' (1991: 2). If we interpret feminism as a movement which necessarily embodies resistance with the aim to end 'sexism, sexist exploitation, and oppression', works of fiction that grapple with the aforementioned themes would then be qualified as *feminist* (hooks, 2000: viii). South Asian anglophone women's fiction, a term that has predominantly been deployed to refer to works by Indian and, to a lesser extent, Pakistani writers, *has* often displayed an abiding concern with patriarchal oppression in its various guises, not always but frequently in the context of middle-class domesticity, notably in novels such as *Inside the Haveli* (1977) by Rama Mehta, *The Dark Holds No Terrors* (1990 [1980]) and *The Binding Vine* (1992) by Shashi Deshpande, Anita Desai's *Fire on the Mountain* (1977), Githa Hariharan's *The Thousand Faces of Night* (1992), as well as the Sri Lankan-Australian writer Chandani Lokugé's *If the Moon Smiled* (2000).[3] Other works, such as Attia Hosain's *Sunlight on a Broken Column* (1961), Desai's *Clear Light of Day* (1980), Bapsi Sidhwa's *Ice-Candy-Man* (1988) and Shauna Singh Baldwin's *What the Body Remembers* (1999), have a broader canvas, dealing with British colonialism in India and the consequent communal strife, but are primarily concerned with female subjugation and the difficult negotiation of female identities and roles.

Introduction

Malashri Lal's seminal 1995 monograph *The Law of the Threshold: Women Writers in Indian English* identifies the line dividing the private, so-called feminine from the public, 'masculine' sphere as a central concern in female-authored texts. Resistance for a female protagonist then primarily entails transgressing this boundary and contending 'with prejudices against her attempts to appropriate her own space in the name of personal dignity' and, effectively, all 'descriptions of her new identity are evaluated as extensions or rejections of the patriarchal norm' (Lal, 1995: 19–20). In drawing in particular on Anita Desai's novels published in the 1970s and 1980s, Lal charts how the female protagonists, being unable to bridge 'the gap between their aspiration to be free and their inability to cope with [the] societal isolation' resulting from their transgressive actions, would often either return to conventional domesticity or fall prey to mental illness, with madness functioning 'as a meta-language for their rebellion and helplessness' (1995: 21). Appearing a few years after the publication of Lal's book, Usha Bande's *Writing Resistance: A Comparative Study of the Selected Novels by Women Writers* drew our attention to the continuing presence of 'the self-effacing, self-sacrificing female' populating the pages of English-language novels by Indian women writers, but also pointed to an equally significant number of works of fiction that feature 'self-questioning women protagonists struggling to locate their autonomous self, asserting their individuality and rejecting male domination', thus lending themselves to being read as feminist texts (2006: 20).[4]

But, as Susie Tharu and K. Lalitha, the co-editors of the now-classic anthology *Women Writing in India*, point out, 'even when the writing is specifically feminist ... opposition to the dominant ideologies of gender can be discomfitingly class or caste bound and draw on assumptions about race or religious persuasion that reinforce the hold of those ideologies and collaborate in extending their authority' (1991: 34–5). Rajeswari Sunder Rajan too alerts us to the pitfalls of considering women 'definitionally subaltern, and their writing, therefore, as always already a resistant practice' (1993a: 75). In a similar vein, I have argued elsewhere (Mirza, 2016) that novels such as Sidhwa's *Ice-Candy-Man* (1988), Moni Mohsin's *The End of Innocence* (2006) and Brinda Charry's *The Hottest Day of the Year* (2001), while remaining trenchant in their condemnation and contestation of patriarchal oppression, appear to shy away from articulating a discourse of resistance that challenges the socio-economic status quo, thus exhibiting a degree of class conservatism. This suggests that certain texts by female South Asian authors have chosen to prioritise a particular kind of resistance, namely resistance to patriarchal oppression, sometimes to the detriment of a recognition of other kinds of resistance that women can and do exercise.

My contention in this book, however, is that a growing number of works by Indian, Pakistani, Sri Lankan and Bangladeshi resident and diasporic women writers have begun to display a sustained preoccupation with a much broader spectrum of often interlinked forms of oppression and injustices, without neglecting gendered violence or colonial/neo-imperial subjugation. Consequently, they present us with a fascinating range of possible resistances, and highlight the array of meanings and connotations that the term resistance can carry. As we will see, when taken together, far from striking a simplistically triumphalist note, the literary works under consideration, including works which have won lucrative prizes and have been commercially successful, address the complexities underpinning both resistance and power. Huggan's work, which I invoked earlier, is a useful reminder of how resistance can be deployed as a marketing ploy within the neoliberal publishing industry, but his observations also open up a space for distinguishing the way in which postcolonial novels are marketed from the novels themselves. As my analysis of the selected texts will demonstrate, many of these works, including bestsellers that have won prestigious literary awards with substantial prize money, *are*, to quote Harlow, 'involved in a struggle against ascendant or dominant forms of ideological and cultural production', even if the struggle is not (necessarily) anti-colonial or anti-imperial in nature (1987: 28–9). Moreover, if Ketu Katrak has contended that postcolonial women writers, unlike their male counterparts, 'explore the personal dimensions of history rather than overt concerns with political leadership and nation-states', the female-authored texts examined in this book invite us to read 'the intimate and bodily as part of a broader sociopolitical context' while also more explicitly engaging with broader socio-political questions (1996: 234). The works under consideration are as preoccupied with how the personal is political as they are with the ways in which the political is personal. As I will demonstrate, they not only bring to the fore the artificiality of the divide between the public and the private spheres, but also interrogate the resistance/ acquiescence, erotic/pragmatic and action/inaction binaries, thus complicating our understanding of what constitutes 'the political'.

Contributing to what Sunder Rajan has referred to as '[r]esistance studies', one of the aims of this book is 'to identify what counts as resistance' in South Asian women's fiction and 'to decide what the meanings of resistant action might be, taking neither as given' (2000: 154).[5] While clearly situating dissent and subversion at the heart of questions of power and oppression, this book brings to the fore the ways in which the texts under discussion compel us to grapple with the emancipatory politics as well as the contradictions and slipperiness of the term 'resistance'. As will become clear, the works of fiction considered here demand a broad understanding of the concepts of both resistance and oppression. They require readers to move beyond, without neglecting the significance of discourses of resistance developed in response to British colonial modes of oppression, or, indeed, as a reaction to male dominance. My discussion is undergirded by sustained attention to the historical and contemporary linkages between various forms of oppression and to the multiplicity of systems of social stratification, based on gender, class, caste, ethnicity, sexuality and other identity markers, which may or may not complement each other. In examining the relationship between these identity markers, I draw on Jasbir K. Puar's concept of 'assemblage' (after Gilles Deleuze and Pierre-Félix Guattari) which she presents in opposition to 'an intersectional model of identity', presuming 'components – race, class, gender, sexuality, nation, age, religion – are separable analytics and can be thus disassembled' (2005: 127–8). Unlike an intersectional approach which 'demands the knowing, naming, and thus stabilizing of identity across space and time, generating narratives of progress that deny the fictive and performative of identification', my study adopts the lens of a 'resistant' identity assemblage and perceives figures of resistance, and acts of resistance, as inseparable from myriad 'interwoven forces that merge and dissipate time, space, and body against linearity, coherency, and permanency' (2005: 128).

Lying at the interstices of the fields of postcolonial literary studies, gender studies, sociology and political philosophy, this interdisciplinary book not only examines the depiction of the divergent modes of contestation provoked by a wide range of injustices but also addresses the expectations, contradictions, anxieties and even inaction that the idea as well as the practice of resistance can generate.

Conceptualising resistance

Along with *resistance*, the terms *subversion*, *defiance*, *disobedience* and *activism* (when referring to organised collective resistance) will be evoked in the following chapters. The lines between these concepts might often appear blurred, and they will, on occasion, be used interchangeably, but I find the term resistance to be the one that responds most meaningfully to the nuances of the works of fiction under discussion, particularly when considered in conjunction with the concepts of power, oppression and injustice.

Given its fluid, wide-ranging and polysemic nature, it is important to specify the theoretical underpinnings of my understanding of the term for the purposes of this study. Michel Foucault's reflections on resistance are central to my analysis since, for him, it is inextricably linked to the notion of power, as highlighted by his dictum, 'where there is power, there is resistance' (1998 [1978]: 95). Foucault's *The Will to Knowledge* sheds light on the relational, but also the shape-shifting quality of both power and resistance. He sees power relations as only existing via a 'multiplicity of points of resistance' which play 'the role of adversary, target, support, or handle' (1998 [1978]: 95). Foucault throws into doubt the Marcusian notion of the 'Great Refusal', which privileges revolutionary change, speaking instead of 'resistances' in the plural and seeing them all as special cases, capable of displaying a wide range of attributes.[6] For Foucault, resistances can be:

> possible, necessary, improbable; others that are spontaneous, savage, solitary, concerted, rampant, or violent; still others that are quick to compromise, interested, or sacrificial; by definition, they can only exist in the strategic field of power relations. But this does not mean that they are only a reaction or rebound, forming with respect to the basic domination an underside that is in the end always passive, doomed to perpetual defeat. (1998 [1978]: 96)

Like power, Foucault argues, resistances are 'distributed in irregular fashion' with its 'points, knots, or focuses ... spread over time and space at varying densities, at times mobilizing groups or individuals in a definite way, inflaming certain points of the body, certain moments in life, certain types of behaviour' (1998 [1978]: 96). As a starting point then, taking its cue from Foucault, this book calls for an all-encompassing conceptualisation of resistance and concerns itself with a diverse range of expressions of agency, if we take agency to be the 'socially constructed capacity to act' (Barker, 2000: 237). In engaging with the idea of resistance, defiance and agency, my project necessarily grapples with 'willful subjects', to borrow the title of Sara Ahmed's 2014 book and, therefore, not only with characters who are 'unwilling to obey', but also with the notion of willfulness, as Ahmed defines it, in terms of 'the labor required to reach that no, which might even require saying yes along the way' (2014: 140–1). I will also read as manifestations of resistance moments where the characters realise, in the words of Foucault, that 'there is a power relation' and, therefore, 'there is the possibility of resistance', while also considering why this sort of resistance may not culminate in visible or collective action (1996: 224).

Moreover, echoing José Medina, 'resisting', will be understood as '*contending with*, and not exclusively or fundamentally as *contending against*' (2013: 16; italics in the original). Therefore, I will explore the depiction not only of concrete acts of resistance, but also of the characters' internal, psychological struggles as well as their attempts to understand the workings of power and their own relationship with the concept of resistance. I will analyse the representation of acts of resistance in response to 'structural injustices' which Iris Marion Young has defined as harms, perceived or otherwise, 'that come to people as a result of structural processes in which many people participate' (2003: 7). I am equally interested in resistance to individual injustices, where 'undeserved harms can be traced to the wilful or negligent acts of identifiable "culprits"' (Eckersley, 2016: 346). This book is concerned with the representation of 'public' and 'private' acts of subversion, with the temporal fluidity of resistance, whether it entails sustained activism over many years or fleeting moments of defiance, as well as with the portrayal of individual and collective modes of resistance. In questioning the private/public, fleeting/sustained, collective/individual binaries, my intention is not to homogenise vastly divergent acts of defiance or to discount the significance of activism which, by definition, 'seeks to bring about a change for the collectivity' (Sunder Rajan, 2000: 158). Rather, I wish to explore how the authors under discussion grapple with the forces that inform the construction of these binaries. My analysis is also sensitive to Cathy J. Cohen's argument that while 'cumulative acts of individual agency are not the same as collective agency', in 'this counter normative space exists the possibility of radical change, not only in the distribution of resources, but also definitional power, redefining the rules of normality that limit the dreams, emotions, and acts of most people' (2004: 38). Furthermore, the essays by Judith Butler et al. which appear in the volume *Vulnerability in Resistance* are relevant to this study, since they counter the assumption that 'vulnerability and resistance are mutually oppositional' (2016: 1). Rather than perceiving vulnerability as being synonymous with victimhood and passivity, the contributors to this collection of essays conceive of 'resistance as drawing from vulnerability' and 'as part of the very meaning or action of resistance itself' (2016: 1). In particular, such a conceptualisation of resistance necessarily disrupts stereotypical readings of female agency which vacillate between 'the passive downtrodden South Asian woman' (Puwar, 2003: 25) and, especially in the case of '"the Indian Woman" in popular imagination', a 'triumphant feminist hero', as Raka Ray has observed in her discussion of the film *Bandit Queen* (1999: 1–3). I am interested not only in physical but also affective vulnerability and I assess how ties between individuals, whether romantic, sexual, familial or otherwise, can inform, disrupt or complicate a character's resistant agency and socio-political engagement.

My book is explicitly concerned with various kinds of subaltern resistance, where, following Ranajit Guha, I take the term 'subaltern' as 'a name for the general attribute of subordination in South Asian society whether this is expressed in terms of class, caste, age, gender and office or in any other way' (1982: vii). Within Subaltern Studies, and specifically in Guha's work on resistance in colonial India, a sharp distinction is often made between 'elite politics', which he sees as being 'relatively more legalistic and constitutionalist', and 'subaltern' politics as more 'violent', often manifesting itself in 'peasant insurgency' (1982: 4–5). My analysis, however, will highlight the polyvalent nature of subaltern politics and will demonstrate how the distinction between 'elite' and 'subaltern', as well as between violent and non-violent modes of resistance, can become blurred. Moreover, if Gayatri Chakravorty Spivak's articles 'Subaltern studies: deconstructing historiography' (1985) and 'Can the subaltern speak?' (1988) arguably conceive of gendered subalternity as being more or less inseparable from discursive silence, I am interested in examining the complex ways in which subaltern silence and subaltern speech acts inform and constitute subaltern resistance. Relatedly, my conceptualisation of subaltern resistance also draws on Nancy Fraser's notion of 'subaltern counterpublics' as arenas where subaltern groups 'invent and circulate counter-discourses ... to formulate oppositional interpretations of their identities, interests, and needs' (1997: 81).

In the ensuing chapters, I examine the depiction of a diverse range of manifestations as well as omissions of resistance including, but not limited to, public defiance against military dictatorships, imperial rule and patriarchal oppression sanctioned by the state, the fight for better working conditions, the multiplicity of battles waged in the 'private' sphere, as well as the choice of expressing one's sexual, gendered, creative or linguistic identity. The chosen literary texts present us with depictions of 'counter-hegemonic work' carried out by subjects of a range of genders and sexualities (Parry, 1994: 172). Therefore, this book is as concerned with questions of female and feminist resistance as it is with other interwoven forms of contestation; it seeks to come to grips with not only the positive, but also the ambiguous and disturbing connotations that the notion of 'resistance' carries in contemporary works of fiction by South Asian women writers, as well as the host of affective responses that it can provoke, including anxiety, apathy and shame.

Texts, modes and genres

The primary texts examined in this book include works of fiction by popular and critically acclaimed writers but also by authors whose work has so far drawn relatively limited attention. Moreover, I have consciously chosen to investigate fiction by authors who either reside in India, Pakistan, Sri Lanka and Bangladesh or have roots in these countries to chart their shared concerns and to underscore the exciting diversity, both thematic and aesthetic, that characterises contemporary South Asian women writers' preoccupation with resistance. My study demonstrates that by virtue of the kinds of resistances represented, the wide array of socio-political contexts explored and the range of poetics deployed therein, contemporary anglophone fiction by South Asian women writers compels us to revisit well-worn ways of imagining and enacting resistance. The novels under consideration are Tahmima Anam's *A Golden Age* (2007) and *The Good Muslim* (2011), Abha Dawesar's *Babyji* (2005), Ru Freeman's *A Disobedient Girl* (2009), Meena Kandasamy's *The Gypsy Goddess* (2014), Manju Kapur's *Difficult Daughters* (1998) and *A Married Woman* (2002), Jhumpa Lahiri's *The Namesake* (2003) and *The Lowland* (2013), Suneeta Peres da Costa's *Homework* (1999), Arundhati Roy's *The God of Small Things* (1997) and *The Ministry of Utmost Happiness* (2017) and Kamila Shamsie's *Broken Verses* (2005). I also examine the following short stories: 'A day for Nuggo' (2014) by Rukhsana Ahmad, 'Of bread and power' (1994) by Chitra Fernando, Mridula Koshy's 'Almost Valentine's Day' (2014) and 'The treatment of Bibi Haldar' (1999) by Lahiri.

Given that the English language continues to be the language of the privileged classes in South Asia, and that consequently English-language literature is inaccessible to the majority of the citizens of these countries as well as, in some cases, to the figures of resistance portrayed in the texts under discussion, South Asian fiction in English emerges as an ambiguous site for subversive politics. It cannot boast of the same degree of accessibility as the vernacular dramatic traditions which, as Ashis Sengupta has outlined, include the Bhand performance and Lok theatre in Pakistan, the Madar Pirer Gan in Bangladesh and the rural, folk and ritual theatre of India, encompassing traditions such as Raslila, Ramlila, Kathakali and Nautanki (2014: 4). Anglophone fiction arguably also lacks the immediacy of poetry, oral or otherwise, in 'indigenous' languages; Elias Khouri has deemed poetry as being 'more powerful than other forms of writing as a means of political mobilization' and as means of sustaining, 'within the popular memory, national continuity' (quoted in Harlow, 1987: 34). But, as few and far between as they still are, it would be remiss not to invoke here the significance of Dalit anglophone writings, both fiction and non-fiction, since they complicate the conceptualisation of English as a language that necessarily serves elite interests in the region. With increasing frequency, Dalit writers and thinkers are writing about the relationship between caste privilege and the English language, not to then call for a rejection of this language, but instead to advocate its wider accessibility and to champion its use as a mode of Dalit resistance. In her moving essay, 'On translating the yet unwritten: A Dalit perspective from India', the short story writer and poet Mimi Mondal notes that 'English is the language that saved [her] life', while observing that in India, '[i]t is not fashionable to mention that the English fluency that grants one admission to those hallowed circles at all, *only after which* one starts learning postcolonial discourse, cannot be taken for granted in every household' (2017: n.p.; emphasis in the original). Furthermore, in his article 'Claiming the English language as a Dalit poet', Chandramohan Sathyanathan lists the ways in which the English language can work as a liberatory linguistic force in Dalit lives:

> First, the English language is a lingua franca within India and also provides access to London or New York. Hence, denting the discourse of the nation could be easier in English. Second, while Dalit literature in translation is a fad in academia, we tend to overlook the violence that is meted out to the cultural text in the process of translation. A Dalit writer of the vernacular may not have control over which of his [sic] works is chosen for translation or who is translating it. Thus, knowledge of English can illuminate the contours of exclusion. Third, the English language does not foreground a semantic bias against the anti-brahminical expression conceived in English, unlike when the Dalit writer needs to manoeuvre from his own dialect to the print (mainstream) versions of many vernacular languages. There could be spiritual injunctions against the learning of Sanskrit by the subaltern, but no such reins tether English. Fourth, strife in our social lives happens mostly in the vernacular cultural milieu. The onus is on the Dalit writer, especially if he earns a philosophical-contesting position in the English language to reconstitute himself in the new tongue, and creates a springboard for anti-caste linguistic and cultural praxis. (2021: n.p.)

Anglophone Dalit literary works by women include Yashica Dutt's *Coming out as Dalit* (2019), Sujatha Gidla's *Ants Among Elephants:*

An Untouchable Family and the Making of Modern India (2017), Mondal's speculative short fiction, nonfiction and poetry and Kandasamy's poetry, autofiction and novel *The Gypsy Goddess*. (I will have more to say about Kandasamy's Dalit positioning in particular, and about Dalit identity and the English language in general in Chapter 6.)

I am aware that by focusing on fiction, my book does not engage with life writing, which is a significant mode of resistant writing for queer writers;[7] I would also like to acknowledge the centrality of autobiographical writing in Indian vernacular languages for Dalits, even if, as Sathyanathan's recent article reminds us, an engagement with Dalit writing in translation in academic circles brings in its wake the possibility of epistemic violence. In grappling with fiction, specifically anglophone fiction, this book does not seek to deny the affinity between resistance and life writing or between resistance and poetry, or indeed between resistance and drama, to which the 'Theatre of the Oppressed' techniques developed by Augusto Boal (2008 [1974]) attest, nor does this study attempt to underestimate the significance of sociological, linguistic and genre-related specificities. Rather, a focus on anglophone fiction, a genre that has become a sort of shorthand for postcolonial literature itself, allows for an exploration of the complex and contradictory forms that resistance to various kinds of power can assume in English; the English language is indeed the language of the socio-economically privileged in South Asia but it is also, as demonstrated by my discussion of Dalit writings above, a language that can facilitate the contestation of age-old hierarchies. Such a focus permits scrutiny of the ways in which imbalances of power, and contestations of these imbalances, are bound up not only with language, but also with education and literary production (whether in English or in a vernacular language), which, as we shall see, are important thematic concerns in several of the texts under discussion, including *Difficult Daughters*, *Broken Verses* and *The Gypsy Goddess*.

If only two of the novels, Peres da Costa's *Homework* and Kandasamy's *The Gypsy Goddess*, are written in 'nonrealist' narrative modes, the other texts under consideration in this study, while realist in sensibility, collectively underscore the striking variations that realism as a category can encapsulate and the different kinds

Introduction 15

of realism that exist; these include critical realism, a form of literary representation which is 'socially engaged' and 'depicts social reality so as to analyze and critique' it (Vargas, 2011: 29), domestic realism, focusing on 'issues of home and family, courtship and marriage, interwoven with gender, power, and class conflict' (Dabundo, 2012: 371), as well as a 'subjective' form of realism, which permits the 'depiction of dreams, fantasies, flights of the imagination as part of its conception of the real' (Felski, 1989: 82). Amongst the works examined in this book is Roy's *The God of Small Things*, which has been classified by critics such as Richard J. Lane (2006: 97) and Alexandra Podgórniak (2002: 255–63) as a magic realist text; other literary critics, including myself, argue against such a categorisation of the novel and consider its surreal aspects to be a reflection of the 'heightened, imaginative perceptions of [the] child protagonists' (Tickell, 2007: 57).[8] Moreover, while not suggesting that Lahiri's 'The treatment of Bibi Haldar', a first-person plural narrative, is a magic realist short story, Brewster E. Fitz does raise a valid point when he urges us to evaluate 'what exactly is realistic about an anonymous, nonindividuated group of Bengali housewives, who have no particular identity, speaking in one voice, either in Bengali or in English' (2005: 117). Fitz contends that the use of an unusual narrative voice can be seen as an 'experiment that encourages us readers to willingly suspend our belief that Lahiri's narrative is realistic and mimetic' (2005: 117). However, I argue that the effect of the first-person plural narrative is to lend the short story an allegorical quality.[9] While allegory as a 'register of meaning beyond the purely mundane' can be seen to be 'antithetical to realism', it can also be, as Ulka Anjaria has pointed out, 'a potentially intersecting mode of signification', and can alert us to the meaning of realism 'beyond one individual story and its particularized circumstances' (2012: 62). If Lois Parkinson Zamora posits that 'the characteristic instability of strata – individual, community, cosmos – impels magic realism toward allegory' (1995: 508), Lahiri's short story, which is explicitly concerned with identitary instabilities and contestations, provides us with an example of an allegorical text which is distinctly realist in its sensibility.

As my discussion in the following chapters will demonstrate, the literary works under consideration compel us to dispute the view, 'both popular and academic', which until fairly recently deemed that 'realism and resistance do not converge' (Moss, 2000: n.p.). Indeed, in the 1980s, postcoloniality and magic realism became increasingly intertwined to the extent that Bhabha described magic realism 'as the literary language of the emergent post-colonial world', despite the fact that anglophone writers such as Vikram Seth, Anita Desai, Bapsi Sidhwa and Rohinton Mistry have all produced realist fiction and have come to define the postcolonial canon as much as Salman Rushdie and his magic realist texts have (1990: 7). Indeed, a continuity of realist South Asian narratives can be detected across the nineteenth, twentieth and twenty-first centuries with the pioneers of the Indian English novel, Bankimchandra Chatterjee (1838–94) and Krupabai Satthianadhan (1862–94), writing realist texts. Moreover, social realism was the dominant mode in writings by authors belonging to the Progressive Writers' Association in colonial India as well as in the new state of Pakistan and in independent India until the 1950s.

Of course, as Paul Sharrad correctly points out, 'postcolonial scholarship did not always dismiss realist fiction as simplistic or as a "colonialist" fictional mode' since 'most anti-colonialist writing was dedicated at some point to presenting a realist counter to colonial stereotypes' (2015: 624). Moreover, magic realism itself as a mode has not been immune from criticism; notably, Tabish Khair has argued in *Babu Fictions* that magic realism can help the novelist to 'deny final authority to any extra-literary reality, while appropriating those aspects of that reality which are useful and accessible. It also enables the author to present his/her own "fabulous" version of even those aspects of extra-literary reality that *are* appropriated' (2001: 338; italics in the original). The wariness of, and perhaps the sense of weariness in some quarters towards, the concept of resistance in postcolonial literary studies which I invoked earlier in the Introduction can partly be seen as an unfortunate consequence of the fetishisation of magic realism in postcolonial scholarship in recent decades, which often entailed insisting on a necessary link between 'political or social resistance and non-realist fiction' (Moss, 2000: n.p.). As Laura Moss warns us, the conflation of postcolonial resistance and the magic realist mode often brought in its wake the assumption that '[i]f a text does not fit the profile of postcolonial resistance, as realists texts seldom do, it is generally considered incapable of subversion' and, consequently, its engagement with resistance was often overlooked or dismissed, though the tide has been turning (2000: n.p.).¹⁰ In conjointly addressing nonrealist fiction, realist texts which, in some instances, are dramatically different from each other, as well as fictional works that do not lend themselves to easy categorisation, this book brings to the fore how resistance as a preoccupation in South Asian women's fiction resists being confined to a single narrative mode.

Since the number of novels far exceeds the number of short stories under discussion, this book arguably does not contest '[t]he hegemony of the novel' within postcolonial South Asian anglophone literature (Srivastava, 2016: 253); rather, it acknowledges 'the genre's remarkable portability, flexibility and adaptability to myriad social and political contexts' (Farag, 2016: n.p.). Frank O'Connor has argued that 'Time' is the greatest advantage that the novelist has over a short story writer; when taking 'a character of any interest and set[ting] him [*sic*] up in opposition to society', it allows the novelist to chart 'the chronological development of character or incident' which 'is essential form as we see it in life' (1963: 21). The novel form, by dint of its very length, is a 'capacious form that exceeds borders and rules' and does appear to have an affinity with complex narratives of resistance, particularly narratives that seek to capture the ebb and flow of the process of contestation and to chart a resistant agent's journey, sometimes spanning several years, if not decades, undertaken often in response to complex sociological and political challenges (Chambers, 2018: 203).

For O'Connor, unlike the novel which can evoke 'man [*sic*] as an animal who lives in a community', the short story form is characterised by the presence of 'submerged population groups' and remains 'by its very nature remote from the community – romantic, individualistic and intransigent', with its characters displaying 'an intense awareness of human loneliness' (1963: 19–21). However, as my discussion of ordinary defiances in Chapter 3 demonstrates, short story characters placed in opposition to societal norms can embody forms of resistance that are not necessarily lonely, and that *do* mobilise collective identities as well as the idea of community formation, even if the communities in question may be far smaller or considerably larger in scale than national or regional ones. Moreover, by looking at ordinary acts of resistance in what is 'a form of "minority literature"' within 'postcolonial South-Asian literatures in English' (Srivastava, 2016: 253), I aim to show that precisely because the short story writer's 'frame of reference can never be the totality of a human life' and because she must be 'forever selecting the point at which [she] can approach it', the short story allows for an exploration of the accompanying tensions and transience of certain kinds of resistance, especially in micro-settings (O'Connor, 1963: 21).

Outline of this book

The first chapter of this book focuses on the female protagonists of *Difficult Daughters* and *Broken Verses* who resist involvement in collectivist struggles against socio-political injustice. Set against the backdrop of two significant moments of female activism in pre-Partition India and in 1970s and 1980s Pakistan respectively, the two narratives bring to the fore the tensions that the idea and practice of protest politics can elicit, particularly for women. But precisely because the protagonists are shown to be in close proximity, emotional as well as physical, to women who are actively engaged in political affairs, the two texts resist being read as allegories of female political inaction. The two characters' rejection of protest politics and their ostensible distance from the notion of 'the political' appear to be deeply personal and invite an examination of the ways in which political apathy is intimately tied in not only with the concepts of freedom, choice and agency, but also with fundamental questions of self-identity.

The second chapter addresses the intersection of romance and resistance in four novels: *The God of Small Things*, *The Ministry of Utmost Happiness*, *The Lowland* and *Broken Verses*. Each of the four texts features a heterosexual couple whose amorous trajectory is intertwined with public acts of resistance, including (in the case of three of the four novels under discussion) violent militancy. I am particularly interested in evaluating the significance of 'the romance of resistance' in these relationships, and in analysing the construction of the activist identity of the female characters (Abu-Lughod, 1990). I assess the extent to which the depiction of female activism in the four novels is shown to be informed by gendered imperatives, notably those pertaining to beauty, the institution of marriage and motherhood; I also evaluate what the death of the male partner reveals about the construction of (gendered) resistance in these texts. Finally, I consider whether the romantic relationship itself can be read as an act of resistance which challenges gendered roles and other hierarchies.

Through the lens of four short stories by Indian, Pakistani and Sri Lankan writers, the third chapter examines the depiction of a range of 'ordinary' defiances by women in micro-settings, such as the so-called domestic sphere and the small town. I show that, while underscoring the emotional vulnerabilities that come with the contestation of the domestic status quo and the negotiation of affective ties that are deeply hierarchical, the texts act as a warning against interpreting women's agency as a necessarily 'individualist endeavour' (Banerjee, 2017: 35). As we will see, these 'ordinary' acts of contestation compel us to reconceptualise the relationship between individual and collectivist resistance and to come to grips with the unexpected ties that exist between the two. More broadly, the chapter reflects on the relationship between 'everyday forms of resistance' as depicted in the works under discussion and the short story as a genre (Scott, 1985: 32).

The fourth chapter grapples with representations of resistance enacted by homosexual and intersex characters in *Babyji*, *A Married Woman* and *The Ministry of Utmost Happiness*, and it addresses the multi-layered relationship between queerness and anti-heteronormativity, as well as between queerness and anti-normativity. Engaging with the large-scale collectivist protests and social upheavals in recent Indian history which serve as a backdrop for each of the three novels – the 1990 protests against the Mandal Commission, the demolition of the Babri Mosque in 1992 and the 2002 anti-Muslim riots in the state of Gujarat respectively – the chapter examines the diverse, even contradictory, forms that queer resistance assumes in these works and it unpacks the ways in which they complicate our understanding of the relationship between freedom, equality and identity. In particular, the chapter brings to the fore the importance of examining the subversive contours of sexed, sexual and gender identities in relation to questions of caste, class, age and religion in contemporary India.

In analysing three troubled and troubling figures of resistance, the fifth chapter evaluates some of the ways in which contemporary fiction by South Asian women writers problematises the purely positive and emancipatory connotations of nonviolent resistance as a concept and as a practice. The figures of distorted resistance considered in this chapter are consciously disparate: a middle-aged Indian male immigrant in Australia in *Homework* who agitates, often comically, for Goa's liberation following its annexation by the postcolonial Indian state; Moushumi in *The Namesake*, whose ostensibly transgressive decisions confound the line between (self-)destructive and constructive defiance and need to be understood in terms of her deep malaise about her identity as a second-generation Bengali-American; and finally Latha in *A Disobedient Girl*, who works as a domestic servant in Colombo and for whom the erotic emerges as the primary source and form of agentic behaviour while attempting to contest the socio-economic and affective status quo.

In the sixth and final chapter of this book, I turn to the act of writing itself and to the figure of the female writer by focusing on Maya's character in *A Golden Age* and *The Good Muslim*, set against the backdrop of Bangladesh's brutal war of independence and its aftermath, and the author-narrator of *The Gypsy Goddess*, which grapples with the 1968 massacre of Dalit peasants in Kilvenmani. I analyse the meanings assigned to writing, publishing and reading as activities in these novels and evaluate the representation of the intricate social, emotional, intellectual and economic forces that are shown to underpin the practice of writing as well as the dissemination of the written word. Moreover, as I demonstrate, in pluralising our understanding of both 'writing' as a construct and 'woman' as a social category, the three novels problematise the relationship between resistance and writing, as well as the relationship between violent and non-violent forms of resistance.

In consciously deploying a transnational approach and exploring literary works by Indian, Pakistani, Sri Lankan and Bangladeshi women writers in conjunction with, rather than in isolation from, one another, *Resistance and Its Discontents in South Asian Women's Fiction* not only draws attention to the protean nature of resistance in South Asia today, but also underscores its pressing relevance as a lens for understanding, appreciating and responding to contemporary South Asian realities and imaginaries.

Notes

1 For the most part, the term 'postcolonial' has been deployed in this book to refer to the time period in the Global South and to the literary production by authors from the Global South after the end of European colonial rule in the 1940s and in the following two decades or so, as well as to theories and literary scholarship grappling with these texts. But the term and its use remain problematic, not least because, as Anne McClintock has pointed out, it 'confers on colonialism the prestige of history proper; colonialism is the determining marker of history' (1992: 86). The usefulness of the label 'postcolonial' is further thrown into doubt, since much, if not all, of the Global South is 'caught in the cross hairs' of a 'New Imperialism' led by the United States, most potently represented by 'the American cruise missile and the IMF checkbook' (Roy, 2006: 196). 'Postcolonial' also emerges as a misnomer given the 'colonizing' impulses of former European colonies such as India, 'occupying land and capable of inflicting its own humiliations and hurt' (Gopal, 2009: 183).

2 I am not suggesting that all postcolonial scholars have abandoned, or indeed that they *should* abandon, lines of enquiry which engage with various forms of anti-colonial resistance; Neelam Srivastava's 2018 monograph *Italian Colonialism and Resistances to Empire, 1930–1970*, for example, which explores the role of Italian colonialism in the development of anti-colonial movements, is a testament to the continuing importance of grappling with European colonialism and its aftermath, as is Priyamvada Gopal's *Insurgent Empire: Anticolonial Resistance and British Dissent* (2019); to take another example, Elleke Boehmer's essay 'Revisiting resistance: Postcolonial practice and the antecedents of theory' charts Nelson Mandela's fight against apartheid as a 'dynamically evolving anti-colonialism' (2013: 319).

3 Kamala Markandaya's *Nectar in a Sieve* (1954) is one of the rare examples within early South Asian anglophone fiction by women that departs from this norm by grappling with the severe financial hardships faced by a female villager Rukmani and her family.

4 It is worth pointing out here that bell hooks is emphatic about not reducing patriarchal oppression to male dominance, making it clear 'that the problem is sexism. And that clarity helps us remember that all of us, female and male, have been socialized from birth on to accept sexist thought and action' (2000: viii).

5 With its focus on hitherto neglected 'transverse forms of anticolonial (and postcolonial) alliances', the special issue of *Interventions: International Journal of Postcolonial Studies* entitled 'Postcolonial

studies and transnational resistance' is one example of efforts within postcolonial literary studies to shift 'a rigid "centre-periphery" conceptual mapping' and to contest the privileging of 'nationalist modes of resistance' (Boehmer and Moore-Gilbert, 2002: 7–11). The essays included in the *Journal of Postcolonial Writing* special issue entitled 'Postcolonial thresholds: Gateways and borders' also seek to 'move away from the resisting strategies and counter-discourses associated with the earlier paradigm of "writing back to empire"' (Wilson and Tunca, 2015: 2).

6 See Herbert Marcuse's *An Essay on Liberation* (1969).
7 See, for instance, Suniti Namjoshi's 'autobiographical myth' *Goja* (2000) and the anthology *Facing the Mirror: Lesbian Writing from India* (1999), edited by Ashwini Sukthankar.
8 See also Mirza (2016).
9 In a not dissimilar vein, Noella Brada-Williams argues that the 'lack of representation of [Bibi Haldar's] individual thoughts, memories, and motivations ... lends the title [character] a mythic or allegorical quality' (2004: 460).
10 See, for instance, Anjaria's discussion of what she sees as the emergence of a 'new social realism' in contemporary Indian literature in English (2015: 114).

1

Resisting activism: the politics of apathy and disengagement in *Difficult Daughters* and *Broken Verses*

> Disuse involves decay, physical, mental, spiritual. The powers of the will, the positive forces of the individual which make up character, are no exception to this rule.
>
> – Sara Ahmed, *Willful Subjects*, 2014

The novels under discussion in this chapter are set against the backdrop of two significant moments of female activism in contemporary South Asian history: in Kapur's *Difficult Daughters*, it is the anti-colonial nationalist movement of 1930s and 1940s India and, in Shamsie's *Broken Verses*, the resistance to the military dictatorship of General Zia-ul-Haq and his Islamisation campaign in 1970s and 1980s Pakistan. While both texts present us with convincing portrayals of feisty women activists, they also, almost paradoxically, feature female protagonists, Virmati in Kapur's novel and Aasmaani in Shamsie's, who resist becoming politically engaged and are manifestly apathetic towards the idea of political activism. In examining these representations of disengagement, I aim to demonstrate the ways in which they help us to tease out the tensions that the idea and practice of protest politics can generate, particularly for women. But, as we will see, precisely because both Virmati and Aasmaani are shown to be in close proximity, emotional as well as physical, to women who are actively engaged in political affairs, especially Swarna in *Difficult Daughters* and Samina in *Broken Verses*, the two texts resist being read as allegories of female political inaction. In this context, I will analyse Virmati's relationship with her married lover Harish and Aasmaani's with her activist mother Samina to come to grips with how, for these two characters, the notion of 'the political' and their ostensible distance from it are deeply personal, and how political apathy is intimately tied in not only with the concepts of freedom and choice but also with fundamental questions of self-identity.

My understanding of disengagement in this chapter draws on Thomas DeLuca's conception of political apathy which he defines as 'a loss or suppression of emotional affect with regard to, a listlessness, a loss of interest in, some issue, set of issues, or perhaps politics itself' (1995: 191). Also of relevance here is Benjamin Berger's discussion of the notion of 'engagement' which he interprets as 'activity and attention, an investment of energy and a consciousness of purpose' (2009: 340). By extension, *dis*engagement implies a lack of 'attention to political affairs and processes' but also a lack of 'activity aimed at actualization' (2009: 341). My analysis of the kinds of political disengagement, apathy and 'failures of will' that Virmati and Aasmaani display will be carried out in conjunction with, and in contrast to, the diverse range of political activities in which the other female characters in the two novels are shown to be involved (Ahmed, 2014: 111). These activities often take the form of what in political science is understood to constitute 'participation', characterised by 'attempts to influence the authoritative allocations of values for a society, which may or may not take place through governmental decisions' (Verba and Nie, 1987 [1972]: 2). The 'authoritative allocations of values' that the female activists in *Difficult Daughters* challenge are informed by both colonial discourse and indigenous patriarchal practices, and in *Broken Verses* by a deeply repressive military dictatorship working in concert with Islamic fundamentalist factions.

Wilful failures of will?

Virmati ostensibly lives a wilful life, to deploy Ahmed's terminology. In falling in love with and later becoming the second wife of Harish, a married man and a professor of English literature, Virmati defies her family's demands and expectations to submit to an arranged marriage.[1] Arranged marriages in north India, as Perveez Mody has pointed out, are 'rhetorically described as a religious ritual, sanctified and validated by kin and community', while love marriages are synonymous with rebellion as they entail 'choosing one's own spouse and thus exercising autonomy' and 'ignoring the obligation' to marry the person of one's parents' choice, thereby contravening one's filial duty (2008: 8). Virmati's rejection of her fiancé (a man chosen by her family) represents a deeply transgressive act, incurring her family's furious displeasure. When she gets married to Harish (without first consulting her family or seeking their approbation), Virmati's mother disowns her; she is banished from the familial house and shunned by her siblings.[2]

Moreover, much to her mother's chagrin, as a young girl, Virmati has 'aspirations for learning (initially identified as a masculine terrain)', and goes on to acquire a number of academic degrees; she eventually becomes, as Ida, Virmati's daughter and the novel's narrator, discovers, the most educated girl in the family (Boehmer, 2005: 212). Virmati's grandfather is shown to be an exponent of the Arya Samaj, a Hindu reformist movement which was in 'favor of widow remarriage, against child marriage, and scornful of almost the entire corpus of Hindu myths, epics and scriptures' (Prakash, 2020 [1999]: 92). The family's embrace of this movement, however, does not in any tangible way displace its belief that an arranged marriage is a girl's destiny and her duty, and this is evident in the path that is clearly set out before Virmati since she was thirteen: 'The first class she had to join was the special class for those girls who were weak in English. After that, classes IX and X, and then two years to get a Fine Arts degree. And then marriage, said the elders' (Kapur, 1998: 5). The narrator charts the trailblazing quality of Virmati's scholastic efforts as she resists patriarchal pressures to become the seventh girl to enter AS College, the 'bastion of male learning' (5). But, as the text also makes clear, Virmati's ability to successfully pursue higher education, despite her family's disapproval, rather than a result of her wilfulness (which manifests itself in the form of weeping and sulking), results primarily from the unexpected death of her fiancé's father. It compels the two families to postpone the wedding and greatly contributes towards her family's decision to allow her to study for a bachelor's degree.

More importantly, Virmati's eventual refusal to submit to an arranged marriage, her scandalous romance with Harish and her unconventional educational trajectory are robbed of their subversive power as they will become, to a large extent, dictated by Harish's whims and desires, and his demands which, though couched in the language of love, passion and benevolence, will prove to be no less tyrannical than her family's. Without addressing the implications of being already married, Harish exhorts Virmati to call off her wedding, and is shown to be profoundly insensitive to the familial pressure weighing on her as a young woman. That the day before her wedding Virmati makes an attempt to end her life by drowning is a testimony not only to her feelings of powerlessness before her family, but also before Harish upon whom, she is painfully aware, she cannot depend 'to sort out any domestic situation' (Kapur, 1998: 68). Her attempted suicide, which will result in her affair with Harish being discovered by her family, who then imprison her for several weeks in the basement of the house in which she grew up, will set the tone for her relationship with Harish in the years to follow. Virmati will be compelled to make numerous difficult sacrifices, including forgoing a flourishing teaching career and undergoing a painful abortion, while Harish defers marrying her as it would necessitate bringing Virmati into his home to live with his deeply unhappy first wife Ganga and his mother, who disapproves of his taking a second wife, and thus complicate his otherwise comfortable domestic arrangement.[3]

Just as her ostensibly transgressive romance fails to liberate Virmati, her pursuit of higher education, as emblematic as it might be of female autonomy, does little to enhance her agency as a woman. As Ananya Kabir has pointed out, '[e]ducation becomes the means of both escape and entrapment for Virmati. She staves off arranged marriage by accumulating higher degrees, but these degrees trap her into emotional reliance on the Professor' (2001: 128). This is especially true since Harish also becomes her teacher when, early in their romance, Virmati joins AS College to study English literature. The teacher–pupil hierarchy continues to define their relationship in the years to come, with Harish not only actively shaping her appreciation of literature and art, but also dictating her choice of subjects for future study and deciding where she should live. As we see in Chapter 21 of the novel, during a visit to a cemetery with Virmati, Harish waxes lyrical about the picturesque charm of the gravestones, while she tries to 'see through his eyes when he pointed things out to her. After all these years she was getting quite good at the exercise' (Kapur, 1998: 190). Virmati and Harish's relationship and its hierarchical tenor are steeped in male privilege and pedagogical superiority, but also colonial authority in the shape of the discipline of English literature. As Gauri Viswanathan has argued, 'British colonial administrators, provoked by missionaries on the one hand and fears of native subordination on the other, discovered an ally in English literature to support them in maintaining control of the natives under the guise of a liberal education' (1987: 17). Harish's love of Virmati is bound up with his love of romance, which in turn is underpinned by his reading and teaching of Romantic literature and his embracement of Romantic aesthetics, as attested by his letters to Virmati; English literature, particularly 'Wordsworthian Romanticism', is indeed 'the force that sustains the mutual attraction between the protagonists' (Kabir, 2001: 128–31). Moreover, in his letters addressed to Virmati while she is imprisoned in the family home, Harish adopts an ostensibly feminist language and vocabulary. He stresses the differences between 'Western' culture, in particular its permissiveness with respect to romantic love, and traditional Indian society which he presents as being particularly injurious to women:

> Who is responsible for this state of affairs? Society, which deems that their sons should be educated, but not their daughters. Society that decides that children – babies really should be married at the ages of two and three as we were.[4] As a result, both of us suffer through no fault of ours. I cannot be an adherent to stultifying tradition after this, but Viru, you must make up your own mind about these matters. You are intelligent and capable. (Kapur, 1998: 103)

It is the 'nexus between colonialism, patriarchy and pedagogy', as well as the rhetoric of a feminist and liberating romance that will make it particularly difficult for Virmati to not only come to grips with the various forms of power that inform her life, but also, consequently, to exercise her agency in a manner which will best serve her interests (Kabir, 2001: 128). If for the colonial Englishman, 'the strategy of locating authority in these [literary] texts all but effaced the sordid history of colonialist expropriation' and 'material exploitation', Harish's teaching of English literature, inseparable as it from their love story, dilutes, if not effaces, his exploitative behaviour in Virmati's eyes (Viswanathan, 1987: 22). Despite his condemnation of British rule in India,[5] the weight of Harish's colonial pedagogical authority dulls Virmati's ability to imagine anti-colonial resistance as well as other forms of resistance, even if, as I will discuss below, we do see her later in the narrative attempting to half-heartedly adopt the strategies of the nationalist movement in her personal life.

After her failed suicide attempt and in the face of her staunch refusal to marry, her family see no choice but to allow Virmati to leave Amritsar to pursue a teaching degree at a conservative Hindu college for women in Lahore. Her move to Lahore brings her in close proximity to women who are deeply involved in the anti-colonial and feminist movement of the time, in particular her roommate Swarna Lata, who actively participates in rallies and demonstrations. Over the ensuing decade, Swarna attempts, time and again, to draw Virmati into these activities, but Virmati resists becoming an activist, despite at times desiring that role; she sees herself as lacking the intellectual wherewithal that she feels is required for political participation. In response to Swarna's invitation in the first few months of their friendship to join her and other women in drafting petitions addressed to the colonial government regarding the need for rationing and fair-price shops, Virmati informs her: 'I can't be like you, knowing what to say. I don't know how to convince people. I'm not clever' (Kapur, 1998: 132). Virmati's resistance to activism stems not only from her lack of confidence in her own intelligence (despite her many skills, both practical and intellectual), but also from her awareness that any political activity on her part would be inimical to her romance with Harish, with the text making clear that Virmati's lack of self-confidence and her relationship with Harish are closely interlinked.

In *Broken Verses*, Aasmaani's political disengagement comes about at a clearly identifiable moment in her life. The novel's narratological present is set in Karachi in the early 2000s, fourteen years after the disappearance of her activist mother Samina who spent her adult life fighting various forms of injustice. Samina was a combative defender of women's rights when they came under brutal attack by General Zia's military dictatorship and his Islamisation reforms, epitomised by the promulgation of the Hudood Ordinances.[6] But the adult Aasmaani shows no desire to address the political issues of the time. Instead, she chooses to drift from one job to another, each having nothing in common with the previous one except that it suggests a clear distance from the values that served as an impetus for her mother's activism.[7] When the novel opens Aasmaani has recently resigned from a position at an oil company, prior to which she 'taught a school for the educationally disinclined children of the elite, edited a monthly cricket magazine' and 'translated the Urdu diaries of a nineteenth-century, narrow-minded, petty bureaucrat from an Indian princely state for an Anglophone historian' (Shamsie, 2005: 27). Unlike Virmati, Aasmaani is highly articulate and very conscious of her own intelligence. She clearly does not see herself as being too simple-minded to be involved in protest politics: at twelve years of age, Aasmaani already had a profound and, indeed, precocious understanding of patriarchy and how its language, especially when internalised by women, serves to pigeonhole their lives and their actions. When other women, thinking that the young Aasmaani resented her mother's political activism as it took her away from the home so frequently and often landed her in jail, tried to assure her that Samina's work was driven by the desire to make the world a better place for her daughter, Aasmaani categorically rejected this conservative justification for female political activism, couched as it was in culturally accepted terms that privilege and celebrate motherhood as a woman's primary calling in life:

> I looked at the woman in contempt and told her I didn't need to invent excuses or justifications for my mother's courage, and how dare she suggest that a woman's actions were only of value if they could be linked to maternal instincts. At twelve, I knew exactly how the world worked and I thought that by knowing it I could free myself of the world's ability to grind people down with the relentlessness of its notions of what was acceptable behaviour in women.
> (Shamsie, 2005: 254)

If Virmati's identity, as defined by her family, hinges on her marital status, as a member of an upper-class liberal and, for the most part, secular family, thirty-one-year-old Aasmaani's single status is shown to draw no disapprobation, and she enjoys an unusual degree of freedom and choice, with her father having 'never done anything other than support [her] right to be single' (2005: 25). In fact, her relationship with her immediate family (her father, stepmother and half-sister Rabia), rather than conflict-ridden, is fraught with their anxiety over her apparent listlessness, which contrasts sharply with her passion as a teenager for the causes that her mother had so enthusiastically championed. Rabia wistfully reminds her of her belief as a teenager in 'political ideals, notions of inspirations and activism and all that good stuff which you used to lecture me about in response to a question as seemingly apolitical as "Can I borrow your Walkman?"' (2005: 137).

While Virmati's life as a woman comes to be shaped above all by Harish's essentially exploitative desire for her, and by her own desire to see the affair legitimised through the institution of marriage, until she meets Ed (the owner of the television station where she works), Aasmaani's existence is striking for its lack of any manner of a drive, whether political or sexual. She explains her drifting from one job to another to Rabia, who runs a non-governmental organisation addressing problems faced by women, in the following words: 'Why the oil company, she wanted to know. Because why not, Rabia? Because it made no difference ... I get through the day' (Shamsie, 2005: 134–5). Aasmaani's socio-political apathy is accompanied by the belief that her life is devoid of meaning and purpose, and is marked by the loss of her younger politicised self. As she attempts to explain to Rabia:

> Some people, Rabia, have the luxury of doing things they love. Of knowing, this is what I want to spend my life, in pursuit of, and then being in pursuit of it. Whether it's Shakeel through his art, or you with your women's upliftment projects ... you're the lucky ones. You don't have to spend the greater proportion of your life in an office somewhere, unable to remember quite why it is that you're doing this particular thing than any of those other things out there, rather than any of those things you wanted to do when you were eleven years old. (2005: 134)

Aasmaani is able to trace back her loss of faith in activism to a precise moment in her country's history: 17 August 1988, a month after her mother's disappearance, and more than two years after her mother's lover The Poet's brutal murder, when 'General Mohammad Zia-ul-Haq boarded a plane in Bahawalpur, which exploded minutes after take-off' (2005: 135–9). Her belief in activism is shaken by what she interprets as the failure of various non-violent, 'noble means of resisting' such as 'speeches, rallies and poems', because ultimately what brought an end to Zia-ul-Haq's tyrannical regime was 'a bomb on a plane' (139).[8] Since, rather than as a direct consequence of civil disobedience, Zia's reign of terror ended through an act of violence, Aasmaani concludes that her mother's 'activism amounted to nothing' (141). What follows is Aasmaani's belief that, by extension, her own life can and will amount to nothing, and that she cannot contribute to society in any way that her mother would have deemed meaningful. Unlike Virmati's, Aasmaani's apathy 'constitutes a kind of moral anti-politics', stemming from the inferences that she has drawn from her mother's life and disappearance, and the manner in which Zia's dictatorship came to an end; her political disengagement is a consequence of her understanding of 'political participation as entailing untenable compromises', and she appears to experience politics as 'a failed route to moral-cultural regeneration' (Natanel, 2016: 8). Aasmaani's choice of aimless careers paradoxically reveals a consciousness of purpose, a wilful or 'strenuous disengagement' to quote Nina Eliasoph (1998: 154); it suggests a continued, albeit reluctant and resentful conversation with politics as her mother saw and lived it, and it clearly continues to inform her life choices.

Desiring resistance

In *Difficult Daughters*, it is primarily Swarna Lata's passionate activism which underscores Virmati's political inertia. More often than not, Virmati's reaction is one of astonishment and envy at the sight of Swarna and other women assembling, voicing their opinions and making concrete demands in the public sphere. The very act of making a demand goes against how she has been taught to conceive of womanhood and therefore, despite defying her family in matters of marriage and education, Virmati is unable to shed the language of submission that was bequeathed to her by her family and which, as we will see later in greater detail, is further nurtured by Harish. This is brought sharply into focus in Chapter 18 of the novel when Virmati reluctantly finds herself at a women's political meeting, watching Swarna and other Indian women of different ages and faiths making speeches and voicing their demands with conviction and clarity:

> Virmati was amazed at how large an area of life these women wanted to appropriate for themselves. Strikes, academic freedom, the war, peace, rural upliftment, mass consciousness, high prices due to the war, the medium of instruction, the Congress Committee, the Muslim League, anti-imperialism, Independence Day movement,

rally, speeches. *Virmati's head was swimming*. They were talking a *language* she was yet to learn. (Kapur, 1998: 144; emphasis mine)

The novel presents protest politics and self-assertion as a language, a kind of socio-cognitive skill that has to be learnt and practised. In this scene, Virmati's awareness of her lack of proficiency in 'the language of willfulness' (Ahmed, 2014: 133) echoes her description of herself later in the narrative as a woman who has 'no words', as she sits 'on the margin' marvelling at the confident 'flow of words' between Harish and his friend (Kapur, 1998: 254). In bringing home to the reader the physical discomfort that Virmati's poor command of the language of wilfulness causes her (as mentioned in the just-cited extract, her head begins to swim during the speeches, and she goes on to fall physically ill after the meeting), Kapur's novel alerts us to the extent to which self-expression and women's emotional and physical well-being might be intertwined.

Furthermore, through its portrayal of Swarna, Kiran and other female activists, *Difficult Daughters* reflects the diverse array of political activities in which women became involved during the years leading up to Partition, throwing into sharp relief Virmati's passivity.[9] As Suruchi Thapar explains, in the 1930s, departing from his earlier discourse, 'Gandhi began to encourage the emergence of women into public space, and the sanctity of the home that he had earlier stressed was disturbed' (1993: 86). In addition to nationalist activities within the home, such as spinning and weaving, women became involved in protest politics beyond the domestic sphere:

> Outside the home *Prabhat feris* were organized in which women from all castes and classes would walk to the local temple singing songs to rouse the nationalist and patriotic feelings of the people. In addition they held meetings and demonstrations, took part in *satyagraha*, picketed toddy and foreign-cloth shops, went to prison and also suffered brutalities at the hands of the British police. Lastly, when the nationalist leadership were in gaol, the women took over the leadership roles and provided guidance to the movement. (Thapar, 1993: 81)

But if Mahatma Gandhi's endorsement of women's presence in the public sphere was context-specific and bound up with the anti-colonial movement, the causes that animate Swarna and her friends are far more wide-ranging, and are directly concerned with women's positioning in Indian society.[10] The sight and sounds of Swarna and other women in action prompt Virmati to momentarily wonder about her own single-minded devotion to Harish that leaves no time or space for other passions and convictions. Though she returns to this questioning on a few more occasions in her life and does attempt to assert herself, particularly when frustrated with Harish's sluggishness in marrying her, Virmati is also quick to brush aside these moments of doubt and to resume the role of Harish's submissive partner. In her book *Fields of Protest: Women's Movements in India*, Raka Ray sheds light on the factors that determine Indian women's 'participation in a matrix of political possibilities', and underscores the weight of their multiple identities, based on markers such as class, race, religion and their roles as 'daughters, mothers, lovers, wives, and sisters', but also as 'soldiers, communists, prime ministers, street cleaners, and prostitutes', thus arguing that women 'have interests that sometimes coincide and sometimes clash' (1999: 19). Virmati perceives being an activist as a role clashing with the role of lover that Harish has assigned her, and which she never challenges with any serious conviction. She is surprised to discover, when she meets her years later, that Swarna is just as politically active as before, despite being a wife and a mother. But Virmati seems unable to imagine herself capable of fulfilling multiple roles. Following Virmati's marriage to Harish, when Swarna urges her to participate in yet another demonstration, on this occasion to protest against the Draft Hindu Bill which allowed men to not share family wealth with women, Virmati declines the invitation by alluding to her status as a married woman. Instead, she finds herself examining a scar that she got from cooking and 'a ring that Harish had given her, a ruby set in a round of small pearls' and wonders, 'hands like hers, should they be raised in sloganeering? Would Harish like it?' (Kapur, 1998: 252).

During the political meeting described above, feeling 'out of place', and seeing herself as an 'outcaste' and an 'imposter' amidst confident, self-possessed women, Virmati turns her thoughts to 'Harish who loved her. She *must* be satisfied with that' (1998: 144; emphasis mine). As the use of the modal verb of necessity in the citation suggests, Virmati forces herself to define her identity solely in relation to Harish, but this decision also provokes mental anguish as part of her recognises that her life can and should be more than what Harish demands of her. 'Her heart felt heavy and dull' as she leaves the meeting; indeed, she resents Swarna and the other women for their 'fruitful engagement with the world', of which she deems herself inherently incapable, but which she also perceives as a danger to her relationship with Harish, a view that is actively encouraged by him (1998: 145–6).

Ray contends that '[w]e may not be able to tell a priori which aspect of a woman's identity will assert itself as primary, but we can, if we pay close attention to the construction of the political field, understand the process by which certain identities become salient' (1999: 19). The political field comprises 'such actors as the state, political parties, and social movement organizations, who are connected to each other in both friendly and antagonistic ways, some of whose elements are more powerful than others, and all of whom are tied together by a particular culture' (1999: 7). Patriarchy and male dominance are important components of Indian culture, but while, as Ray urges us to do, it is important to pay close attention to 'the political field' and its cultural setting in order to understand why and how certain identities become salient, it is equally important to examine how the individual character is shown to interact with the political field and the culture in question. As my discussion above of the force of Harish's pedagogical (colonial) authority and of the ideological emancipatory power of romantic love indicates, I do not attribute Virmati's political disengagement solely to patriarchal norms: Swarna Lata, who appears to belong to a family not too dissimilar from Virmati's, incurs the displeasure of her parents, especially her mother, by pursuing higher education and refusing to agree to an arranged marriage, and her political activism is neither endorsed nor encouraged by them. When Virmati first meets her, she cannot help but notice that Swarna is a woman who has wrested control of her life from her parents, and her self-confidence stems from her political convictions. As she relates to Virmati:

> I was clear that I wanted to do something besides getting married. I told my parents that if they would support me for two more years I would be grateful. Otherwise I would be forced to offer satyagraha along with other Congress workers against the British. And go on offering it until taken to prison. Free food and lodging at the hands

of the imperialists ... they agreed because they knew I meant what I said. (Kapur, 1998: 118)

It is at the political meeting described earlier that Virmati repeatedly hears the women employ the word 'freedom' in relation to their struggle against British rule, and briefly questions her relationship with Harish and wonders about the pitfalls of romantic love: 'I came here to be free, but I am not like these women. They are using their minds, participating in conferences, politically active, while my time is spent being in love. Wasting it. Well, not wasting time, no, of course not, but then how come I never have a moment for anything else?' (1998: 131). As DeLuca points out, an exploration of the phenomenon of political apathy serves as a clue 'about how free we are, how much power we really have, what we can fairly be held responsible for, whether we are being well-served – by others or even by ourselves' (1995: 8).

While Swarna and her colleagues are demanding freedom from colonial rule, but also from religious strife, patriarchal oppression and economic deprivation, Virmati cannot help but think of freedom in narrower terms, emotionally shackled as she is to Harish. The political is almost always personal for Virmati, as I argue in greater detail below, rather than vice versa. Moreover, as Priyamvada Gopal has pointed out,

> [f]reedom has multiple meanings, and even if the personal is not always at one with the national, each inflects the other, at times, in indeterminate and evasive ways. Like national freedom, choices made in matters of love and desire, even transgressive ones, are never simple nor do they take place in a vacuum. (2009: 149)

As noted earlier, despite the socially transgressive nature of Virmati's affair, her relationship with Harish is deeply hierarchical, underpinned by the belief, held by both parties, that he should decide what is to become of Virmati. A poignant reminder of this dependency and of her acute lack of self-belief is a question that Virmati addresses to her married lover, as her teaching degree in Lahore draws to a close: 'And what are your plans for me?' (Kapur, 1998: 149).

Virmati's construction of her own identity is undeniably inflected with the definition of her needs and desires according to Harish, which is crucial in helping us to understand her disengagement from political matters. As she watches women who are ostensibly like her make speeches and demands, she tells herself that 'the larger spaces were not for her' and her focus moves away from the women's words to recollections of lovemaking with the Professor: 'She could feel the pressure of the Professor's thighs against her own. At such moments the meaning of her life seemed perfectly plain. She just *had* to follow that memory upwards, to feel him thrusting inside her' (1998: 144; emphasis mine). Here too, the use of a modal verb of necessity underscores the extent to which Virmati feels compelled to define sex and marriage with the Professor as her primary need, and the degree to which she commits herself to this role. Like Aasmaani, she is aware of a lack of purpose in her life, but if Aasmaani defends her lack of political commitment by evoking what she perceives to be the futility of her mother's struggle as an activist and, by extension, the meaninglessness of life in general, Virmati convinces herself that Harish is the rightful centre of her emotional and intellectual universe. Despite the divergent nature of their political apathy, both Virmati and Aasmaani feel compelled to offer justifications to themselves and to others around them for their status as disengaged, depoliticised citizens, and this rationalisation seems to emerge as a way to resolve 'conflicts about their identity and of finding meaning in their lives', which 'is an important independent reason as to why depoliticized roles can be so resilient and so difficult to break free from' (DeLuca, 1995: 183).

Virmati's apathy is actively cultivated by Harish, who considers himself to be the arbiter of what constitutes the appropriate degree of political awareness for Virmati to possess. In *Fortunes of Feminism*, Nancy Fraser draws our attention to the 'politics of need interpretation', and argues that '*who* gets to establish authoritative, thick definitions of people's needs is itself a political stake' (2013: 56; emphasis in the original). Fraser's focus on 'needs politics' compels us to ask 'what sorts of social relations are in force among the interlocutors or co-interpreters?' (2013: 56). Moreover, as she warns us, 'members of subordinated groups commonly internalize need interpretations that work to their own disadvantage' (2013: 63). On the one hand, Harish wants Virmati to keep abreast of political events so that in her, unlike his illiterate first wife Ganga, he will have a ready audience when he holds forth on literature, art and current affairs, and so that he can parade her in front of his friends, who are poets and professors, as proof of his liberal values and progressive stance on women's education. On the other hand, he clearly does not believe that Virmati needs to think for herself, and wants her involvement in political matters to be kept to a bare minimum. In fact, he sees an active need for Virmati to be only marginally politically aware, so that she remains dependent on him for intellectual guidance and direction. He frames his desire for her continuing dependence on him in a language of benevolent concern for her physical and mental health, and admonishes her 'lovingly': 'And what was she doing going to women's meetings anyway? She was in Lahore to study, not fritter away her energies. Though it was important that Virmati be exposed to the latest in political and social trends, she must not overdo it' (Kapur, 1998: 148). Virmati's compliance to Harish's will becomes a habit; she learns to silence the need to contribute to society that she experiences in Swarna's presence and in the company of other female activists. As Virmati's daughter observes, like her mother, she has had to learn to tailor her needs to what she has been taught a woman can realistically achieve in life: 'That is my female inheritance. That is what she tried to give me. Adjust, compromise, adapt. Assertion, though difficult to establish, is easy to remember. The mind goes soft and pulpy with repeated complying' (1998: 256).

In the initial years of their marriage, in order to make the fraught living arrangements more tolerable for himself,[11] Harish compels Virmati to pursue a degree in philosophy in Lahore (a subject she has no interest in or aptitude for), unilaterally deciding that 'Virmati and he had been at their happiest when he had been teaching, and she learning' (1998: 247). So limited becomes the space within which she can assert her identity and so shrivelled becomes her sense of self that Virmati, a woman with multiple educational degrees and not inconsiderable talents,[12] finds herself battling with Ganga over who would have the honour of washing Harish's dirty clothes and, in spite of the autonomy that she experienced and enjoyed as a single woman in Lahore and in Nahan, she unthinkingly recycles inherited patriarchal 'truths': '"A woman's happiness lies in giving her husband happiness", remarked Virmati, a language she learned long ago' (1998: 227).

In 'The political is personal', the final chapter of her book *Romancing the Vote*, which explores the literary depiction of feminist activism in American fiction, Leslie Petty contends that, unlike the other works under consideration in her study, which 'rely on the feminist notion expressed in the slogan "the personal is political" – the characters' activism grows out of their individual experiences and affective relationships', in Henry James's *The Bostonians*, the opposite is true (2006: 171). She argues that 'both Olive and Verena must learn that their political ideals must have relevance to their personal lives' and '[b]ecause they do not understand this connection at the outset, their attempt at forming a feminist oppositional community is doomed to fail' (2006: 171). If, as it is for Olive and Verena, for Virmati too the 'political is personal', this equation in *Difficult Daughters* takes on a different tenor in that Virmati's understanding of the 'political' almost always evokes the personal and *only* the personal in the form of her all-consuming relationship with Harish. So, for instance, when she sees Kiran protesting in the streets during the Indian National Army trials,[13] she decides that 'she too must take a stand. I have tried adjustment and compromise, now I will try non-cooperation', and decides to 'resist' by postponing her return to the marital home in Amritsar where she faced the undisguised hostility of Ganga and her mother-in-law (Kapur, 1998: 259). But interpreting the political in terms of her personal dilemma does not lead to sustained resistance even in her personal life, and this consciousness emerges in spurts only to disappear quickly, always keeping her firmly at a distance from collective action. To return to an example I cited earlier, when Swarna invites Virmati to join her in demonstrating against the Draft Hindu Bill, Virmati's response is to first wonder whether a new Hindu Code would 'remove inequalities between two wives', and then to remind herself that 'she had to think of her husband's good name, how he would appear to others, how his absent ears would react to any confidences she might reveal' (1998: 252). It is not surprising then that as the rioting and violence leading up to Partition intensify, she elides 'the public conflicts of emergent India when she is pregnant, choosing to bask in a dry swimming-pool, an anomalous island in the storm', and effectively, for Virmati, as Boehmer argues, 'both romance and the nation signify the unwelcome surrender of self to the collective will' (2005: 214).

Maternal legacies

Virmati's legacy of acquiescence and political apathy stands in marked contrast to the language of willfulness that Samina bequeaths to her daughter. For Aasmaani, the political is arguably even more personal than it is for Virmati or, rather, it is the *a*political that is especially personal for her, since, instead of an embodiment of patriarchy (in the form of a traditional family or a lover) or of an oppressive colonial presence, it is inextricably bound up with her unconventional mother's activism and her disappearance. Shamsie's novel is striking for its many passages devoted to Aasmaani's as well as her family's attempts to better understand the reasons behind her disengagement. If Virmati feels the weight of Swarna's expectations, which are in sharp contrast to the demands made on her by her family, and more importantly by Harish, in Aasmaani's case, it is her apolitical way of life that her family see as a cause for concern. While they realise that the mother–daughter relationship lies at the heart of her depoliticisation, they are unable to pinpoint the exact source of her disengagement. As her half-sister asks her: 'Is it that you don't want to be your mother, or that you're afraid you'll fail so dismally to live up to her that you don't even try?' (Shamsie, 2005: 28). Aasmaani's response underscores the extent to which her mother looms large in how she perceives herself and how she is perceived by others despite the years that have elapsed since her disappearance: 'Either way, you've proved my point. All that I am, all that I believe or try not to believe, it's got nothing to do with larger truths and everything to do with being the daughter of Samina Akram' (2005: 28). It is worth noting that her very name, Aasmaani Inqalab, which was chosen by her mother and which means 'Celestial Revolution', brings with it the expectation of not merely an activist, but a revolutionary sensibility (2005: 3). As Amaya Fernández-Menicucci has observed, '[a]lways shadowed by her mother's celebrated activism, her successes, political visibility and personal charm, Aasmaani has had to fight all her life in order to construct an identity of her own', and this construction entails, as I discussed earlier, adopting various professional roles which belie her activist roots with a distinct vehemence (2012: 78–9).

But I would argue that Aasmaani's rejection of a political life as an adult does not solely stem from a desire to have an identity that is separate from her mother's, though it is evident that she does feel burdened and stifled by the expectations that come with being the daughter of an internationally renowned activist. The novel's opening coincides with the arrival of the digital revolution in Pakistan, and Aasmaani's sister attempts to bring to her attention the potential that the Internet and cable television hold to change lives, especially after the dominance of the deeply conservative state-owned Pakistan Television (PTV) under General Zia-ul-Haq for many years: 'It's such a powerful medium, television. Think of all you could do ... [i]nfluence people's thinking' (Shamsie, 2005: 27). Instead, Aasmaani chooses to work on a quiz show, and pities her colleagues who are energised by their role in television and their engagement in the political climate of the time. While Aasmaani's disdain for her colleagues contrasts sharply with Virmati's often starry-eyed admiration of politically engaged women, it does echo her sense of detachment from them:

> They had light in their eyes, those girls did, of believing that they were part of something bigger than their own lives. They were going to beam youth culture, progressive thought, multiple perspectives, in-depth reporting to a nation which until so recently had only known news channels which spoke with the voice of the government. For a moment I tried to step into their minds, to remember what it was to be that *hopeful*. Poor enviable fools. (Shamsie, 2005: 4–5; emphasis mine)

Aasmaani's apathy in political matters cannot be separated from her sense of utter hopelessness which, as I pointed out earlier, is rooted in the manner in which Zia's brutal regime ended, leading her to conclude that non-violent civic obedience was a futile exercise. Virmati's passive relationship with protest politics remains more or less stagnant during the course of the narrative, and the earlier inner conflict that she experienced over her political inaction appears to dissipate, if not entirely vanish when, just before Partition, she allows Swarna to drop out of her life. Towards the end of *Broken Verses*, however, unlike her earlier professional avatars, Aasmaani adopts what Ruvani Ranasinha has called 'a more activist role' as she offers to work as a researcher for a documentary about the women's movement in Pakistan, which is to be broadcast in time for the twentieth anniversary of the Hudood

Ordinances (2016: 142). For Ranasinha, '[t]his philosophical arc perhaps represents a nation that needs to engage with the more challenging terrain of the present, rather than remain fixated on the grandeur of idealistic visions of the past' (2006: 142). In a review of the book, the novelist Rana Dasgupta makes the opposite argument, contending instead that Aasmaani's involvement in the making of the television documentary suggests that she is 'still fixated on the grandeur of the past, and still anxious about the trivialising influence of foreign places and modern life', and that it would have been 'gratifying to see this heroine's search open up newer and more challenging terrain, and thus end slightly further away from where we began' (2005: n.p.). Ranasinha arguably overstates the 'national' and allegorical significance of Aasmaani's new role by not recognising that, while Aasmaani might have been socio-politically disengaged for many years, other women (including her own sister) were clearly not. Conversely, Dasgupta downplays the importance of Aasmaani's philosophical journey and the resulting recalibration of her perceptions with respect to protest politics. Moreover, to suggest that a documentary about the Hudood Ordinances harkens back to a bygone triumphant struggle belies the role that these laws continue to play in women's lives as well as the support from fundamentalist groups that they enjoy in Pakistan today, and certainly did in the narratological present of *Broken Verses*. As Aasmaani points out, television executives had initially baulked at the idea of producing such a documentary, fearing backlash from 'the religious parties in the Frontier' (Shamsie, 2005: 335). Furthermore, while the passage of the Protection of Women Act of 2006 did introduce certain, primarily procedural, improvements to the Hudood Ordinances, it did not, as Human Rights Watch reports, address or repeal 'the discriminatory provisions that criminalize sex outside of marriage, value women's testimony as half that of a man's, and fail to recognize marital rape' (2006: n.p.).[14] Therefore, Aasmaani's engagement with these laws as a researcher *is* timely and relevant, and does signal a return to a more politically engaged sensibility, however modest it might seem compared to her mother's more dramatic contributions.

It is undeniable that Aasmaani's rediscovery of her identity as an engaged and hopeful individual, much like her earlier disengagement, comes about because of her mother, and hence the past, but it is a consequence of a fresh understanding of her mother's life in particular, and of activism in general. This shift is prompted by archival access to her mother in action, by means of an old audio recording of a public debate that Samina held with a male religious scholar, contesting, among other things, his dubious interpretation of the Quran with respect to women's obligation to wear some form of head covering:

> But now I had her voice echoing in my ear, the laughter of the women in the audience echoing with it. And then all the sound of the world fell away and I was left in that silence – that almost holy silence which had grown upon her, sentence by sentence, as she artfully moved the debate to the exact space in which she had all along intended it to exist – that accountable space. How could I call that nothing? And the thrum of my own blood as I heard her speak, how could I repudiate that? (Shamsie, 2005: 287–8)

Upon hearing the joyous laughter of other women as her mother sparred with the cleric and outwitted him on his own terrain, and upon recognising her own irrepressible excitement as she hears her mother compel the cleric to offer some semblance of intellectual accountability, Aasmaani is in turn compelled to re-evaluate her long-held assessment of her mother's political engagement as futile and farcical. This is followed by conversations with her father and her mother's friend, the actress Shahnaz, which bring her face to face with her mother's crippling depression following the Poet's politically motivated brutal murder, a possibility that she had consistently rejected in the past, choosing instead to remember Samina as invincible and indestructible. She recognises now that her mother had not merely disappeared but was dead, having in all probability killed herself. It is only now, fourteen years after Samina's departure, that Aasmaani will allow herself to acknowledge that her mother 'wasn't an unbreakable creature of myth. She was entirely human, entirely breakable, and entirely extraordinary', and that she refused to see Samina's 'collapse for what it was' because that would have meant recognising that her mother, along with her many strengths, had her weaknesses (2005: 331–2). Tellingly in the concluding pages of the novel, Aasmaani discovers a home movie dating back to 1983, which shows her mother in conversation with a journalist. It is a poignant passage that is worth quoting at length, not only because of the profound effect it has on Aasmaani but also because it is a powerful reminder of the necessity of organised resistance when tyranny leaves little room for hope and makes the world seem 'senseless':

> It's not about the ultimate victory. It's just that a nation needs to be reminded of all the components of its character. That's what we do when we resist ... remind people, that this, too, is part of your heritage and, more importantly, it can be part of your future. Be this rather than those creatures of tyranny ... in concrete battles the tyrants may have the upper hand in terms of tactics, weapons, ruthlessness. What our means of protest attempt to do is to move the battles towards abstract space. Force tyranny to defend itself in language. Weaken it with public opinion, with supreme court judgements, with debates and subversive curriculum. Take hold of the media, take hold of the printing presses and the newspapers, broadcast your views from pirate radio channels, spread the word. Don't do anything less than all you are capable of, and remember that history outlives you. It may not be until your grandchildren's days that they'll point back and say, there were sown the seeds of what we've now achieved.
> (2005: 335–6)

Samina's words stress the need to pit the intangibility of non-violent resistance, with its reliance on language, education and dialogue, against the terrifyingly tangible aspects of oppression, in particular, the use of physical force and weapons; as Ahmed has also pointed out, '[v]oices can be arms, raised in the hope of disturbing the ground' (2014: 141). Moreover, Samina compels Aasmaani (and the reader) to perceive non-violent resistance as a necessarily long process, binding past, present and future together, and making the abdication of responsibility unfeasible, not only in moral but also in practical terms. Samina makes a case for perceiving 'wilfulness' as 'an archive of incompletion' and demands that failure and disappointment be understood as part and parcel of political struggle (Ahmed, 2014: 141); she necessarily allows for what Butler et al. (as discussed in the Introduction) have referred to as the phenomenon of 'vulnerability in resistance' (2016). In the closing paragraph, Aasmaani stands on the beach, letting her mother's name and the sand 'stream out between [her] fingers' and permitting them to be 'carried away' by the waves (Shamsie, 2005: 335). She thus succeeds in moving away from a dichotomous and reductive understanding of Samina's life and of collectivist resistance, as well as of herself as a being who must either reject or be defined by her mother's choices and her activist legacy.

In subtly delineating two politically disengaged female characters who, albeit in different ways and for very different reasons, resist the call to political action and social engagement, *Difficult Daughters* and *Broken Verses* compel us to grapple with the tensions and conflicts, both internal and relational, that activism can provoke. Moreover, the two novels invite us to reflect on the complex and shifting relationship between hope and resignation, between roles that have been inherited and those that ostensibly have been chosen and, more broadly, between the political and the personal. They bring home to the reader the extent to which even, or perhaps especially, when dismissed or elided, not only the practice but also the idea of activism has the power to shape identities and selves.

Notes

1 If, as Leslie A. Baxter and Chitra Akkoor have pointed out, 'arranged marriages in some form are still the norm' in India and represent 'an estimate of 95% of the marriages' in the country, this percentage is likely to have been even higher in the 1930s and 1940s, during which much of Kapur's novel is set (2008: 34).
2 Virmati is allowed back into the parental home by her mother several years later when the sectarian violence in Amritsar in the weeks following Partition reaches a frenzied pitch.
3 Until the promulgation of the Hindu Marriage Act of 1955, polygamy was permissible among Hindus in India.
4 Harish is alluding to his marriage to Ganga, which was arranged while they were infants.
5 In one of his letters to Virmati, Harish makes the following observation: 'How can the British claim to be sincere about defending democracy when they refuse to give up their control over India?' (Kapur, 1998: 98).
6 Promulgated in 1979, the Hudood Ordinances include the Zina Ordinance, which pertains to crimes of rape, abduction, adultery and fornication. Under this ordinance, no distinction is made between rape and non-marital fornication, therefore women filing a complaint for rape could effectively be convicted of adultery. Moreover, this law

stipulates that the testimony of four adult Muslim male witnesses is required for a rape conviction. As Shahnaz Rouse points out, '[n]ot only are these laws weighed heavily against the victims, that is, women, but because the Hudood Ordinances privilege the testimony of male Muslims over female Muslims and all non-Muslims, they also legally sanction discrimination and secondary status on the basis of gender and religion' (1998: 62).

7 Samina's activism will be discussed in greater detail in Chapter 2.

8 General Zia-ul-Haq, Arnold Lewis Raphel (the US Ambassador to Pakistan) and numerous top military personnel died in an air crash on 17 August 1988 and investigations revealed that the plane crashed as a result of an explosion 'caused by a bomb placed in the plane while it was parked at the airport near Bahawalpur' (Burki, 1991: 68).

9 Kiran is the daughter of the woman in whose home Harish, a few months into their marriage, arranges for Virmati to stay, while she (on his instructions) is studying for a degree in philosophy in Lahore.

10 As Malashri Lal has pointed out, 'the intervention of the Indian National Movement and Mahatma Gandhi disturbed social order for a limited period of patriotic zeal but even there, none had questioned the old premise that a woman's place was essentially at home and her language was one of silence' (1995: 6).

11 Once married to Harish, Virmati moves into his house in Amritsar where also live his two children, his first wife Ganga, his elderly mother and younger sister.

12 Consider, for instance, the immense skill and ease with which Virmati runs a school for girls in Nahan upon completion of her teaching degree in Lahore. But this professional idyll comes to an abrupt end when, despite her remonstrations, Harish visits her at her cottage. This leads to her dismissal, as she is unmarried and a male visitor (especially one who stays overnight) seriously compromises her reputation within the local community.

13 The Indian National Army (INA) was organised by Subhas Chandra Bose in 1943 with the aim of fighting for India's liberation from the British. Alongside the Japanese army, it entered British India in 1944 but was forced to retreat. However, the INA reappeared in the public spotlight when the British put three officers of this army on public trial in 1945–46 for treason. While the court martial sentenced them to deportation for life, the British, aware of the support for the INA among the public and among the ranks of the British Indian Army, released the three men. As Kirsten Sellars points out, 'the trial of the three accused – who, fortuitously, happened to be Hindu, Moslem and Sikh – not only became a rallying cry for the already aroused independence movement

but also managed to temporarily unite this movement across political and religious lines' (2016: 46).

14 Moreover, to appease the Muttahida Majlis-e-Amal, an alliance of five ultra-conservative Islamic political parties (and Taliban sympathisers), which rose to power in 2002 in the province of Khyber Pakhtunkhwa (or the North West Frontier Province as it was then known), and which was vehemently opposed to the Protection of Women Act, the Pakistani government introduced a 'fornication' (defined as sex between a non-married couple) clause into the penal code.

2

Revolutionary love and the romance of resistance: *Broken Verses, The Lowland, The God of Small Things* and *The Ministry of Utmost Happiness*

> Really being in love means wanting to live in a different world.
> – Lucy Goodison, 'Really being in love means wanting to live in a different world', 1983

This chapter grapples with the relationship between romantic love and activism in Shamsie's *Broken Verses*, Lahiri's *The Lowland* and Roy's *The God of Small Things* and *The Ministry of Utmost Happiness*, each featuring a heterosexual couple whose trajectory is entwined with collectivist acts of resistance, including violent militancy. Given the prevalence of arranged marriages in the Indian subcontinent and the weight of 'endogamous codes that ensure social distance across caste and class boundaries', in flouting social divisions or in failing to subscribe to familial expectations, or both, a romantic relationship can present a dramatic challenge to the status quo (Virdi, 2003: 73). This helps to explain the popularity of the star-crossed lovers trope in subcontinental cultural production, ranging from Punjabi Sufi poetry to Bollywood films to English-language fiction. The affinity between romantic love and defiance is also rooted in prevalent patriarchal strictures which seek to limit expressions of female sexuality to the institution of heterosexual marriage and prescribe female chastity by designating women as 'repositories of familial and communitarian honour' (Mirza, 2016: 62). In this chapter, I evaluate the ways in which each of the texts under discussion binds its portrayal of collectivist action to heterosexual romance, and the extent to which the authors address the gendered politics of both resistance and romance. I then examine how romantic love, motherhood and resistance intersect in the four texts and complicate our understanding of the female protagonists' resistant subjectivity. Finally, I assess the significance of the end of the romantic relationship, resulting from the male activist's death, and evaluate how it shapes the politics of resistance in each novel as a whole.

Before commencing my analysis, given the not immaterial contextual and ideological divergences amongst the texts under discussion, a brief discussion is in order about how the novels position themselves with respect to the political movements that they chart and how they conceive of violent resistance. In both *Broken Verses*, which is narrated in the first-person by Aasmaani, and *The God of Small Things* (henceforth *Small Things*), which is narrated in the third person, the narrator's ideological values are aligned with those of the activist-protagonists. Even if Aasmaani does question the efficacy of her mother's activism, as we saw in Chapter 1, the text is a celebration of the modes of resistance that Samina deploys: she and her lover Omi practice what Butler refers to as 'aggressive nonviolence', displayed by their vociferous contestation of gendered oppression and autocratic rule through legal recourse, speeches, poetry and debates, despite facing incarceration, police violence and exile (Butler, 2020: 21). In *Small Things*, Ammu and Velutha's romance takes place against the backdrop of communist power struggles and the emergence of Naxalism in late 1960s Kerala. The narrator's sympathies indubitably lie with the Dalit carpenter Velutha and his fellow marchers at the demonstration where Ammu's daughter catches sight of him. We are meant to feel the full weight of 'the keg of ancient anger' that the marchers carry on their shoulders; moreover, we are invited to understand why this rage against centuries of crippling class and caste oppression found itself 'lit with a recent fuse' and to see this new, Naxalite 'edge' to the anger as a logical response to that oppression (Roy, 1997: 69). Naxalism was an armed uprising that began in 1967 in the village of Naxalbari in West Bengal; it quickly spread to several other Indian states including Kerala and Bihar. Inspired by Maoist teachings, the manifesto of the movement included 'comprehensive demands like the abolition of landlordism, redistribution of land through peasant committees, wage increase for agricultural labourers, distribution of government land to the landless, control over forest resources and political mobilization of peasants, dalits and tribals' (Deshpande, 2003: 386). In *Small Things*, the narrator does not dwell on the politics of the violence practised by the Naxalites against landlords, usurers and state authorities. Instead, the novel foregrounds the desperate plight of the dispossessed and lays stress on the failure of the two communist parties – the Communist Party of India and the Communist Party of India (Marxist) – in particular, and parliamentary democracy in general, to address the structural inequalities that led to the uprising. However, 'the pros and cons of violent and nonviolent resistance' have been enduring preoccupations of the author as is evident from her numerous interviews, essays and, more recently, her second novel (Barsamian and Roy, 2004: 125).

In *The Shape of the Beast*, Roy argues that the rise of armed insurgencies in India compels us to interrogate not only the efficacy, but also the feasibility of Gandhian nonviolent resistance for impoverished groups. These militant struggles, according to Roy, ask:

> how the hungry can go on hunger strikes, how people with no incomes can refuse to pay taxes, how those with no possessions can boycott foreign goods. They ask whether these are not tactics only available to middle-class people and are meaningless to truly radical struggles. They believe the threat of offering themselves up for harm (a practice fundamental to the principles of Satyagraha) cannot prevail over an Indian state that would be only too happy to see millions of poor people annihilate themselves. (2008a: viii)

But Roy has also stated that she does not think 'there can be any doubt that violent resistance harms women physically and psychologically in deep and complex ways' (Barsamian and Roy, 2004: 125). In 'Gandhi but with guns', she further asserts that the 'violent excesses' of the Naxalite movement are 'impossible to defend' and has decried the fetishisation of 'violence, blood and martyrdom' by Charu Mazumdar, 'the chief theoretician of the Naxalite Movement' (Roy, 2010: n.p.). While agreeing with the interviewer that the use of violence perverts any movement, no matter how just, in a recent video interview, Roy deems it 'very dangerous' to argue that 'only the state is the legitimate perpetrator of violence' (*Wire*, 2019), hence alerting us to how condemnations of armed resistance to state power are often underpinned by a conveniently narrow understanding of what constitutes violence and by a disturbing acceptance of the physical atrocities committed by the state as well as of state policies and 'other forms of coercion' which 'indirectly cause physical harm' to certain sections of the population (Banerjee, 2010: 35).[1]

Echoing the unequivocal condemnation of caste, class and patriarchal violence in *Small Things*, the narrator of Roy's second novel *The Ministry of Utmost Happiness* (henceforth *Utmost Happiness*), deplores, in no uncertain terms, the Indian military occupation of Kashmir which, as Pankaj Mishra writes, is 'the biggest, bloodiest and also most obscure military occupation in the world', exposing the Valley's four million Muslims not only to 'the everyday regime of arbitrary arrests, curfews, raids, and checkpoints', but also 'to extrajudicial execution, rape, and torture' (2011: 1).[2] Armed resistance to Indian rule began in 1989 and Indian-administered Kashmir has since been the site of a pro-independence insurgency, with heightened Indian militarisation and increased interference from Pakistan-sponsored militants in the Valley. Roy's second novel not only charts the brutality of the oppressor, but also, unlike *Small Things*, addresses head-on the treacherous consequences of subjugated populations resorting to violent resistance. In the novel, the Kashmiri freedom fighter Musa asks his Indian lover Tilo to hide weapons for him in her flat in New Delhi, suggesting that he does engage in some form of armed resistance, but we, as readers, never witness it. We do, however, learn how Musa deploys *psychological* warfare against his enemies. For instance, he 'didn't kill' the Indian officer Amrik Singh, who perpetrated horrific acts of violence in the Valley; instead, when the latter moved to the US, Musa and other Kashmiris 'turned up at his workplace, at his home, at the supermarket, across the street, at his children's school. Every day. He was forced to look at [them]. Forced to remember … Eventually it made him self-destruct' (Roy, 2017: 433).

Although Musa is never shown to commit an act of violence, Roy does devote considerable textual space to exposing the pernicious and self-defeating contradictions that have riddled the Kashmiri armed insurgency. The narrator foregrounds not only the self-serving role that Pakistani (state-sponsored) militants have played in this struggle, but also the paradoxical nature of the insurrection itself, which, in order to become a force that the Indian authorities could not afford to ignore, had to be indiscriminate and welcome 'black marketeers, bigots, thugs and confidence-tricksters' into its fold (2017: 314). We are alerted to how, ironically, the language of resistance itself can become a casualty as an armed movement gains strength: 'They grafted the language of God and Freedom, Allah and Azadi,[3] on to their murders and new scams' (2017: 314). Particularly through her depiction of Tilo's preoccupation with gendered oppression, Roy draws our attention to how certain inequities and prejudices have either emerged in Kashmiri society or have become calcified since the inception of the armed struggle.

Indeed, both *Utmost Happiness* and *The Lowland* present us with ambivalent representations of resistance movements, although I argue that the ambivalence is consciously constructed in *Utmost Happiness*, while in *The Lowland* it emerges as a result of unresolved narratological tensions between resistance and heterosexual romance. Lahiri's novel has been criticised for not fully recognising that the 'roots of the Naxalite movement' lay 'in the gross inequalities of Indian society' (Walonen, 2019: 1) and for colluding with 'pedagogic nationalist aspirations for stability, unity and continuity' by constructing the familial 'disunity' resulting from the middle-class protagonist Udayan's Naxalite politics as an 'allegorical representation of the threat posed by Naxalism to the desired homogeneity of India' (Malreddy, 2016: 227). The novel's condemnation of Naxalite violence centres on one particular episode – the killing of a policeman, and Udayan's witting, and his wife Gauri's unwitting, role in it:

> He had not been to wield the dagger, only to stand watch. But his part in it had been crucial. He had gone as close as he could, he had dipped his hand in the fresh blood of that enemy, writing the party's initials on the wall as the blood leaked down his wrists, into the crook of his arm, before he ran from the scene. (Lahiri, 2013: 339)

At different points in the narrative, the movement is described as 'rudderless', 'misguided' and as having caused 'nothing but damage', and while its denouement does represent a rejection of Naxalite politics, *The Lowland* is not oblivious to societal injustice and is more wavering in its assessment of the movement than Pavan Kumar Malreddy and Michael K. Walonen suggest (Lahiri, 2013: 115, 275). The narrator fluctuates between a recognition of the defensible emancipatory impulse that triggered the Naxalite insurgency and an unqualified indictment of it and, as I demonstrate below, this vacillation is bound up with the depiction of Udayan and Gauri's romantic relationship.

Gendered identities and politicised heterosexual romance

Turning now to the gendered politics of resistance and heterosexual romance in the works under consideration, I begin with a discussion of Roy's *Small Things*, arguably the best-known of the four novels and featuring the most obviously taboo-breaking romantic relationship. In the now considerable body of scholarship on *Small Things*, often a clear line is drawn between the kinds of resistance that Ammu, an upper-caste Syrian Christian woman, and her Paravan lover Velutha, embody: Velutha is a card-holding member of the Communist Party of India (Marxist), and we see him demonstrating at the Naxalite rally invoked earlier, raising 'his knotted arm in anger' (Roy, 1997: 176).[4] While she does enjoy some of the privileges of a middle-class identity (for instance, the ability to speak English), Ammu, as a divorcee with two children resulting from an inter-faith marriage that was not sanctioned by her family, is an outcast in her milieu. Moreover, given the sexist inheritance laws in place at the time, she is not entitled to inherit any familial property, making her financially vulnerable and dependent on her brother Chacko. Her most transgressive and resistant act is her sexual relationship with Velutha. Challenging Aijaz Ahmad's contention that Ammu's resistance, because of its 'libidinal' nature, is less political than Velutha's involvement in the Naxalite movement (2007 [1997]: 116), Brinda Bose has convincingly shown that, in loving a Dalit, Ammu challenges an oppressive 'caste/class/gender/sexuality' nexus and her resistance is thus no less significant than Velutha's (2007 [1998]: 125).

While Ammu does not explicitly voice her opinion in relation to the Naxalite movement, as I have argued elsewhere (Mirza, 2016: 64), it is Velutha's presence at the protest that leads Ammu to realise that Velutha might share an aversion to the 'the smug, ordered world that she so raged against' (Roy, 1997:176). Moreover, Ammu possesses an acute and, it is suggested in the text, an inborn understanding of the manipulative power of various ideologies, be it patriarchal dogma, Orientalism or even Marxism. In the questions that her former sister-in-law, an Englishwoman, asks about the amorous habits of Indians, Ammu is able to read the disturbing impulse to exoticise people of colour, despite the fact she 'had not had the kind of education, nor read the sort of books, nor met the kind of people, that might have influenced her to think the way she did. She was just that sort of animal' (1997: 180). Unlike the other women in her family who act as enablers in Chacko's sexual exploitation of the female workers at his factory, whom he accosts under the guise of an egalitarian ethos, Ammu uses her sharp tongue to expose the superficial and self-serving nature of Chacko's commitment to Marxism. Ammu is aware that Velutha's Naxalite politics, itself an off-shoot of communist politics, stands in stark opposition to her brother's Marxism which is essentially a shallow posture, fulfilling his appetite for drama and performativity: 'a princeling playing Comrade, Comrade' (1997: 65).

Small Things stands out from the other three novels because of the striking disparity in the caste and class positionings of the lovers, and because of the rabid commitment of their families to the status quo. Samina's lover in *Broken Verses* may be lower down the class hierarchy than her in economic terms, but his educational and cultural capital amply compensate for his financial inferiority. In contrast, Velutha's male identity is an example of what R. W. Connell refers to as 'marginalised' masculinity: his severe class and caste marginality effectively diminishes any privileges that he may have enjoyed as a man in a patriarchal society (2005: 81). Even Velutha's immense skill as a carpenter does little to alleviate his class positioning, since Ammu's mother Mammachi pays him less than she would a skilled non-Dalit carpenter. It is important to note that inter-caste, inter-class coupling is anathema not only to Ammu's family but also to Velutha's; it is, after all, Velutha's father who exposes the affair to Ammu's family. Moreover, Mammachi, who accepts Chacko's dalliances with lower-class (and possibly lower-caste) women as an expression of 'natural' male urges, is filled with disgust and rage at the very thought of Ammu's coupling with Velutha, which is a breach not only of class boundaries and the laws of untouchability, but also of patriarchal strictures: 'Her tolerance of "Men's Needs" as far as her son was concerned, became the fuel for her unmanageable fury at her daughter. She had defiled generations of breeding' (Roy, 1997: 258).

Of the four novels, *Small Things* most powerfully dramatises the *romance as resistance* trope, which is further accentuated by the violence directed against Velutha. If all four male protagonists meet violent deaths, it is only Velutha who is punished for both his political leanings *and* his transgressive sexuality. With its final love-making scene, *Small Things*, more consciously than the other three texts, foregrounds heterosexual erotic love as a significant form of defiance and the body as a key site of resistance; it exposes the artificiality not only of the boundary separating familial and societal oppression, but also of the boundary separating private and public acts of defiance. While the romance may ostensibly appear to be an individualised form of resistance, it is inseparable from Ammu and Velutha's desire for a more just society, and this is despite Ammu's ambiguous resistant subjectivity as a mother, which I discuss below.

Although Samina and her lover, known for his anti-establishment poetry and translations, are united in their nonviolent opposition to the abuses of power by the Pakistani military, the trajectory of their relationship is by no means predictable: it goes through several phases which broadly coincide with Samina's various incarnations as an activist. When she first meets him, as a young woman of twenty-three, Samina has made a name for herself internationally and amongst the country's English-speaking elite as 'Pakistan's Gypsy Feminist' following an appearance in a Canadian documentary in which she discussed the plight of a female villager (Shamsie, 2005: 87). At this early stage, her celebrity has much to do with her extraordinary physical attributes. We are told that 'on camera, she was ablaze with beauty – and with a sense of justice so newly minted it shone through her eyes' (2005: 87). Omi is instantly smitten with her and very publicly casts her in the role of his muse, a role that Samina initially enjoys: 'he made her a figure of rebellion, of salvation, she played into it' (2005: 88). But Samina soon recoils from the predictable literary configuration of male poet/female love-object or muse. It is worth noting that, rather than a subcontinental literary trope, this gendered template can be far more easily traced back to European medieval poetry, specifically the concept of courtly love, as well as the Petrarchan convention, which, as Julia Straub explains, sees the female 'beloved as exalted', but 'all the gestures of veneration and deification which the male poets use to praise their lady are rhetorical, based on an understanding of the woman as object of poetic idolatry, whom the poet can mould according to his own ideas' (2009: 56). Historically, in the Urdu ghazal, reflecting cultural mores in relation to female modesty, both the beloved and the speaker have been male and, as Hoshang Merchant points out, it was not until the nineteenth century that 'Lucknow poets dared to introduce a woman as muse' (2010: xix). While Omi writes in Urdu, his literary appetites extend far beyond the Indian subcontinent: '[H]e wrote sonnets, pantoums, villanelles, canzones. For those who loved his ghazals this was a profound betrayal, particularly in the light of the nationalistic, anti-colonial feeling that ran high among young Pakistanis in the early 1950s, and they mockingly took to calling him "The Poet" rather than "Nazim"' (Shamsie, 2005: 84).[5] Whether it is the influence of Western poetic traditions or more recent subcontinental ones, a combination of the two or quite simply a reflection of a male-centred sensibility, Omi does initially objectify Samina in his writings; he attempts to reduce her to a symbol and, even more unoriginally, to a national allegorical figure, by changing the year of her birth in his poems 'so that she was the same age as Pakistan' (2005: 87).

Refusing to play the role of a literary device, Samina leaves the Poet 'in search of an identity that wasn't caught up in his shadow' and returns to him a few months later having married and become pregnant by another man (2005: 88). The two never marry, which puts them, but especially Samina as a woman, at odds with the prevailing patriarchal values in Pakistan where live-in relationships are strictly taboo. However, in sharp contrast to Ammu, Samina faces no hostility from her immediate family or even her former husband, as they profess progressive values with respect to gender and religion, making her unorthodox relationship with Omi far less transgressive than Ammu's with Velutha, and consequently far less vulnerable, though not immune, to external attack. Unlike *Small Things*, *Broken Verses* focuses primarily on how the female figure of resistance negotiates the contours of the romantic relationship itself and attempts to keep her romantic, maternal and activist commitments in balance.

Samina's reunion with Omi marks the second phase of her activism: she moves beyond her elite roots by speaking out vociferously against his unjust imprisonment for having 'condemned the generals and politicians he held responsible for the tragedy of the 1971 civil war'; Samina's efforts to have him released are clearly an act of love, but it is a love that encompasses 'other women who were engaged in similar fights for husbands or brothers or sons. Even after the Poet was released she continued to seek out ... women in search of justice ... pointing them in the direction of sympathetic lawyers and journalists or explaining their legal rights to them' (2005: 90). Samina in a sense becomes the saviour in the relationship, disrupting what Diana Reep has labelled 'rescue conventions' which 'affirm traditional male dominance and female submission' (1982: 89). Samina and the Poet's struggle against injustice is echoed and strengthened by the eventual gender parity in the relationship, reminding us of Ann Ferguson's observation that '[r]omantic love, even it if is re-defined as a mutual love that breaks down patriarchal gender norms, can only be radical in a progressive way if it is tied to social justice struggles against all forms of social domination' (2017: 26). The gender parity in their romantic relationship extends to Samina and Omi's public personas and unsettles the public/private divide: if Omi is tortured by state operatives, Samina is attacked by policemen at public demonstrations, leaving her body covered in 'vicious bruises' (Shamsie, 2005: 95). Despite the emphasis in the text on the contrast between Samina's show-stopping beauty and the Poet's underwhelming looks, their relationship also troubles the aesthetic/pragmatic binary, in that Samina's activism, centred as it is on 'practical' measures such as fighting an oppressive legal system, also takes on more aesthetic forms. While she is not a poet herself, her efficacy as an activist owes much to her immense talent as a public speaker, possessing the ability to both captivate and galvanise hundreds of people into action.

Shamsie has acknowledged that when she imagined the Poet's 'poetry and national stature', she thought of the revolutionary Pakistani poet Faiz Ahmed Faiz (Chambers, 2011: 227). 'An archetype in Urdu poetry', the Beloved 'can mean friend, woman, God' and, as Agha Shahid Ali has pointed out, 'Faiz not only tapped into these meanings but extended them so that Beloved could figure as the revolution' (1995: 80). In condemning the assault on democracy in Pakistan by the imposition of martial law, first by General Ayub Khan (1958–71), and then by General Zia-ul-Haq (1977–88), Omi, too, extends the meaning of the Beloved in his poems to the political. His poetry is marked by a preponderance of 'the absence of the Beloved is Hell' trope; 'sometimes the absent beloved is a woman, sometimes it is democracy, sometimes it is the dreams of youth' (Shamsie, 2005: 326–9). This celebration of Omi's humane revolutionary spirit notwithstanding, just as it refuses to romanticise Samina's activism, as we saw in Chapter 1, the novel rejects an idealisation of the male figure of resistance. It does so not only by describing Omi's initial attempts to objectify Samina and by bestowing an unattractive physical appearance upon him, but also by showing that the Poet is capable of gratuitous cruelty which he directs against Samina's former husband. His artistic prowess came with a degree of contempt for those who do not resist through the act of writing. He was given, as Aasmaani's father reminds her, to 'laughing at those of us who had to go to work for a living. Vertical readers, he used to call us. Because we'd spend our days poring over numbers in columns instead of words written across a page' (2005: 250–1).

In *Broken Verses*, Shamsie presents us with a heterosexual relationship which, after some negotiation, is essentially egalitarian in financial as well as intellectual terms. This is demonstrated by how, upon receiving 'the first major cheque of his life, as prize money for the Rumi Award', Omi promptly transfers the money to Samina's account and she responds 'by signing over the house he lived in to him' (2005: 171).[6] Furthermore, when the Zia government's crackdown on dissenting voices intensifies, knowing that Omi's imprisonment is inevitable, Samina and Omi work together to devise a secret code that would prevent the state from intercepting their letters. In breach of prevailing conventions, they are also united in their disdain for the institution of marriage. But the novel also foregrounds the relational calibrations that Samina has to constantly effect as a female activist. In addition to her initial resistance to being cast in the subservient role of her lover's muse, later in their romance, her independence of spirit collides again with the Poet's when he decides to go into exile for a second time and asks her to accompany him; but, on this occasion, she refuses to join him. Coinciding with the beginning of the final phase of her activism, her refusal is a feminist decision stemming from her desire to remain in Pakistan and to work with the Women's Action Forum to challenge the new Hudood Ordinance, which would further disenfranchise women.[7] However, she soon begins to 'pine' for Omi; upon hearing news of his illness, she leaves immediately, telling her daughter that 'she'd be back in a few weeks', but her absence lasts no less than three years (2005: 93). After a year in Colombia, at her insistence, Omi and Samina move to Egypt to 'discover the feminist traditions within Islam that would allow her to battle the hard-liners' back home in Pakistan (2005: 95). But if Samina is quick to recognise the ideological tensions between her various roles, as I will demonstrate below, her grasp of the practical implications of her identity as a lover, mother and activist is less acute.

Utmost Happiness features a romance between Tilo and Musa who fall in love as college students in Delhi. In sharp contrast to *Small Things*, religious, class and caste identities are strikingly insignificant factors in the romance. Musa is a progressive Muslim while Tilo is the product of an affair between her (estranged) Syrian Christian mother and a Paravan, a man Tilo has never met. It is Tilo, rather than their families or the state, that stands in the way of a traditional happy ending to the couple's love story. She rejects Musa's marriage proposal since she wants to remain 'free to die irresponsibly' (Roy, 2017: 159). Musa then returns to his hometown in Kashmir and becomes a freedom fighter. He falls in love with another woman and has a daughter, both of whom are killed by the Indian military. Months later, at his invitation, Tilo meets Musa in Kashmir, while informing him in no uncertain terms that she is 'not a Kashmiri nationalist'; Musa, however, predicts her conversion to the cause: 'You soon will be. You will be, because I know you. When you see what you see and hear what you hear, you won't have a choice. Because you are you' (2017: 360). Tilo is soon arrested by the armed forces for being an accomplice of a terrorist, and only escapes prosecution by calling upon an old classmate, Biplab Dasgupta, who is Deputy Station Head for the Indian Intelligence Bureau in Srinagar.

Tilo's Kashmiri activism takes several forms: although she rejects the possibility of marriage with Musa, she consents to marry Naga, another former classmate of theirs, for cover. Since he is a journalist with ties with the Indian Intelligence Bureau, their marriage allows her to obscure not only her own involvement in the Kashmiri freedom struggle but also Musa's activities. Her flat in Delhi acts as a repository of notes, witness reports and counterfeit passports for Musa's many identities as an underground militant, as well as a few weapons that he sends her for safekeeping. Then there is the archive that Tilo herself develops, consisting of her own notes and musings about Kashmir over the course of a decade during which she travels back to Kashmir 'obsessively'; it is important to note that these trips are not romantic trysts, but are spent collecting

> scraps of stories and inexplicable memorabilia that appeared to have no purpose ... She had no set task, no project. She was not writing for a newspaper or magazine, she was not writing a book or making a film. She paid no attention to things that most people would have considered important. Over the years, her peculiar, ragged archive grew peculiarly dangerous. (2017: 270)

Tilo's unruly collection of documents can be read as a sort of 'willfulness archive', privileging stories that are not deemed worthy of official accounts of history (Ahmed, 2014: 1). The archive, like the political situation in Kashmir, Tilo notes, is neither orderly nor polished: 'I would like to write one of those sophisticated stories in which even though nothing much happens there's lots to write about. That can't be done in Kashmir. It's not sophisticated, what happens here. There's too much blood for good literature' (Roy, 2017: 283). Just as the Kashmir insurgency, the region and its history resist precise narration, Tilo's romance with Musa defies romantic conventions because of its intermittent nature and its rejection of a joint identity for the lovers, imbued as Tilo is with a sense of independence so fierce that it overshadows even Samina's formidable determination to forge her own identity. Even when Tilo comes to sympathise with the Kashmiri cause, she is oblivious neither to the contradictions within the movement nor to the marginalised positioning of women in Kashmiri society. For instance, when she is told that, as a woman, she is not permitted to attend Musa's friend's funeral, defiant thoughts seethe through her, taking the form of a chant ('*Women are not allowed. Women are not allowed. Women are not allowed*'), puncturing the rhetoric of benevolence that accompanies most patriarchal prescriptions, including those central to her lover's culture and his fight for freedom (2017: 387; emphasis in the original). Upon seeing a photograph of Musa's dead daughter, she does not fail to notice her headscarf; while her tone is light-hearted, the questions that she addresses to Musa are undeniably confrontational, and underscore her acute awareness of how women's clothing often functions as an instrument of patriarchal control:

> 'Did she like wearing a headscarf?'
> 'Arifa?'
> 'No, your daughter.'
> Musa shrugged. 'It's the custom. Our custom.'
> 'I didn't know you were such a customs man. So if I had agreed to marry you, you'd have wanted me to wear one?'
> 'No, Babajaana. If you had agreed to marry me, *I'd* have ended up wearing a hijab and you would have been running around the underground with a gun.'
> Tilo laughed out loud. (2017: 368; emphasis in the original)

Although also light-hearted in its tone, Musa's response suggests that he understands only too well that Tilo is unwilling to compromise on her commitment to gender equality, regardless of the strength of her feelings for him and the Kashmiri cause. Both Tilo and the narrator, then, reject a hierarchy of resistances, whereby a political struggle such as the Kashmiri fight for liberation would take precedence over Tilo's abiding preoccupation with prescriptive gender roles and expectations.

Gauri's relationship with both (militant) collectivist politics and rigid gender roles in *The Lowland* comes across as more ambiguous than Tilo's (and indeed that of the other female characters examined in this chapter). This ambiguity forms part of the novel's broader ambivalence about Naxalism and is reinforced by the relatively limited textual space devoted to Gauri's thoughts on gendered cultural scripts. Lahiri's novel focuses in greater detail on the contours of Udayan's involvement in the Naxalite movement, which serves as the backdrop for his romantic relationship with and eventual marriage to Gauri. In Roy's *Small Things*, we are not given details of the genesis of Velutha's Naxalite identity, only that he suddenly 'disappeared' from Ayemenem for four years, his absence giving rise to the 'inevitable rumour' that he had become a Naxalite; upon his return 'he never talked about where he had been, or what he had done' (1997: 77). The narratological silence with respect to

Velutha's initiation into Naxalite politics arguably suggests that, given his status as an impecunious Dalit, there is little need for an origin story to explain the appeal that such a movement would have for him. Studying at one of Calcutta's top colleges, and although not wealthy, Udayan is by no means disadvantaged like Velutha, making his decision to become a Naxalite far less predictable. Through her portrayal of Udayan's politics, Lahiri relays an important historical fact: the Naxalite movement not only spoke to the impoverished and subaltern classes, but also 'cast a spell on the youth and the students' as well as on members of 'well-to-do families' (Rai and Prasad, 1972: 456). Theirs, as Haridwar Rai and K. M. Prasad argue, 'was a personal penance, an identification with the people' (1972: 456). Udayan's stay in the Bengali countryside, much like Supratik's in Neel Mukherjee's 2014 novel *The Lives of Others*, proves to be crucial to his understanding of the injustices embedded in the Indian economy:

> He'd gone to the countryside to further *indoctrinate* himself … He met tenant farmers living in desperation. People who resorted to eating what they fed their animals. Children who ate one meal a day.
>
> Those with less sometimes killed their families, *he was told*, before ending their own lives.
>
> Their subsistence was contingent *on* arrangements with landowners, moneylenders. *On* people who took advantage of them. *On* forces beyond their control. He saw how the system coerced them, how it humiliated them. (Lahiri, 2013: 336; emphasis mine)

Lahiri's repetitive use of the preposition 'on' and the adverb 'how' is worth noting as it draws attention to the dense web of disadvantageous power relationships that the peasants are trapped in as well as the myriad ways in which the structure of the economy disempowers them. Indeed, these lines complicate Walonen's assessment of *The Lowland* as 'a bourgeois humanist appraisal that largely sidesteps the economic injustices and human rights abuses impelling the movement's challenge to India's inegalitarian capitalist status quo' (2019: 7).

As the just-cited passage indicates, the novel does not shy away from recognising structural oppression, but certain linguistic choices also suggest a narratorial distance from, and discomfort with, the movement and its convictions. To a certain extent, the use of the verb 'indoctrinate' in the passage belies the otherwise sympathetic description of the plight of tenant farmers, conveyed in Lahiri's characteristic matter-of-fact tone. Moreover, the indictment of structural injustices is diminished by the editorialising remark ('he was told'), which casts doubt on the veracity of the statement. Later, on the same page, when Udayan is confronted with the corpse of a young peasant woman, the text tells us that 'here was more proof that the system was failing, that such poverty was a crime'. But, once again, the force of this assertion is deflated by the following sentence, written in the passive voice, which questions the very possibility of restructuring the Indian economy: 'They were told that there was an alternative' (Lahiri, 2013: 336). The novel's equivocal stance on Naxalism is evident also in the passages focusing on Udayan's altruism and innate humanity. For instance, in Chapter 5, the narrative unexpectedly shifts to the consciousness of a neighbour who saw Udayan grow up and recalls his activist compassion for the downtrodden. As a young boy, he took to giving lessons to the children of domestic servants who worked for middle-class families in his neighbourhood: '[H]e befriended these children, eating beside them, involving them in his games, giving them meat from his plate ... he collected worn-out items, old bedding and pots and pans, to distribute to families in colonies, in slums ... But the police had called him a miscreant, an extremist' (2013: 183). However, despite this focus on Udayan's humanitarian instincts and despite the revolutionary backdrop of Gauri's relationship with him, in gendered terms, their budding romance is a fairly conservative one. It adheres to what Suzanna Rose has referred to as the 'adult romance script' in Western literature and popular culture, whereby 'the romantic heroine is a virtuous and unappreciated woman, waiting to be validated and consumed by love' (1985: 254). Until her meeting with Udayan, a college friend of her brother's, Gauri saw herself as an unremarkable woman, not worthy of attention: 'Always at the end of a queue, in the shadow of others, she believed she was not significant enough to cast a shadow of her own. Around men she'd felt invisible' (Lahiri, 2013: 60). Given the importance accorded to fair skin as a criterion of beauty, especially female beauty, in the Indian subcontinent, Samina's lack of melanin makes her conventionally beautiful. In the eyes of 'most Indians', Tilo's dark complexion 'disqualified her straightaway from being considered good-looking' (Roy, 2017: 153). Ammu, too, is dark skinned, but both Tilo and Ammu are still desired and considered attractive by men. In fact, Ammu's beauty draws the unwanted attention of her husband's British employer who encourages him to prostitute Ammu in order to retain his job on the tea plantation. But in Gauri's case, her dusky beauty is something that only Udayan notices and appreciates. It is Udayan and his love for her that renders Gauri distinctive to herself, bestowing upon her a degree of confidence that had always eluded her: 'But Udayan regarded her as if no other woman in the city existed. Gauri never doubted when they were together that she had an effect on him' (Lahiri, 2013: 60). It is also Udayan who reorients her reading tastes, reminding us, to a certain extent, of Virmati's relationship with Harish in *Difficult Daughters*: 'When marches sprouted along College Street, he brought her along. He started giving her things to read. From the bookstalls he bought her Marx's Manifesto and Rousseau's Confessions. Felix Greene's book on Vietnam' (2013: 58). The presence of a chain of knowledge, however, does not preclude a genuine exchange of ideas between them: 'They exchanged the limits of political freedom, and whether freedom and power meant the same thing. About individualism, leading to hierarchies. About what society happened to be at the moment, and what it might become. She felt her mind sharpening, focusing' (58). Gauri is not a mere receptacle for Udayan's ideas and beliefs and her relationship with him thus seems more egalitarian in intellectual terms than Virmati and Harish's. But it is difficult to ignore that, during their courtship, even as she delights in the honing of her mind, this intellectual activity helps Gauri, above all else, to feel 'closer to Udayan' (2013: 58). By 'thinking about the things that mattered to him', she is able to 'bridge the physical distance between them during the days that they are apart' (2013: 59). As Pierre Bourdieu wonders, is heterosexual love 'an exception … to the law of masculine domination, a suspension of symbolic violence, or is it the supreme – because the most subtle, the most invisible – form of that violence' (2001: 109)? When Udayan asks her if she would support his decision to leave for the countryside 'to live among the peasants', the power imbalance is visible to both Gauri and us as readers (Lahiri, 2013: 59). He is subjecting her to a sort of love test, gauging her commitment to him and to the cause, effectively preventing her from voicing her thoughts for fear of alienating his affections:

> She was aware that he was testing her. That he would lose respect if she turned sentimental, if she was unwilling to face certain risks. And so, though she did not want him to be away from her, did not want any harm to come to him, she told him she would. (2013: 59)

Since Gauri is an orphan, she is not shackled by the strictures of familial pressure and expectations, and their marriage is arguably more transgressive for Udayan than it is for her. He marries 'a woman of his own choosing', rather than showing respect for custom which dictates that it was his 'parents' place to decide'; moreover, he disrupts cultural and familial norms by taking a wife before his elder brother does (2013: 47). The parents grudgingly accept Gauri as their daughter-in-law, and it is only after Udayan's death that they unleash their fury upon her. Paradoxically, Udayan's decision to marry at all is subversive in itself since matrimony seemed too conservative a life choice for someone 'so dedicated to his politics, so scornful of convention' (2013: 47). In showing how Udayan can inhabit both convention *and* conventional male behaviour, alongside radical politics, *The Lowland*, like *Broken Verses*, troubles the perhaps too-neat equation between revolutionary politics and enlightened romantic love that we find in *Small Things*.

At Udayan's behest, Gauri gathers intelligence and delivers notes that allow the Naxalites to orchestrate the policeman's killing. But the narrator casts Gauri as primarily an unsuspecting cog in the militant machine. She is willing to accept 'the benign version' of events that Udayan offers her and smothers 'the stray particle of doubt, the mute piece of her that suspected something worse' (2013: 320). The novel actively foregrounds Gauri's innocence, but also, contradictorily, provides us with evidence that throws into doubt the extent of her ignorance, not least because she is also shown to be highly intelligent. The injuries that Udayan sustains in the weeks before his death – one of his hands and eardrums are damaged while assembling a pipe bomb – testify to the violence that characterised his contribution to the Naxalite cause, and while he takes care to keep his parents in the dark, he *does* tell his wife 'what had really happened' (2013: 107). Moreover, despite the description of the movement in the novel as 'misguided', paradoxically, some of

Gauri's memories and thoughts recounted towards the end of the novel imply that first, Gauri was *not* entirely indifferent to communist politics and, second, that Udayan's values (and thus the movement) *were* rooted in a legitimate desire for a more just society. As an older woman, Gauri wistfully recalls participating in a rally with Udayan, listening to the communist politician Kanu Sanyal, and the euphoria that his words elicited in her: she 'remembered the single emotion she'd felt a part of. She remembered being thrilled by the things he'd said' (2013: 281). I would argue that the indictment of Naxalism in the novel comes into conflict with the narratological demands of relating a convincing love story which would preclude constructing Gauri as a blind follower of Udayan's instructions and her work for the Naxalite movement as resulting from traditional notions of female submission. In the just-cited extract, by allowing Gauri to express a degree of sentimentalism for the Naxalite movement, and by mobilising what Lila Abu-Lughod has referred to as the 'romance of resistance' (1990), the novel does not so much dilute its critique of Naxalite politics (for in the very next paragraph, in the voice of an academic, the movement is dismissed as 'unrealistic'), but rather seeks to bestow an ennobling tenor upon Gauri and Udayan's essentially inegalitarian and fairly conventional relationship (Lahiri, 2013: 279).

Motherhood, romance and resistance

Alerting us to the ambiguous relationship between motherhood and activism, Annalise Orleck argues that 'it is impossible to speak about motherhood without speaking of social systems of power and domination' (1997: 5). While acknowledging that motherhood 'is an individual and highly personal experience', she contends that it can be 'the basis for inclusion in an activist community, the inspiration for and the foundation of visions of large-scale social change' (1997: 3–5). However, a conservative, preserving-the-peace approach can also accompany motherhood, 'quieting and grounding even the most rebellious of women' (1997: 3). Ammu, Samina and Gauri are biological mothers, while Tilo adopts a young baby girl who was abandoned by her activist mother. Only Gauri gives birth to a child, Bela, who was fathered by her activist partner. But romantic love, the idea and practice of maternity, and resistance are closely interlinked in all four novels.

In *Small Things*, despite Ammu's contestation of class-, caste- and gender-driven hierarchies, her parenting style, though by no means devoid of love and tenderness, can be remarkably unforgiving of her children's deviations from a rigid code of conduct which she demands they live by, with homework corrections shot through with intimidatory language: 'I will punish you very severely if you disobey these instructions' (Roy, 1997: 158–9). Moreover, when the twins fail to show the necessary amount and form of deference to Ammu and resist her parental authority in public, she threatens them with banishment: 'I will see to it that you are sent away to somewhere where you will jolly well learn to behave' (1997: 148). Given her own marginalised positioning in Keralite society, it is through her children that Ammu attempts to prove her worth in society. She is committed to demonstrating that, if nothing else, she is a capable mother who possesses the skills required for raising well-behaved children, in defiance of the cultural logic that dictates that a paternal presence is necessary for the well-being of the children, no matter how ill-equipped the male may be to assume a parental role. The at-times punitive tenor of her parenting, whereby she makes her love for the twins conditional upon their compliance with her commands, deepens her children's existing insecurities. Rahel is especially prone to monitoring and attempting to quantify the amount of love that Ammu feels for her: '"D'you know what happens when you hurt people?" Ammu said. "When you hurt people, they begin to love you less..." A cold moth with unusually dense dorsal tufts landed lightly on Rahel's heart ... A little less Ammu loved her' (1997: 112). Ammu's clampdown on her children's innocent defiance brings home to us not only her own imperfect parenting, but also her feelings of powerlessness from which much of this style of parenting seems to stem. She lashes out against her children who are even more marginalised than her, sometimes alternating between hypercritical overparenting and an impatience with the obligations of maternal love. In fact, one of the sources of her aunt Baby Kochamma's hostility towards Ammu is that motherhood *did not* quiet and ground her rebelliousness, as she continues 'quarrelling with ... the fate of the wretched man-less woman', refusing to accept her divorce as the end of her sexual existence (1997: 149). In one scene, where Estha and Rahel play with her body, Ammu reasserts her right over her physical being and resists the demands of motherhood: 'Ammu grew tired of their proprietary handling of her body. She wanted her body back. It was hers. She shrugged her children off the way a bitch shrugs off her pups when she's had enough of them' (1997: 224). She seeks refuge in the bathroom from this suddenly invasive filial love and subjects her body to close scrutiny, deeply preoccupied with the spectre of her waning desirability: 'Withered breasts that hung like weighted socks. Dry as a bone between her legs, the hair feather white. Spare. As brittle as a pressed fern. Skin that flaked and shed like snow. Ammu shivered' (1997: 222). By turning the lock in her bathroom door, Ammu shuts out the twins to dwell on her sexual identity, inviting a reading of erotic love and maternity in oppositional terms. But Roy does not see motherhood, resistance and erotic love as being mutually exclusive since Ammu comes 'to love by night, the man her children love by day' (1997: 44). As I have noted elsewhere (Mirza, 2016: 66–7), Ammu recognises Velutha as a sexual being and a potential lover when she sees him playing with her daughter: 'The man standing in the shade of the rubber trees with coins of sunshine dancing on his body, holding her daughter in his arms, glanced up and caught Ammu's gaze' (Roy, 1997: 175). Velutha and Ammu's radical politics are thus aligned and their love for each other brings with it the ultimately thwarted hope of a more fulfilling kind of parental and familial love. *Small Things*, as Anuradha Dingwaney Needham explains, 'situates Ammu and Velutha's relationship within a nexus of another set of relationships, which could (in a not yet possible future) come to constitute an alternative, more enabling family and form of community' (2005: 385).

The tensions between mothering, romantic love and activism are far starker in *Broken Verses*. Samina does not abdicate motherhood the way that Gauri does in *The Lowland*, but in leaving Aasmaani's father to live with Omi, and in embracing activism with gusto, she becomes at once a semi-absent and a ubiquitous mother: as a child and then teenager, Aasmaani's primary carers are her father and kindly step-mother, yet her mother's activism, and her revolutionary lover, make her the more exciting of the two parents in Aasmaani's eyes. The young Aasmaani loves Samina as much as she hero-worships her, which also prevents her from expressing her resentment at having to, on numerous occasions, play second fiddle not only to Samina's public commitments but also to the Poet whom she joins while he is in exile. Aasmaani recalls her mother's words, dismissing the validity of a cultural narrative which sees motherhood and activism as being incompatible: 'I would not allow them to tell me there was a choice to be made between motherhood and standing up for justice' (Shamsie, 2005: 90). Certainly, while Aasmaani was an infant, romantic love, maternity and activism did overlap relatively easily, with Samina taking baby Aasmaani with her to 'courtrooms, prisons, lawyer's offices' as she fought to have the Poet released when he was arrested for criticising the army's atrocities in East Pakistan (2005: 90).

Patricia Jeffrey has highlighted the pitfalls of political mobilisation around motherhood, including the ease with which 'motherhood may be turned against women ... when domestic mismanagement and social chaos are blamed on "bad" mothers' and the limited space that such activism leaves 'for negotiating the conditions under which women become (or choose not to become) mothers' (Jeffrey, 1998: 225). But, like Orleck, Jeffrey also acknowledges how 'motherhood has sometimes been a very effective vehicle for women's political mobilization' (1998: 225). No doubt influenced by Samina's strong views on the subject, even as a young girl (as pointed out in Chapter 1), Aasmaani refused to accept that the cultural 'truth' that the *only* legitimate justification for a woman's decision to pursue activism – resulting in long absences from her child's life – was that her activism would make the world a better place for her offspring. But, by extension, both Samina and Aasmaani also discount the validity of motherhood-driven, and even motherhood-informed, activism, privileging instead an almost romantic notion of 'pure' activism; they paradoxically undermine what has been one of the main tenets of modern feminist thought, that the personal *is* political, which surely calls for an acknowledgement of the political potential of motherhood.

Samina not only refuses to equate motherhood with activism, but she also rejects the mother/sexual being dichotomy, not concealing her appetite for sex from her daughter: 'She laughed her wonderful, unabashed laugh. "Sweetheart, I can't stop being a woman just because I'm your mother"' (Shamsie, 2005: 203). Aasmaani's use of the adjective 'wonderful' while describing her mother's lack of embarrassment indicates that she was in resounding agreement with her about women's sexual needs. But the intrusion of romantic love upon their mother–daughter relationship in terms of time as well as energy is clearly something that Aasmaani struggles to accept and, while her mother was still alive, she could never bring herself to ask her: 'But what about the choice to be made between motherhood and romantic love?' (2005: 90). In its absorbing meditation upon the competing pull of motherhood, romance and activism, the novel sheds light on how, for Samina, a woman who defied binary identities and reductive gendered roles, and whose irrepressible social conscience informed so many of her life decisions, recognising the *practical* rather than the ideological tensions between her various roles proved to be more challenging.

Gauri's abandonment of her child in *The Lowland* has been the focus of numerous reviews and articles, with Delphine Munos arguing that, through Gauri's character, the author has sought to 'give voice, representability, and legitimacy to a female character for whom motherhood can only intensify the catastrophic loss represented by Udayan's execution' (2017: 362). I would contend that Gauri's response to motherhood needs to be read not only in the context of her husband's execution but also of her complicated activist past in India. Facing hostility from her parents-in-law, Gauri, who is pregnant at the time of Udayan's death, drifts into marriage with Subhash and moves to the US. She harbours mixed feelings for her late husband, which include love and longing, as well as anger at being implicated in the policeman's death. Moreover, she is racked by guilt in the early years of Bela's life as she struggles to bond with her: 'She was not only ashamed of her feelings but also frightened that the final task Udayan had left her with, the long task of raising Bela, was not bringing meaning to her life' (Lahiri, 2013: 164). The memory of the brutal fate suffered by Udayan and his fellow activists colours how she perceives her daughter and contributes to her decision to abandon her daughter; Bela reminds her not only of the love that she shared with Udayan, but also of their failed activism. The narrator draws attention to the disturbing discordance between the apparently uncomplicated joys of her familial life with Subash and Bela and the violence that the Naxalites in Calcutta were subjected to:

> Gauri remembered how happy he had been ... for a whole week he'd stayed home with Bela, making a holiday of it ... Then she remembered another thing. How, at the height of the crackdown, the bodies of party members were left in streams, in fields close to Tollygunge. They were left there by the police, to shock people, to revolt them. To make clear that the party would not survive.
> The school bus was approaching. (2013: 169)

As she sees Bela off on an uneventful day of the week in Rhode Island, her American present is invaded by violent images from her Indian past. For Gauri, the requirements of motherhood and the minutiae of her hastily cobbled-together nuclear family can gloss over neither the specific pain of Udayan's death nor the general trauma resulting from the failure of the Naxalite movement.

Kalyan Nadiminti sees Gauri's resistant subjectivity as emerging only *after* her immigration to the US and her decision to dedicate her life to 'intellectual labor' as her primary act of resistance, arguing that it represents 'a willful rebellion from the expectations of reproductive labor and maternal caregiving' in the context of post-1965 United States (2018: 241–3). While Gauri's abandonment of Bela and Subash can arguably be seen as a refusal to 'overwrite her first husband's death at the hands of the postcolonial state', it is more difficult to also see it, which Nadiminti invites us to do, as a refusal to subscribe to 'national ideations of immigrant kinship' fostered by the US Immigration and Nationality Act of 1965 which prioritised family reunifications (2018: 243). In fact, in choosing a career in academia, Gauri does not cease to be a 'caregiver'; as the narrator tells us: 'her job was not only to teach students but to mentor them, to know them' (Lahiri, 2013: 233). She comes to adopt a quasi-maternal role with her students, inviting them to her apartment, 'making tea for them on Sunday afternoons', listening to their personal problems, 'telling them not to worry', effectively becoming 'an alternate guardian to a few', which makes it difficult to perceive her rejection of Bela as a conscious, wilful response to US policy making (2013: 233). Moreover, Gauri's is a largely apolitical existence in the US as she remains detached from collectivist contestations of the status quo around issues of race, gender, sexuality and immigration. In fact, we see Gauri eventually lamenting her 'Western' research interests, centred as they are on the work of male European philosophers such as Schopenhauer and Horkheimer, bearing little relation to her activist past in India:

> Her ideology was isolated from practice *neutered* by its long tenure in the academy. Long ago she'd wanted her work to be in deference to Udayan, but by now it was a betrayal of everything he had believed in. All the ways he had influenced and inspired her, shrewdly cultivated for her own *gain*. (2013: 234; emphasis mine)

The use of the word 'gain' occurs in condemnatory tones in this passage which lends itself to being read as an implicit critique of neo-liberal capitalism (of which the university is very much a part), and perhaps as an acknowledgement of the more humanist goals underpinning communist thought, if not practice. Similarly, the term 'neutered' is a charged one, suggesting Gauri's dissatisfaction, rather than contentment, with her life in academia and her abandonment of Naxalite politics.

In fact, it is Bela, the daughter he did not live to meet, who arguably keeps Udayan's legacy alive through her social work. Reading it as a sign of Udayan's 'inspiration' and 'influence', Subhash observes with some alarm that 'there was a spirit of opposition to the things' Bela did; she is shown to be deeply sensitive to the 'unequal distribution of wealth' and the lives that it destroys: 'She was spending time in cities, in blighted sections of Baltimore and Detroit. She helped to convert abandoned properties into community gardens. She taught low-income families to grow vegetables in their own backyards, so that they wouldn't have to depend entirely on food banks' (2013: 224–5). Bela's activism can be described as 'developmental social work' with its emphasis on organising locals and promoting 'their involvement in community projects that improve health, nutrition, literacy and infrastructure' (Midgley, 2011: 24–5). While both characters are driven by unhappiness with inequality and the human suffering it causes, Udayan's political activities did not preclude recourse to violence and represented a direct challenge to state power, while Bela's social work operates within existing societal parameters. Moreover, Bela embraces single motherhood, her parenting style fiercely different from Gauri's and aligned with her activism. I do not mean to underestimate the importance of the kind of social work that Bela does or to belittle the activist sensibility that she embodies. However, it is worth noting that the novel holds up Bela's activism, which does not challenge the moral legitimacy of the modern American state, as not only humane and ethically sound, but also as visibly effective, in contrast to her father's failed Naxalite resistance. By tying in Bela's political concerns solely with the 'unequal distribution of wealth' and hence ignoring how class inequality in the US intersects with other forms of oppression, notably racism, the novel avoids addressing the limitations of Bela's variety of activism, particularly in the context of the harrowing and multifaceted structural oppression faced by peasants, Dalits and other subjugated groups in India who found hope in the Naxalite movement. Arguably, in inviting us to see the affinities between father and daughter, the novel seeks to further validate Udayan and Gauri's romance since it produces Bela: the 'right' kind of activist, and the possibility of a reunion between Bela and Gauri, which is hinted at towards the end of the text, is meant to further erode the tensions between Udayan's politics and romantic love, to which I return in the final section of the chapter.

In *Utmost Happiness*, Tilo chooses to 'adopt' a baby girl, years after having an abortion when she became pregnant by Musa. Tilo kidnaps the baby who has been abandoned by her biological mother at Jantar Mantar in Delhi. Thus Tilo's activist motherhood, much like her activism in support of the Kashmiri cause, is steeped in illegality. In naming her Miss Jebeen the Second (Miss Jebeen being the moniker that Musa chose for his daughter), Tilo creates a network of familial links that bind her not only to Musa, but also to everything and everyone that he loves, even the child that he fathered with another woman. In addition to this activist genealogy that Tilo bestows upon her, Miss Jebeen the Second comes with her own inheritance of protest politics: her mother was a Maoist who fell pregnant following her gang rape by the Indian military.[8] The novel thus extends its critique of the postcolonial Indian state and further exposes its fictional unity by drawing attention to movements other than the Kashmiri liberation struggle that it has sought to quash, strategically deploying gendered violence to silence dissent.

We learn that Tilo's decision to terminate her pregnancy and not have a child with Musa stemmed from her unhappy childhood and the neglect and abuse that she suffered at the hands of her mother: 'She did not trust that she would be a better mother than Maryam Ipe. Her clear-eyed assessment of herself was that she'd be a far worse one. She did not wish to inflict herself on a child. And she did not wish to inflict a replication of herself on the world' (Roy, 2017: 391). Her love for her adopted child is strikingly devoid of proprietary feeling; having found her, Tilo realises that 'she could not remember when last she had been this happy. Not because the baby was hers, but because it wasn't' (2017: 138). It is telling that the ending of the novel leaves us with an image of communal mothering, with Miss Jebeen the Second finding a home in Jannat Guest House, a makeshift shelter located in a graveyard and run by Anjum, an intersex character. The inhabitants of Jannat Guest House, all marginalised beings, 'close ranks around Miss Jebeen the Second like a formation of trees, or adult elephants – an impenetrable fortress in which she, unlike her biological mother, would grow up protected and loved' (2017: 426). It is a form of mothering that defies the compulsory logic of biology, and Roy's conscious recasting of motherhood is bound up with her atypical conception of romantic love in the text, which I discuss below.

Death, doomed love and 'failed' resistance

Each of the four texts under consideration presents us with an example of an ostensibly doomed romance, with either one or both of the lovers dying prematurely. In all four novels, the male protagonist's death is a result of state violence; however, in contrast to Shamsie's and Roy's novels, despite its ambivalence towards the Naxalite movement, Lahiri's text ultimately does not challenge the legitimacy of this violence. In contrast to the other three novels, the lovers' relationship in *Small Things* is particularly short-lived, ending with Velutha's killing soon after his affair with Ammu is discovered, the swiftness of which can be read as a searing indictment of the combined power of patriarchal, casteist and classist prejudice.

While both the Poet's and Samina's deaths take place off-stage, and their bodies are not identified, Omi's extrajudicial execution represents a politically and narratologically unequivocal death – he is a martyr to his cause, his murder by state agents retribution for his anti-establishment poetry. Samina's depression and suicide, on the other hand, not only highlight the ultimately debilitating primacy of romantic love in Samina's life, but also bring to the fore the ways in which the trajectory of a female activist eludes a precise ending: having lived an unconventional life as the Poet's unmarried lover, Samina's grief is not considered 'legitimate' as she is denied the public solace that would have been extended to her as his widow. Her grief, because of its unconventional nature and its consequent lack of recognition, is reminiscent of Sara Ahmed's definition of 'lesbian grief'. As Ahmed argues, 'when lesbian grief is not recognized, because lesbian relationships are not recognized, then you become nonrelatives. You become unrelated; you become not. You are alone in your grief. You are left waiting' (2016: 219). And this waiting, this *becoming not*, compounds Samina's suffering following Omi's death. In fact, following their lovers' demise, both Ammu and Samina fight to perform what can perhaps be described as precarious mothering, which entails carrying out, or attempting to carry out, their duties as mothers, despite not being mentally and/ or physically equipped to do so. The Poet's death reduces Samina to 'an almost coma-like state, lying in bed, her eyes fixed on nothing'; she hangs on to 'an intolerable existence for two years' because of Aasmaani, before she is seen 'walking towards the sea' (Shamsie, 2005: 273). I argue that, despite her feminist credentials, because Samina's activism is shown to be so closely entwined with her love life, the Poet's death signals the end of her activism *and* presages her death. The text thus invites us to see romantic love as both empowering and limiting because of its all-consuming nature.

In *Small Things*, once Velutha's relationship with Ammu is exposed, a trio of public and private institutions (the police, the Communist Party and the family) join forces to eliminate his threatening presence. The narrator's description of the injuries that the 'posse of Touchable policemen' inflict on him is distinctly clinical in its tone:

> His skull was fractured in three places. His nose and both his cheekbones were smashed, leaving his face pulpy, undefined. The blow to his mouth has split open his upper lip and broken six teeth, three of which were embedded in his lower lip, hideously inverting his beautiful smile ... His spine was damaged in two places. (Roy, 1997: 310)

The lone reference to Velutha's beautiful smile briefly punctures the detached quality of the narration, accentuating the viciousness of the attack. His battered body dramatises his physical vulnerability resulting from his resistance to the status quo – the kinds of resistance that Velutha enacts are performed through the body: most obviously in his sexual relationship with Ammu, but also through his active, shouting presence at the Naxalite demonstration. As Butler reminds us, 'those who gather to resist various forms of state and economic power are taking a risk with their own bodies, exposing themselves to possible harms … vulnerability is enhanced by assembling'; yet vulnerability necessarily 'emerges earlier, prior to any gathering' (2016: 12). It is Velutha's acute awareness of his own socio-economic vulnerability in Keralite society that leads him to become a Naxalite and to participate in protests, which in turn accentuates his bodily vulnerability by making him a visible target, but also allows him to overcome it 'at least provisionally' by carving out not only a 'platform for political expression' but also for a tangible embodied political presence that the state cannot ignore (2016: 12–13).

In the penultimate chapter of the novel, the bourgeois family and the police collude to destroy his reputation: Velutha dies in a filthy cell at the local police station, after Estha is manipulated by Baby Kochamma into falsely claiming that Velutha abducted him, his sister Rahel and their English cousin Sophie Mol. Velutha is also held responsible for Sophie's accidental death, and his consensual relationship with Ammu is recast as rape, which, for Ammu's family, is a more palatable version of events. Thus, the institutional powers not only seek to eliminate him physically, but also to effect an erasure of his resistant subjectivity. Through its depiction of Velutha's death, the novel alerts us to how resistance movements in the so-called public sphere are inseparable from the artificially demarcated private sphere, and how recorded accounts of subaltern resistance are themselves reflective of the threat that it represents; manipulation, blackmail and spectacular lies of omission and commission are deployed by institutional forces, as readily as brute force, in an attempt to not only physically squash any challenge to their authority, but also to overwrite and expunge the very memory of that challenge.

Ammu's death in a hotel room follows a few months later and is also closely entwined with the workings of institutional power. Her 'Unsafe Edge' becomes blunted and 'the reckless rage of a suicide bomber' that she appeared to inhabit instinctively seems all but gone in her last days, blighted as they are by the loss of her lover, the trauma of separation from her children and the physical ravages of tuberculosis (Roy, 1997: 44). If the Poet's death causes Samina to become clinically depressed, Velutha's death results in the slow and painful disintegration of Ammu's body, with Rahel summing up her impressions of her mother in three adjectives: 'Wild. Sick. Sad' (1997: 159). In Aijaz Ahmad's estimation, Ammu's death is an authorial failing on Roy's part; he argues that '[i]f Ammu were to live on, she would have to face the fact that the erotic is very rarely a sufficient mode for overcoming real social oppressions' (2007 [1997]: 116). I would contest Ahmad's observation that Roy does not let Ammu 'live on' after Velutha's death – she does after all survive her lover by several months – but there *is* a shift in the kind of defiance that Ammu embodies following her lover's murder. If the sharp-tongued, sensuous Ammu seems all but extinguished, she does exhibit considerable fighting spirit in her final months, her resistance aimed at ensuring her own and her children's survival. Once her affair with Velutha is discovered, Ammu is banished from the familial home and is actively de-mothered by her family, with Estha 'Returned' to his father and Rahel sent away to a boarding school (Roy, 1997: 9). In the aftermath of this ostracisation, Ammu's mode of resistance becomes distinctly economic in nature as she enters the labour market and, despite her debilitating illness, tries to hold down a series of low-paid jobs. She is determined to become financially independent, which in turn would allow her to reunite with her children. The description of her corpse and the Church's refusal to bury Ammu 'on several counts' underscore how her body remains a site of resistance even after her death:

> Ammu died in a grimy room in the Bharat Lodge in Alleppey, where she had gone for a job interview as someone's secretary. The sweeper found her in the morning ... She had a blue sac under one eye that was bloated like a bubble. As though her eye had tried to do what her lungs couldn't. (1997: 162)

That Ammu dies while attempting to find yet another job brings to the fore the multi-layered quality of her resistant subjectivity, and, contrary to what Ahmad asserts, both Ammu and the narrator clearly do recognise that erotic love is 'rarely a sufficient mode for overcoming real social oppressions' (2007 [1997]: 116). As such, through its ending, the extended love scene on the banks of a pristine Meenachal river, which would later, following India's adoption of neoliberal economic policies, become heavily polluted, smelling of 'shit and pesticides bought with World Bank loans', the novel foregrounds the magic of resistance and the necessity of it (Roy, 1997: 13). But it also appears to see resistance, whether in the form of an insurgency or erotic love, as only momentarily effective, offering temporary respite in the face of structural oppression.

It could be argued that Samina's and Ammu's resistant subjectivity lives on in their progeny, but such a claim has greater applicability to Shamsie's novel than it does to Roy's. Estha and Rahel's incestuous love-making can be read as an echo of their mother's transgressive eroticism, breaking as it does the Love Laws that 'lay down who should be loved, and how. And how much' (1997: 328). That said, the narrator makes it clear that this is an act born of 'hideous grief' and is largely stripped of the emancipatory power of Ammu and Velutha's coupling (1997: 328). On the other hand, as we saw in Chapter 1, to a large extent Aasmaani reunites ideologically with her mother at the end of the novel; the documentary on the Hudood Ordinances that she is shown to be working on suggests the return of an oppositional sensibility. Moreover, the audio and video recordings of her mother that Aasmaani is able to access leave open the possibility of an enduring legacy of feminist resistance, one that could extend beyond the familial and become part of the country's heritage. Therefore, despite the tragic deaths of the two lovers, Shamsie's novel is more optimistic, though by no means sanguine, about the power of resistance, as compared to *Small Things*.

Like the Poet and Samina, Musa's is an off-stage death, in that his death is not described in the novel. But it is also an 'off-stage' death in that, rather than narrating it as an event in the past, Roy makes use of free indirect discourse and prolepsis, 'marked by a tense which indicates a future event in relative terms while remaining in the past' (Currie, 2007: 34), to present us with Musa's passing as seen through his own eyes, while lying in Tilo's arms during their last night together on his final visit to New Delhi:

> He would leave for Kashmir the next morning, to return to a new phase in an old war from which, this time, he would not return. He

would die the way he wanted to ... He would be buried the way he wanted to be – a faceless man in a nameless grave. (Roy, 2017: 437)

Musa foresees that his imminent death and the passing of his generation will bring in their wake more violent, less sophisticated forms of resistance: 'The younger men who would take his place would be harder, narrower and less forgiving. They would be more likely to win any war they fought, because they belonged to a generation that had known nothing but war' (2017: 437). In her 2008 article 'Azadi: it's the only thing Kashmiris want. Denial is delusion', Roy noted that '[h]undreds of thousands of unarmed people' in Kashmir had come out to 'reclaim their cities, their streets and mohallas',[9] overwhelming 'heavily armed security forces by their sheer numbers, and with a remarkable display of raw courage' (2008b: 16).[10] She saw those protests as a sign of the young generation having discovered 'the dignity of being able to straighten their shoulders and speak for themselves, represent themselves' (2008b: 16). But the nonviolent protests did not pave the way for Kashmiri liberation; as Roy points out in her more recent essay 'India: intimations of an ending': '[t]he Indian government has made it clear that the only option for Kashmiris is complete capitulation, that no form of resistance is acceptable – violent, nonviolent, spoken, written, or sung. Yet Kashmiris know that to exist, they must resist' (2019: n.p.). The novel foreshadows India's growing colonial ambitions in the region marked by the suspension of Article 370 of the Indian Constitution in 2019, signalling the de facto annexation of Kashmir by India and, consequently, the increasingly essentialist and existential nature of Kashmiri resistance.[11]

If Roy's second novel highlights the contradictions of resistance, it also brings to the fore the paradox of oppression: it is not only the colonised Kashmiris who bear psychological scars, but also colonising Indians. On his final trip to Delhi, Musa points out to his erstwhile classmate Biplab who, as an Indian Intelligence Officer, functions in this conversation as a stand-in for the Indian state: 'You may have blinded us, every one of us, with your pellet guns by then. But you will still have eyes to see what you have done to us. You're not destroying us. You are constructing us. It's yourselves that you are destroying' (Roy, 2017: 433). Much more than *Small Things*, without contesting the legitimacy of the liberation movement,

Utmost Happiness ruptures the romance of resistance by pointing not only to the unsavoury aspects of the freedom struggle, but also to how the dichotomy between oppressed and oppressor, coloniser and colonised can become blurred, reminding us of Ashis Nandy's *The Intimate Enemy*, where he argues that:

> modern oppression ... is not an encounter between the self and the enemy, the rulers and the ruled, or the gods and the demons. It is a battle between dehumanized self and the objectified enemy, the technologized bureaucrat and his [sic] reified victim, pseudo-rulers and their fearsome other selves projected on to their 'subjects'. (1983: xvi)

Musa's speech addressed to Biplab has more than a whiff of the performative, as Musa is clearly seeking to provoke him. But Musa's words also convincingly point to the chillingly self-destructive nature of oppression, echoing Roy's observations in her non-fiction: 'India needs azadi from Kashmir just as much – if not more – than Kashmir needs azadi from India' (2008b: 24). Musa's words are meant to be a warning and a threat, and they succeed in unsettling Biplab who, unaware of the doubts riddling Musa, wonders: 'What if he's right? We've seen great countries fall into ruin virtually overnight. What if we're next in line?' (Roy, 2017: 433). This is yet another example of the psychological warfare that Musa deploys by alerting the oppressors to the limits of their power and to the perils of their colonial ambitions which could turn them into 'camouflaged victims, at an advanced stage of psychosocial decay' (Nandy, 1983: xvi). In her review of Roy's second novel, Parul Sehgal observes that '[t]he world she conjures is often brutal, but never confusing or even very complex. Manichaean dualities prevail: innocence (embodied by puppies, kittens, little girls) versus evil (torture, torturers, soldiers, shopping malls)' (2017: n.p.). I would argue instead that Roy's novel, without neglecting the very real implications of power asymmetries, complicates the oppressor–oppressed duality not only by underscoring the many contradictions that characterise the Kashmiri freedom struggle but also by pointing to how the practice of oppression traumatises both the victim and the perpetrator.

In the just-cited excerpt from the novel, Musa denies that the Indian state is destroying Kashmir, but this claim suggests a bravado on Musa's part which is belied by his conversations with Tilo in which he fulminates against the pernicious effects of the Indian military occupation on the Kashmiri psyche. Moreover, the words that he addresses to Biplab imply a level of optimism about the efficacy of the Kashmiri resistance movement that is at odds with Musa's fears about the schizophrenia that the occupation has bred in the Valley, and the 'standardiz[ation]' of Kashmiri identity that it has necessitated (Roy, 2017: 370). Musa laments that the Indian military occupation and the resultant resistance movement has compelled his compatriots to 'think the same way, want the same thing … do away with our complexities, our differences, our absurdities, our nuances … we have to make ourselves as single-minded … as monolithic … as stupid … as the army we face' (2017: 370–1). The novel points to the dilemma faced by identity-based movements which, in order to become a viable political force, feel compelled to foreclose internal debate, dissent and difference. As Biddy Martin and Chandra Mohanty point out, 'stable notions of self and identity are based on exclusion and secured by terror' (1986: 197). Both Tilo's and Musa's discomfort with the reductivist nature of the Kashmiri struggle is reinforced by the novel's many contextual passages which set out the exclusionary terms of the movement with respect to sectarian affiliation and gender. As the narrator tells us, the arrival of Islamic militants in Kashmir from Pakistan sent a clear message to the Kashmiri population:

> No more worshipping of home-grown saints and seers at local shrines … There was one way of praying, one interpretation of divine law and one definition of Azadi … in future, all arguments would be settled with bullets. Shias were not Muslim.[12] And women would have to learn to dress appropriately. (Roy, 2017: 320)

Spivak has famously invoked the utility of *strategically* deploying 'positivist essentialism' in the service of 'a scrupulously visible political interest' (1985: 342).[13] Over the last three decades or so, scholars, particularly those working within the fields of feminist and queer studies, have continued to wrestle with the function that essentialist discourse can serve in political mobilisation. For instance, Joshua Gamson points out that '[q]ueerness spotlights a dilemma shared by other identity movements (racial, ethnic, and gender movements, for example): Fixed identity categories are both the basis for oppression and the basis for political power' (1995: 391). Roy's second novel, I contend, brings to the fore how, rather than choosing to do so, the majority of Kashmiris have been coerced into adopting an essentialist identity by the twin presence of the Indian army and Islamic militants. Nyla Ali Khan notes that, historically, 'Kashmiris have taken pride in inhabiting a cultural space between Vedic Hinduism and Sufi Islam' and in being able to 'synthesize not just cultural but religious practices as well' (2010 [2009]: 40). This 'syncretism of Kashmir' is under direct threat from the militant nature of the Kashmiri struggle with its *compulsory* essentialism which is accompanied by the spectre of self-destruction, rather than political autonomy (Roy, 2017: 320). As Musa muses despondently, the 'standardization' of Kashmiris will make them 'impossible to defeat. First it will be our salvation and then … after we win … it will be our nemesis. First Azadi. Then annihilation. That's the pattern' (2017: 371). Towards the end of the novel, in celebrating Tilo's heterogenous activism, the narrator further points to the ultimate futility of resistance based on rigid identities. But, just as her non-fiction underscores how the well-established tactics of nonviolent resistance are not always available to the poorest of the poor, Roy's second novel underlines how the freedom to practice a non-essentialist, syncretism-friendly variety of resistance may not be available to all oppressed peoples, and this – a nuanced existence and resistance – is partly what Musa is fighting for while, paradoxically, continuing to operate within a framework which only allows for a collectivist resistance based on a reductive notion of Kashmiri identity.

Musa's, then, is a necessarily unsuccessful resistance, not merely because he personally does not live to see his beloved Kashmir rid of the Indian military, but also, as we saw above, because of the self-destructive mode of the Kashmiri freedom struggle itself. But the novel refuses to conflate failed resistance with doomed romance. Lisa Lau and Ana Cristina Mendes have argued that Roy's deployment of the trope of failed or doomed romance in fiction is 'a postcolonial strategy which enables her fiction to engage with India's insistent and oppressive othering of individual [sic] and minority and poverty-stricken groups' (2022 [2019]: 104). This observation has a certain applicability to Roy's first novel, but, in *Utmost Happiness*, rather than mobilising doomed love as a trope, Roy compels us to revisit the very meaning of an ill-fated romance by choosing to highlight the plurality of love and, by extension, the plurality of resistances. As the narrator tells us in the passage describing Musa and Tilo's conversation about his deceased wife: 'It was possible for Tilo and Musa to have this strange conversation about a third loved one, because they were concurrently sweethearts and ex-sweethearts, lovers and ex-lovers, siblings and ex-siblings, classmates and ex-classmates' (Roy, 2017: 267–8). Much like how the novel recasts motherhood as a communal vocation, Roy's depiction of Musa and Tilo's love story challenges the primacy of romantic love by showing how it can jostle with other cherished values and other loves.

At the end of the novel, in joining Anjum's motley congregation at Jannat Guest House, Tilo's activism becomes entwined with a collective identity which, unlike Musa's, is based on difference, rather than on a standardised collective self. In addition to contributing to Miss Jebeen the Second's upbringing, she starts giving lessons to children from impoverished families, but we learn that 'she didn't teach her own pupils to sing "We Shall Overcome" in any language, because she wasn't sure overcoming was anywhere on anyone's horizon' (2017: 398). The narrator leaves us with no doubt that when the time comes, 'Tilo [will] grieve deeply at Musa's passing but [will] not be undone by her grief' the way Samina was, and that she will persevere with her activism (201: 437). The narrator emphasises the strength of the spiritual bond that holds Musa and Tilo together, making it possible for them to communicate beyond death: 'She was able to write to him regularly and visit him often enough through the crack in the door that the battered graveyard held open (illegally) for her' (2017: 437). Jannat Guest House functions as a subaltern counterpublic sphere, to deploy Fraser's terminology, where not only are identities and roles reimagined, but also a plethora of resistant subjectivities are allowed to flourish, allowing Tilo to maintain an almost mystical attachment with Musa while embracing a type of resistance which is very different from his. It is at Jannat Guest House that Tilo finds peace and happiness, with Roy deploying capital letters to highlight her deliberate reconfiguration of the standard happy ending of romances: 'Instinct told her that she may finally have found a home for the Rest of Her Life' (2017: 305).

Finally, I turn to Lahiri's depiction of Udayan's death. While maintaining third-person narration, it is through Udayan's consciousness

Revolutionary love and the romance of resistance 83

that the final pages of the novel are related to us: the closing sections of the novel take the form of an extended flashback homing in on the moment when Udayan finds himself surrounded by paramilitary officers, and then going further back in time as Udayan revisits the circumstances surrounding his involvement in Naxalite politics, the suffering that he witnessed in the Bengali countryside and his budding romance with Gauri, only to return to the day of his death. We see him weighing Che Guevara's words ('Remember that the revolution is the important thing and that each of us alone is worth nothing') and concluding that 'in this case it had fixed nothing, helped no one. In this case there was to be no revolution. He *knew* that now' (Lahiri, 2013: 334; emphasis mine). Factive verbs, as John I. Saeed explains, 'presuppose the truth of their complement clause', and the use of the factive verb *know* in this extract is meant to erase any doubt about the futility and unviability of Naxalism, when, in fact, it has refused to die down (2009: 107). If the insurgency was brutally crushed in the early 1970s, as Pratul Ahuja and Rajat Ganguly explain, 'the Naxalite movement began to revive in the 1980s' (2007: 257). It continues to spread today since the 'the causal conditions – such as poverty, inequity and caste discrimination – which led to peasant discontent and agitation in the first 30 years after independence still remain strikingly pervasive' (2007: 257).

Udayan's is a summary execution at the hands of paramilitary soldiers, but the edge of this extrajudicial violence is blunted in the narrative by showing his acceptance of the justness of his own killing:

> He'd known from the beginning the risk of what he was doing, but only the policeman's blood had prepared him. The blood had not belonged only to the police officer, it had become a part of Udayan also. So that he'd felt his own life begin to ebb, irrevocably, as the policeman lay dying in the alley. Since then he'd waited for his own blood to spill. (Lahiri, 2013: 339)

Malreddy notes that 'the novel invests heavily in the idiom of Udayan's death as the ultimate outcome of Naxalism' (2016: 228). This focus on an urban, middle-class individual effectively elides the suffering of subjugated groups whose involvement in the movement was a direct response to a deeply entrenched and profoundly exploitative *rapport de force* and who went on to bear the worst brunt of the state violence directed against the insurgency. The Naxalite movement becomes ultimately telescoped into this one act of *anti-state* violence, which is deployed to illustrate not only the moral untenability of the movement, but also, and perhaps more problematically, the justness of the state's response to the rebellion. As such, this focus on the policeman's death and Udayan's dismissal of the Naxalite movement pushes the suffering of the subjugated groups to the background, making the policeman's life in the narrative 'disproportionately more livable and grievable than others' (Butler, 2020: 17).

As he surrenders to the paramilitary, Udayan is pained to see the 'look of disillusion' on Gauri's face, a look that leaves no room for anger at *state* oppression; it casts Udayan's involvement in the Naxalite movement as a betrayal of the purity of their romance, 'a revision of everything they'd once shared', proving that he had been 'no hero to her' (Lahiri, 2013: 339). In fact, Udayan's damning assessment of the Naxalite movement before his death combined with his acceptance of his extrajudicial execution works as a cleansing force in the text, returning him to a prelapsarian state: as he lies dying, it is a vision of Gauri and a memory from their early days of marriage that gently enter his consciousness. The closing lines of the novel read as follows: 'Gauri stood in front of him wearing a peach-coloured sari ... His head angled down, his hand forming a canopy between them to shield her face from the sun. It was a useless gesture. Only silence. The sunlight on her hair' (2013: 339). With resistance to structural oppression being dismissed as pointless, Udayan is rewarded with a sunlit vision of uncomplicated heterosexual romance. In ending with this rosy image of their relationship, the novel glosses over the gender disparity that marked Gauri and Udayan's relationship. Ultimately, it not only obscures its, albeit uneven, engagement with the inequalities that led to the Naxalite uprising, but also rejects radical resistance on theoretical, ethical and practical as well as *romantic* grounds.

Despite the at-times stark ideological differences among them, the four novels underscore the aptness of romantic love as a lens for coming to grips with the idea and practice of resistance, not only because of its transgressive potential and the contradictions that it can encompass, but also because its emotional and affective charge finds an echo in any passionate opposition to the status quo. If romance and radical politics are almost seamlessly aligned in *Small Things*, when taken together, the four texts disrupt a reading of romantic love as being inherently and necessarily subversive, presenting us with a complex picture of the affinities as well as the tensions between romance and collectivist action. Moreover, although not always intentionally, and indeed sometimes quite problematically (as shown in my analysis of *The Lowland*), the texts foreground how no discussion of heterosexual romantic love and activism can afford to circumvent a consideration of gendered imperatives, whether literary or extra-literary.

Notes

1 The interview can be accessed at www.youtube.com/watch?v=BOoRjBzGoUE (Accessed: 23 February 2022).
2 The state of Jammu and Kashmir has been a bone of contention between India and Pakistan since the departure of the British in 1947 left undecided the fate of this Muslim-majority area under Hindu princely rule. By signing an instrument of accession in October 1947, the Hindu Maharaja gave India jurisdiction over the state's external affairs, defence and communications; the legitimacy of the instrument was immediately contested by Pakistan. The scramble for Kashmir led to the de facto partitioning of the region in 1949, two-thirds of which came under Indian, and the remainder under Pakistani, rule; this tussle has brought in its wake no fewer than three wars and numerous skirmishes between India and Pakistan over the decades.
3 *Azadi* (Urdu): freedom.
4 The Naxalites formed the Communist Party of India (Marxist-Leninist) in 1969; E. M. S. Namboodiripad, co-founder of the Communist Party of India (Marxist), declared them to be 'completely bankrupt politically and organisationally' (1994: 235).
5 'Nazim' is Omi's pseudonym and is a homage to the Turkish Poet Nazim Hikmet.
6 Samina, unlike Omi, was born into money and inherits two adjoining houses from her father. She and Omi live separately in the two houses that share a gate, effectively living together without co-habiting.
7 The platform of the Women's Action Forum, formed in 1981, was the 'rejection of the Hudood Ordinances, the Law of Evidence, and other religiously-motivated legislation, and of attempts to segregate universities' (Mumtaz and Yameena, 1996: 46).

8 Some of the factions which the original Naxalite movement split into include Party Unity, CPI (ML) People's War and Janashakti. The Communist Party of India (Maoist) was formed in 2004 by the merging of CPI (ML) People's War and the Maoist Communist Center (Bihar). See also Malreddy (2016: 220–2).
9 *Mohalla* (Urdu): neighbourhood.
10 The demonstrations referred to in Roy's essay took place in response to the transfer by the Indian government of forest land in Kashmir to the Amarnath Shrine Board; the transfer led to a dramatic increase in the number of Hindu pilgrims travelling to Kashmir and was seen by Kashmiris, the majority of whom are Muslim as 'an aggressive political statement by an increasingly Hindu-fundamentalist Indian state' (Roy, 2008b: 15).
11 In August 2019, Indian Prime Minister Narinder Modi repealed Article 370 which had given 'Indian-administered Kashmir some autonomy, including the right to craft limited local policy and to deny outsiders the right to acquire land there, which many Muslim Kashmiris saw as protection against Hindus from the rest of India moving to the region, changing its demographics, and undermining its push for independence' (Salam, 2019: n.p.).
12 Kashmiri Muslims predominantly belong to the Sunni sect of Islam.
13 Perhaps equally famously, Spivak distanced herself from the phrase 'strategic essentialism' only a few years later because she felt that it had become 'the union ticket for essentialism' (Danius, Jonsson and Spivak, 1993: 35).

3

'Ordinary' defiances and the short story

> Novels are read by people who have money, and those who have money also have time. Short stories are written for ordinary people, who have neither money, nor time.
>
> – Premchand, translated by Shital Pravinchandra, 2018

> The great thing about a short story is that it doesn't have to trawl through someone's whole life; it can come in glancingly from the side.
>
> – Emma Donoghue, quoted by Ian Seed (2016)

Drawing on the Indian writer Premchand's observations about the short story, Shital Pravinchandra alerts us to the 'fundamental link between socio-economic class and literary genre' (2018: 199). As we will see, the short stories examined in this chapter suggest that this genre, particularly when operating within a broadly realist mode, is especially apt for representing acts of resistance which are executed by ordinary individuals who are confronted with the very concrete implications of being short on either time or money, or indeed both, and for charting defiances which are geared towards the attainment of personal, though not necessarily selfish, goals, rather than 'long-term structural change' (Scott, 1985: 247). These short stories underscore the emotional vulnerabilities that come with the contestation of the domestic status quo and with the negotiation of affective ties; as I will demonstrate, it is often a negotiation that is enacted, to borrow Emma Donoghue's words, glancingly from the side. The short stories under discussion allow us to not only explore the constraints of time and money encountered by women, but also the societal constructions of women's relationship with time and money. This in turn invites us to reflect on the relationship between labour, identity and gendered resistance.

In *Contemporary Feminism and Women's Short Stories*, Emma Young argues that the formal characteristics of the short story that facilitate feminist critique are: open endings, ambiguity, voice, time and brevity (2018: 13). In particular, Young contends that the ambiguity of short stories, stemming from both characterisation and open endings, can work to 'challenge representations of gendered identity and the boundaries of sexuality', making the genre a 'viable literary vehicle for contemporary women writers' negotiation of feminist politics' (2018: 4). In a related vein, the short stories under consideration in this chapter show us how the four authors 'have utilised the short story's capacity of narrative and character ambiguity' to complicate representations of gendered resistance and the boundary separating resistance from acquiescence, vocal and visible forms of resistance from those that are shrouded in secrecy and silence, as well as principled acts of rebellion from morally dubious ones (2018: 13). These short stories also sound a warning against interpreting an individual woman's agency as 'an individualist endeavour', linked as it is to 'relational gender dynamics and the agency of the others within the household' and, I argue, to the wider community (Banerjee, 2017: 35).

The four stories under discussion, Fernando's 'Of bread and power', Ahmad's 'A day for Nuggo', Lahiri's 'The treatment of Bibi Haldar' and Koshy's 'Almost Valentine's Day', are set in Sri Lanka, Pakistan, India and the United States respectively, each featuring a female protagonist. The action of each of the four texts takes place in a micro-setting, which is thrown into relief by the narrative's explicit or implicit interpellation of wider geographical configurations, whether it is the city, the nation-state or diasporic spaces. With respect to time and temporality, however, we see a different tendency at work: even when the short story covers a span of several years, as is the case in 'The treatment of Bibi Haldar', which charts the eponymous protagonist's changing positionality in what appears to be a small town near Calcutta, it still exhibits a 'proclivity to fragmentariness' and tends to describe 'moments instead of processes' (Patea, 2012: 12). Fernando's story unfolds for the most part within the confines of a lower-middle-class home in the city of

Matara, and centres on a few months in the life of Seela, who, to her parents' dismay, 'was still unmarried' at twenty-six years of age (1994: 23). Ahmad's 'A day for Nuggo' charts the several weeks' long struggle of a Christian domestic servant working in an upper-class Muslim home in Lahore as she attempts to assert her right to a day off. And finally, Koshy's 'Almost Valentine's Day' describes the weeks following the arrival of a lower-class Indian woman, Aruna, in the United States to work as a domestic servant for a middle-class Indian family. Writing in 1995, Lal argued that 'while most women's writing around the world over deals with the problematics of domestic relations, Indian women writers in English dwell specifically and unilaterally in this area' (1995: 21). The works considered in this chapter, too, are concerned with 'the problematics of domestic relations', but also with the permeability of the line separating the so-called domestic and public spheres, generating forms of resistance that may be personal in nature, but nevertheless entail a redefinition of the protagonist's relationship with herself and a wider collective identity.

Familial economics, non-conformity and happiness

In 'Of bread and power', Seela faces an aggressive form of othering within her familial home, with her parents seeing her as a 'burden' both in financial and cultural terms (Fernando, 1994: 34). When the short story opens, Seela has already been 'inspected by several prospective husbands', but 'pleased none of them' (1994: 29). Seela's parents' animosity stems from a patriarchal conception of parent–daughter relationships according to which a young girl's parental home is only a temporary abode, her rightful place in the world being her husband's or her parents-in-law's house, and it is the parents' responsibility to ensure that their daughter is married off at a culturally determined 'appropriate' age so that she can fulfil her destiny as well as her duty as a woman of being a wife and mother. As we will see, Seela resists conforming to the narrow gender roles prescribed by her family and the wider community, and her defiance takes the form of an often-painful redefinition for herself of what Cathy Cohen (2004: 38) refers to as 'the rules of normality that limit the dreams, emotions and acts of most people'.

Seela's parents prevent her from pursuing further education, and instead encourage her to learn the conventionally feminine skills of flower making and batik work, skills which are likely to be unthreatening to the patriarchal status quo and (consequently) carry the potential to enhance a woman's value on the arranged marriage market. But, with the help of her seventy-three-year-old grandmother, who suggests that she start teaching, Seela is able to redefine the political and economic significance of these skills:

> Twice a week she was the centre of intense activity on the back veranda. Under her direction, jasmine, roses and lilies bloomed out of stiffened cloth and bits of wire. A tiger, tense with feral power, crouching among spiky plants under a glowing orange sun, sprang to life on ordinary cotton cloth. She felt strength, power rise within her.
> (Fernando, 1994: 30)

Creative work becomes an unexpectedly lucrative source of income for Seela; it also restores her self-confidence and reinforces her faith in her own capabilities. Moreover, the juxtaposition in the just-cited passage of the visual softness of the flowers, the rigidity of the cloth and wire, the regal ferocity of the tiger and the mundanity of cotton work to underscore how closely emotional vulnerability, domestic ordinariness and resistance are entwined for Seela. This is especially so since her newfound independence intensifies her parents', particularly her mother Agnes's, hostility towards her: 'Here was another woman sleeping under *her* roof, eating *her* food, having a life of *her own* which had nothing to do with her, Agnes Hamine' (1994: 32; emphasis mine). As the repetitive use of the possessive pronoun 'her' and her reference to her own daughter as 'another woman' suggest, Agnes sees her adult unmarried daughter as an interloper in the familial home and has decided to abandon the language of parental benevolence and familial love. It is her daughter's agency, both temporal and monetary, which represents a challenge to Agnes's parental authority, rooted as it is in a deeply hierarchal understanding of familial relationships. Agnes resents Seela's teaching activities as they take up 'more and more time' and allow Seela to earn 'good' money from what were essentially hobbies that had been imposed upon her (1994: 30). Seela's parents see her rejection of a marriage proposal as a further affront to the patriarchal order of things, causing her father to wash his hands off her: 'there was nothing more he could do for her' (1994: 31). The parental oppression that Seela faces takes the form of active withdrawal of affection as well as emotional manipulation: Agnes tries to browbeat her into accepting the marriage proposal by accusing her of being 'selfish' and by seeking to diminish her self-worth: 'a woman of nearly twenty-six with your face can't be too particular' (1994: 31).

When these attempts fail, Agnes tries to convince Seela by pointing out that the suitor 'doesn't mind all this cloth-painting and flower-making' and that she would be able to continue working after marriage, an argument which unabashedly subscribes to patriarchal logic which deems that it is a woman's father's, and then upon marriage, her husband's prerogative to decide whether or not she can perform paid labour outside the home (1994: 31). Seela's creative growth is shot through with the discovery of the undeniably conditional nature of her parents' love for her and is marked by a painful sense of loss: 'When she was a little girl, her father used to lift her high in the air, so she could pick the mangoes off the lower branches of the tree. How safe she had felt in his arms then!' (1994: 34). Seela is shown to directly confront her parents and vocalise her resistance on only two occasions (the latter of which I will discuss in greater length below). The first instance is at the beginning of the text when in response to her mother's repeated criticism of Seela's nose and dark colouring and her subsequent lack of desirability on the marriage market, Seela points to the obvious fact of their shared genetic makeup and resulting physical resemblance: 'Is your skin or nose any better than mine, Mother? Tell me that' (1994: 29). Her mother responds by accusing her of being disrespectful and an ingrate (and later a bad Buddhist), a view that her aunt seconds, and together they succeed in silencing Seela. But through its use of indirect discourse, the short story makes us privy throughout to her thoughts which indicate the strength of Seela's resolve not to succumb to familial pressure, despite often saying nothing: 'Seela was not to be crushed. Father, Mother, Auntie – she would never marry just to please them, and they could all stand on their heads if they wanted to. They hadn't wanted her to study, so let them put up with her now' (1994: 30–1).

Seela's contestation of parental authority and, by extension, patriarchal discourse blurs the line separating defiance from negotiation and is reminiscent of Medina's conception of resistance; as

Medina argues, resisting is not 'always a matter of opposing from the outside' and '[i]t can feel more like being pulled in different directions from the inside, like being torn from within' (2013: 16). Even though she does not give in to parental pressure with respect to marriage, she does submit to a number of other demands that her parents circuitously make on her, which include paying her parents for her board and lodging and eventually also covering her grandmother's cremation expenses. Tellingly, her parents do not expect their eldest son Upali, who is a doctor, to make similar financial contributions. Her parents justify their discriminatory behaviour in unapologetically sexist terms and remind Seela of the importance of maintaining Upali's 'status as a doctor' (Fernando, 1994: 35). The use of indirect discourse in the short story poignantly brings to the fore Seela's struggle as she attempts to live up to the image of the 'dutiful daughter' upheld by her parents and the wider community, while also refusing to silence the increasingly loud demands of her own conscience:

> Excepting in the matter of the marriage proposal, she had obeyed her parents all her life; she had been bound to them by all the ties and obligations of a daughter. No, she couldn't leave unless her parents gave her their permission to. On the other hand, she didn't see why she shouldn't leave and have her parents' permission too. (1994: 36)

The strength of Seela's determination not to submit to an arranged marriage is juxtaposed against her desire to spare her parents the indignity of a scandal which her departure from the parental home to take up a job at a batik shop in Colombo would cause. Her parents' opposition to her moving to another city is rooted in a desire to save face in a community where a young woman's independence is perceived as an affront to parental authority and a daughter's departure from the parental home is expected to coincide with her marriage (to a man of the parents' choosing): 'Women of respectable families didn't live in strange boarding-houses far from home. It was a disgrace. Seela was continually trying to rub soot on their faces' (1994: 35). Her father makes clear to her that should she move to Colombo, he would no longer wish to see her. In the face of such blatant emotional blackmail, Seela's enduring desire to maintain ties with her parents makes her resistance less dramatic, though perhaps more realistic, than if she were shown to relinquish what is only an appearance of familial feeling between them by leaving for Colombo without their approval. Seela recognises that while 'she would be among strangers' in Colombo, 'those at home were even greater strangers' and thus is able to see through romanticised notions of family and home (1994: 35). But Seela also rejects the possibility of a clean break from her family, pointing to the difficulty of effecting such a categorical rupture in relationships where biology, love, reputation and duty, but also money and happiness, are inextricably bound up with each other. In her exploration of the role played by the idea of happiness in perpetuating gender inequities, Sara Ahmed alerts us to how 'happiness scripts' in patriarchal societies provide 'a set of instructions for what women and men must do in order to be happy, whereby happiness is what follows being natural or good' (2010: 59). The happiness that Seela yearns for necessarily entails a deviation from the prevailing happiness script, but she is unwilling to jettison this script entirely or to exist hermetically outside it. Her younger brother Tissa's decision to pursue a degree in architecture in Colombo provides a solution to this dilemma as it allows Seela to leave her parental home without precipitating the formal demise of her relationship with her parents. Seela strategically offers to rent a house in Colombo, where Tissa would also reside, thus sparing her parents the expense of paying for his accommodation; she also promises to send them one hundred rupees every month to help cover part of his course fees. This financial offering, coupled with the knowledge that the other residents of the town are aware that, in keeping with patriarchal convention, they oppose Seela's growing independence, results in a temporary softening of her parents' oppositional stance and facilitates Seela's exit: 'The whole town knew how strongly they'd disapproved of Seela's plans. Their reputation as careful conscientious parents was quite secure. So now, if Seela wanted to go, she could go' (Fernando, 1994: 36).

Fernando's depiction of Seela's resistance rests on a recognition of the untenability of a binary understanding of familial politics. It blurs the line dividing appeasement and defiance; it also rejects a simplistic chosen family versus biological family dichotomy and refuses to present familial relationships in necessarily oppositional terms, or indeed the joint family as a necessarily regressive social arrangement. If Seela draws immense strength from her work, her relationship with her younger brother and her grandmother is no less significant: 'Seela squeezed his hand gratefully. He often helped her with her drawings and with the waxing of her batik work … As long as she had her grandmother and him on her side, she felt she could face anything' (1994: 32). Seela's new blended family in Colombo includes friends, but also her younger brother, and her sense of belonging to it is bolstered by her grandmother's memory and values. For Seela's new friend Somie, the struggle for happiness and freedom should entail the disavowal of 'all this grandmother talk of *karma* and *sansara*',[1] but since her grandmother's support played a defining role in the emergence of Seela's resistant subjectivity, she does not see her fight for greater autonomy as an intergenerational conflict: 'Our grandmother was a very wise woman. She knew who she was and what she wanted' (1994: 37). Moreover, if Seela is shown to be subjected to gender-based discrimination in her family home, the short story steers away from privileging solidarity based purely on gender, not only by showing us how Seela's mother actively seeks to curtail her daughter's life choices, but also by presenting both her grandmother and her brother as her allies in her fight for greater autonomy. Indeed, the short story highlights the impossibility of individualist resistance, even in a micro-setting, and makes a compelling case for cross-gender, cross-generational alliance-building to combat patriarchal practices and discourse.

As the short story draws to a close, it becomes evident from the taunts directed at Seela during her visits home that her parents and relatives still find her wanting as a dutiful daughter. They see her happiness, which depends heavily on spatial, financial and creative freedom, rather than on parental approval, to be especially inimical to the fulfilment of her daughterly duties. Her aunt's remarks are meant to be a threat and a rebuke as well as an attack against the happiness script that Seela has forged for herself: 'You may have a bank account but you are a woman with no husband, no children … Leaving your parents' home to lead a *gay life* in Colombo! You're nothing. You'll know it when you have no roof over your head' (1994: 36; emphasis mine). Seela's response signals a subtle turn towards a less placatory form of resistance, attesting to her growing self-confidence: 'Seela laughed. "Don't worry about me, don't worry. Don't you forget, I have a bank account. So I can build my own house, if I want to"' (1994: 37). Seela thus challenges the patriarchal logic underpinning her aunt's observations and punctures the veneer of concern which is meant to disguise her aunt's malice. Seela's confrontational words and laughter notwithstanding, it is clear that her aunt's words succeed in wounding her as, upon returning to Colombo, she hastens to recount this exchange to Somie. When probed by Somie as to whether she agrees with her aunt's assessment that she 'wasn't a dutiful daughter', Seela responds categorically in the negative ('"No", said Seela very firmly, "no I don't"'.), which causes Somie to 'enthusiastically' announce that Seela was 'one of [them]' (1994: 38). She goes on to declare that together they 'would build a society based on justice, freedom and friendship' and all 'be like brothers and sisters' (1994: 38). In fact, Somie misreads the philosophical implications of Seela's response: rather than contesting the importance of being a dutiful child and rejecting familial ties, Seela's resistant subjectivity entails redefining what it means to be a good daughter while also facing up to the very material limitations of familial love. Perhaps it is Somie's reference to familial bonds ('brothers and sisters') as a political ideal that Seela recoils from in particular: '"No", said Seela. "I – I want to be like my grandmother. She had no illusions. And even when she had no money and no power she knew what to do. I want to be a good designer and understand myself and other people"' (1994: 38).

This disagreement between Seela and Somie, however, concludes amicably with neither woman imposing her opinion on the other. The closing lines of the short story see Seela and her friends settling down around a table to eat and 'to talk about what they pleased'; these lines underscore Seela's success in experiencing the kind of happiness and fulfilment which was denied to her in her parental home, but they do not elide the struggles that may well lie ahead of her (1994: 38). The hesitation in Seela's voice as indicated by the initial stuttering in the just-cited passage suggests that the process of self-discovery is far from over for her. In moving to Colombo, Seela succeeds in becoming financially and spatially independent of her parents, but she appears to see this as only one step towards understanding her own place in the world which, for her, remains intimately bound up not only with her work but also with other people, including those who may not share her worldview.

'Disability', speech and silence

For several decades now, fiction by South Asian anglophone women writers has displayed an enduring preoccupation with how an arranged marriage, both the event itself and the expectation of it, can function as a deeply oppressive force in a woman's life. Kapur's *Difficult Daughters* examined in Chapter 1 is only one such example; others include Anita Desai's *Cry, the Peacock* (1963), Bharati Mukherjee's *Wife* (1975), Bapsi Sidhwa's *The Bride* (1983), Jaishree Misra's *Ancient Promises* (2000), Chandani Lokugé's *If the Moon Smiled* (2000), Samina Ali's *Madras on Rainy Days* (2004) and Fernando's 'Of bread and power', as we saw above. In 'The treatment of Bibi Haldar', however, we witness a reversal of this trope with the eponymous character, a young orphaned woman who appears to suffer from epilepsy, shown to often demand, rather than dread, much less resist, an arranged marriage. The *Oxford English Dictionary* defines 'disability' as a 'physical or mental condition that limits a person's movements, senses, or activities' (2022: n.p.). In choosing to use the term 'disability' within quotation marks while discussing Bibi's condition, I wish to recognise that epilepsy, if that is indeed what Bibi suffers from, can be considered a disability when it, as the Epilepsy Society (UK) reports, 'greatly affects someone's ability to do everyday activities … over a long period of time', and to draw attention to the extent to which Bibi's condition is *perceived* as a disability by those around her, limiting the everyday activities she is permitted to carry out and the dreams that she is allowed to dream.[2]

Bibi's disability results in a distinctly gendered form of ostracisation as she is not considered fit or worthy of the milestones that mark the conventional path laid out for the other women in her building: marriage, motherhood and middle-class domesticity. As the sociologist Nandini Ghosh notes, '[t]he ideal type of the good girl, a woman who is physically unimpaired, beautiful and capable of physical labour, plays an important role in the representation of disabled women as un-marriageable' in India (2018: n.p.). Of the four protagonists examined in this chapter, Bibi's life is arguably the most restricted, both spatially and temporally. Her condition, the narrators note, confines 'her world to the unpainted four-story building in which her only local family, an elder cousin and his wife, rented an apartment on the second floor' and 'her daily occupation', which consists of recording inventory and managing her cousin Haldar's cosmetics shop, requires her to 'sit in the storage room on the roof' of the building, further confining her to 'a space in which one could sit but not comfortably stand' (Lahiri, 2000 [1999]: 159). She receives 'no income' for working at her cousin's shop, and 'her cracked plastic slippers' and old housecoat speak of her marginalised socio-economic positioning within the family (2000 [1999]: 159). Bibi's life's trajectory is expected to remain, unlike that of other women, unmarked by either biological reproduction or productive labour. Far from resigning herself to discriminatory social constructions of her time, we see Bibi frequently and noisily voicing her discontentment and demanding that those around her recognise the injustice of the treatment meted out to her: 'I ask you, is it fair for a girl to sit out her years, pass neglected through her prime, listing labels and prices without promise of a future?' (2000 [1999]: 160). If the female speaker in Kamala Das's famous poem 'An introduction' rebels against the social edicts that command her to 'dress in sarees, be girl/be wife ... Be embroiderer, be cook,/be a quarreller with servants', Bibi Haldar yearns for these very trappings of conventional femininity (2014 [1965]: 6). This 'ordinary' aspiration, inflected through the intersection of gender, disability and cultural perceptions of gendered disability, lies at the heart of Bibi's resistant subjectivity: 'She wanted to be spoken for, protected, placed on her path in life. Like the rest of us, she wanted to serve suppers, and scold servants, and set aside money in her *almari* to have her eyebrows threaded every three weeks at the Chinese beauty parlor' (Lahiri, 2000 [1999]: 160).

The narrators describe Bibi's condition in the following words: 'Liable to fall unconscious and enter, at any moment, into a shameless delirium, Bibi could be trusted neither to cross a street nor board a tram without supervision' (Lahiri, 2000 [1999]: 159). The categorisation of Bibi's delirium as 'shameless' testifies to the female narrators' complicity in patriarchal discourse which sees the female body as a repository of communal honour. Moreover, the inadvertent lack of self-restraint that accompanies Bibi's paroxysms, causing her to pound her fists, kick her feet and sweat profusely, invokes the spectre of the hysterical woman.[3] In her discussion of the ever-changing definition of hysteria and the wide range of signs and symptoms associated with it over the centuries, Carroll Smith-Rosenberg has noted that '[t]he one constant in this varied history has been the existence in virtually every era of Western culture of some clinical entity called hysteria; an entity which has always been seen as peculiarly relevant to the female experience, and one which has almost always carried with it a pejorative implication' (1972: 652). While the construction of hysteria in the Indian subcontinent as a distinctly female malady arguably cannot be traced back to Western influence and British colonialism alone, the 'most strident gendering' seems to have happened 'as a result of 19th century encounters with British medicine'.[4] By declaring that 'marriage would cure her' (Lahiri, 2000 [1999]: 161), Bibi's doctor echoes both the Hippocratic texts that declared that hysteria can be 'cured by intercourse and/or childbirth, to which marriage and pregnancy are the necessary precursors' (King, 1993: 24) and the cultural belief in the Indian subcontinent that marriage is 'a cure for different forms of mental disorders ranging from hysteria to psychoses' (Behere et al., 2011: 288). As steeped as this prognosis is in dodgy science and patriarchal constructions of womanhood, it also has the unintentional effect of validating Bibi's deepest desires. It is only now that the narrators, having earlier dismissed Bibi as 'not pretty', suddenly begin to notice 'the clarity of her complexion, the length and languor of her eyelashes, the undeniably elegant armature of her hands' (Lahiri, 2000 [1999]: 160–2). But Haldar and his wife do not consider Bibi deserving of the financial sacrifice ('feeding guests, ordering bracelets, buying a bed, assembling a dowry') that joint families conventionally make to fund the wedding of an able-bodied female relative (2000 [1999]: 164).

Bibi's othering by her own relatives is compounded by cultural perceptions of people with disabilities as inauspicious: Haldar's wife believes that the 'devil himself possessed' Bibi and that she was 'contagious, like the pox' (2000 [1999]: 163–7).[5] When Haldar's wife becomes pregnant, Bibi is no longer permitted inside the flat and is made to sleep in the storage room, and the treatment meted out to her mimics the mores of untouchability which underpin the caste system: 'In the bathroom Bibi was given separate soaps and towels' and 'Bibi's plates were not washed with the others' (2000 [1999]: 167). Later, when the baby arrives, Bibi is forbidden to touch the baby girl, and when the child falls ill, Haldar and his wife accuse Bibi of having 'infected' the child (2000 [1999]: 170). Since marriage, motherhood and domestic duties are upheld as integral aspects of womanhood in her community, Bibi's exclusion from these roles and activities, despite their deeply constraining and limiting nature, represents a denial of her sexuality, especially since a heterosexual (arranged) marriage is often seen as the only legitimate arena where a woman is allowed to exist as a sexual being. As the female narrators note while evaluating Bibi's female credentials and, by extension, her marriageability: 'Bibi had never been taught to be a woman ... She had not been taught to wear a sari without pinning it in four different places, nor could she embroider slipcovers or crochet shawls with any exceptional talent' (2000 [1999]: 163). The veracity of Simone de Beauvoir's famous proclamation, '[o]ne is not born, but rather, becomes a woman' (2014 [2009]: 146), is amply demonstrated in the text which charts the role of socialisation in the construction of gender identities and alerts us to how gender as an identity is 'instituted through *a stylized repetition of acts*' (Butler, 1988: 519; emphasis in the original). But Lahiri's text also suggests that, for a disabled woman like Bibi, the absence of such a socialisation and an exclusion from culturally valid and recognisable ways of existing as a woman can work to magnify her marginalisation within her own community, especially when other models of acceptable womanhood are unavailable.

Lahiri's choice of a first-person plural narrative voice, which I invoked in the Introduction, corresponds to the perspective of a group of women living in Bibi's building. I drew attention to the allegorical quality that the narrative voice lends to the short story without compromising its realism: it allows us to appreciate the wider meaning of Bibi's marginalisation and resistance, beyond her 'individual story and its particularized circumstances' (Anjaria, 2012: 62). Fitz posits that its 'lack of particular identity', 'anonymity' and 'oneness' invites readers 'to question the authenticity of the narrative voice' (2005: 117); I would argue that Lahiri's narrative technique encourages readers to not only question the reliability of the narrative voice, but also to ponder the extent of its complicity in the prevailing norms and values, effectively underlining both the importance and limitations of collective gendered resistance. The narrating women are undeniably sympathetic to Bibi's plight: they attempt to offer her solace and lovingly groom her; when, after the birth of his child, Bibi's cousin's neglect of her takes on cruel overtones, they vote with their feet and cease to patronise his shop, thereby succeeding in driving him out of business. But they, too, clearly see Bibi as the 'Other': '[S]he was not our responsibility, and in our private moments we were thankful for it' (Lahiri, 2000 [1999]: 167).

Lahiri's short story is distinctive not only because of the subversive tenor of Bibi's perfectly conventional desires, but also because of the large number of speech acts that are attributed to her in the text, as well as the remarks made by other characters about Bibi's speech and indeed her language. In 'Can the subaltern speak?', Spivak concluded that '[t]he subaltern as female cannot be heard or read' (1988: 308). In a later interview, she clarified that 'even when the subaltern makes an effort to the death to speak, she is not able to be heard, and speaking and hearing complete the speech act' (Spivak, Landry and MacLean, 1996: 292). In Bibi Haldar we have a subaltern figure who is striking for her determination to be heard. This determination manifests itself in her 'louder than necessary voice', but also in the wide variety of speech acts that she performs (Lahiri, 2000 [1999]: 160). At certain points in the story, we see her exercising what Ruvani Ranasinha refers to as her 'anarchic agency' by entertaining bystanders with private details of her cousin and his wife's life (2016: 189); at others, she presents herself as a figure of pity and expresses hopelessness: 'I will never be cured, never married' (Lahiri, 2000 [1999]: 161). At yet other points, she challenges societal perceptions which seek to reduce her identity to her condition by methodically listing the maladies from which she *does not* suffer, thus foregrounding her *ableness*: '"Apart from my condition I am perfectly healthy", she maintained … "I have never had a cold or flu. I have never had jaundice. I have never suffered from colic or indigestion"' (2000 [1999]: 167). She painstakingly catalogues the responsibilities, tasks and activities underpinning the conventionally defined fantasy of female happiness which has been denied to her because of her disability. Bibi's listing in the form of rhetorical questions what are traditionally held to be female and feminine preoccupations poignantly underscores both the sense of deprivation that marks her life as well as her abiding need for this deprivation to be recognised as unfair by those around her: 'Is it wrong to envy you, all brides and mothers, busy with lives and cares? Wrong to want to shade my eyes, scent my hair? To raise a child and teach him sweet from sour, good from bad?' (2000 [1999]: 160). Bibi does not challenge the patriarchal 'assumption that happiness follows relative proximity to a social ideal' (Ahmed, 2010: 53); instead, her resistance takes the form of vying, *despite her perceived disability*, for the social ideal that other women are expected to achieve as a matter of course. As Ghosh reminds us, disabled young women in India are often 'excluded from gendered notions of sexuality' which affects the way they 'adapt and deal with culturally valued notions of femininity, desirability and attractiveness' (2018: n.p.). Bibi's wilfulness then is a protest against a value system that dictates that she is 'not even entitled to be proximate' to the fantasy of female happiness (Ahmed, 2010: 51).

Through much of the short story, we see Bibi demanding to be treated like what society recognises as an ordinary female and claiming her right to perform acts that are the bricks and mortar of a humdrum female existence in her community. Her cousin Haldar dismisses Bibi's demands by declaring that she speaks 'backward': perhaps rather than implying that Bibi speaks by literally inverting syllables or words, an assertion which is not borne out by the direct speech attributed to her in the text, he is referring to the *content* of Bibi's demands which are incongruous with what society judges is appropriate for a disabled woman to desire (Lahiri, 2000 [1999]: 163). The narrators' description of Bibi Haldar's speech acts echoes that of Haldar: the narrators deploy adjectives such as 'mawkish' and 'maudlin' to describe her soliloquies, and they inform us that Bibi speaks 'in non sequiturs' (2000 [1999]: 160–1). The narrators also report that 'it was rumoured by many that Bibi conversed with herself in a fluent but totally incomprehensible language', without contesting or commenting on the veracity of this rumour (2000 [1999]: 165). Thus, despite their sympathy for her, the narrators' editorialising comments about Bibi's speech suggest an implicit refusal on the women's part to hear her. Or perhaps these comments are indicative of their decision, whether conscious or subconscious, to only partially hear Bibi and thus to extricate themselves from the responsibility of actively challenging societal constructions of gendered disability.

This distance between Bibi and her female neighbours complicates the idea of female solidarity across the (perceived) ability/

(perceived) disability divide, and Bibi's awareness of this divide comes through sharply at the end of the text. Given Bibi's earlier volubility, her retreat into 'a deep and prolonged silence', following the departure of her cousin and his wife, after being driven out of business by the narrators, coincides with a retreat from the community of women (2000 [1999]: 171). And when, a few months later, she is found four months pregnant, in contrast to her earlier, uncensored and obviously resistant speech, she opts not for complete silence and mutism, but for sparser and perhaps more carefully curated speech. The narrating women continue to serve as a much-needed support network for Bibi, helping her deliver her son and teaching her how to 'feed him and bathe him and lull him to sleep'; they also assist her when she sets up her own cosmetics business using the existing stock and a few hundred rupees that her cousin left her (2000 [1999]: 172). But if 'The treatment of Bibi Haldar', as Susan Muchshima Moynihan argues, 'spotlights the formation of communities and the responsibility to the abject figures at their edges' (2012: 112), it also highlights the tensions within and limitations of such communities by alerting us not only to the women's participation, albeit passive and well-meaning, in perpetuating Bibi's otherness, but later also to Bibi's refusal to disclose the name of her child's father: 'She said she could not remember what had happened. She would not tell us who had done it. We prepared her semolina with hot milk and raisins; still she would not reveal the man's identity' (Lahiri, 2000 [1999]: 172).

The narrative does not clarify whether Bibi is genuinely unable to recall who impregnated her, or if she is invoking temporary memory loss as a strategy to ward off further questions from her neighbours. Indeed, Lahiri's entire text is shot through with ambiguity. Not only does it have an open ending, but the enigmatic nature of Bibi's impairment dominates much of the text. We learn early in the short story that the 'treatments offered by doctors' of all persuasions 'only made matters worse', yet at the end of the text, the narrators inform us that, 'to the best of [their] knowledge', Bibi was 'cured' (2000 [1999]: 158–72). Neither the narrators nor we as readers know for certain if Bibi has indeed been cured, not only because of the limited perspective of the narrators, but also because it is not clear what constitutes being cured in this context since the 'mystery' of Bibi's disease is never solved (2000 [1999]: 166). The

'Ordinary' defiances and the short story 103

ending of the short story does, however, suggest a marked broadening of Bibi's spatial and financial horizons as her business is shown to thrive. If at the beginning of the text the women declared that Bibi was not fit to use public transportation 'without supervision', the closing paragraph tellingly sees her travelling alone 'by taxi to the wholesale market, using her profits to restock the shelves' (2000 [1999]: 159–72). She continues to maintain close ties with her female neighbours, but also holds herself apart, not only through her continued refusal to reveal the identity of her child's father, but also through the alternative model of womanhood that she is able to forge for herself as a single, unmarried mother and businesswoman in defiance of her community's patriarchal prescriptions and the prevailing norms and expectations with respect to disabled female bodies.

Of course, the success of Bibi's resistance is complicated by the lack of clarity as to the exact circumstances that led to the pregnancy; it is a success that perhaps *necessitates* the failure of the narrators as detectives: 'A few of our servants were questioned, and in tea stalls and bus stands, possible suspects were debated and dismissed' (2000 [1999]: 172). A class bias informs this investigation which presupposes that only a lower-class man could have 'disgraced' Bibi (2000 [1999]: 172).[6] Notably, the women do not consider the possibility of a middle-class man, and indeed, one of their husbands, fathering a disabled woman's child: in order for the community feeling to remain intact, such a possibility has to be precluded, and this silence, which is not explicitly recognised by the narrators, accentuates the distance between Bibi and the narrating women. Moreover, their use of the term 'disgraced' is not only a nod to the stigma attached to pre- and extramarital sex for women, but also suggests that they do not see Bibi as a sexual being who could have wilfully given consent and participated in the sexual act. By making this observation, I am not seeking to downplay the very valid and worrying question, in view of Bibi's frequent paroxysms, as to how freely and consciously she could have given consent, but am arguing that it is equally problematic to assume that Bibi could *not* have freely given her consent or have initiated sexual intimacy. The possibly deliberate withholding of information on Bibi's part, and the silences and ellipses that punctuate the text because of Lahiri's choice of narrative voice do not diminish Bibi's achievements as a single mother and businesswoman, but they do ambiguate our perception of her successful resistance, which appears to be both bound up with the community of narrating women and at a necessary arm's distance from it, both a product of Bibi's wilfulness and of a situation where perhaps she did not have much of a say.

Domestic servitude, labour rights and resistance

In 'A day for Nuggo' the narrator charts the dilemmas faced by the eponymous character, a lower-caste Christian woman, who works as a domestic worker and is compelled to assert her right to a day off from work when her friend Raagni launches a campaign mobilising Christians in Lahore to fight for better working conditions.

According to Elizabeth Koepping, Chura (Dalit) converts from Hinduism constitute 90 to 95 per cent of the Pakistani Christian community today (2011: 25). More often than not, they remain saddled with their historically designated occupations, which primarily entail refuse collection and sanitation work: despite constituting only '1.6 percent of Pakistan's population of some 200 million, according to a 1998 government census, rights groups believe they fill about 80 percent of the sweeper jobs' (Ur-Rehman and Abi-Habib, 2020: n.p.). The short story grapples with Nuggo's caste inferiority, perceived untouchability and the resulting discrimination that she has to endure by showing us how, upon the birth of her second child, when she decides to take on additional work, the only option available to her is that of a municipal sweeper; we also see Sarwari, a Muslim domestic servant and a friend of Nuggo's, making sure that the saucepan in which she brings milk for her does not touch Nuggo's clay jug, which the prevailing mores deem is ritually polluted.

Domestic servants are omnipresent in middle- and upper-class homes across the Indian subcontinent, and, as elsewhere in the world, domestic work in Pakistan is performed predominantly by women; it forms part of the country's informal economy and is largely unregulated.[7] Therefore, in addition to caste discrimination, Nuggo's work as a domestic servant makes her particularly vulnerable to class exploitation and the lack of state regulation makes collectivist action especially difficult. Nuggo and her family live in 'mud encroachments' along the boundary wall of her employers' luxurious property (Ahmad, 2014: 174). This spatial proximity between Nuggo's makeshift dwelling and her employers' home, despite the vastly dissimilar material conditions, results in a blurring of the line separating the workplace and the home as spatial entities for the domestic worker, which consequently muddies the demarcation between working hours and private time. Nuggo is on call seven days a week, 'dusting, sweeping and washing clothes in lieu of a small salary, her lunch and the privilege of occupying their shabby home' (2014: 177). It is worth noting here that Nuggo's private time is far from synonymous with leisure: having performed a range of domestic chores in her employer's home, and later, having completed her shift as a municipal sweeper, she then does all the housework in her own home, while also attending to her children. In keeping with the sexual division of labour in patriarchal societies which classifies housework as a woman's 'natural' calling (McDowell, 1999: 73), Nuggo's husband Samuel's contribution is limited to minding their sons 'in a rough and ready fashion' in her absence (Ahmad, 2014: 179). The blurring of temporal and spatial lines that the quasi-live-in nature of her work brings in its wake makes it particularly difficult for Nuggo to demand a day off. As Raka Ray and Seemin Qayum point out, domestic labour 'confuses and complicates the conceptual divide between family and work, custom and contract, affection and duty, the home and the world precisely because the hierarchical arrangements and emotional registers of home and family must co-exist with those of workplace and contract in a capitalist world' (2009: 3).

The emotional registers of home and family are especially closely interwoven with that of the workplace for Nuggo because of the affective generational debt that Samuel carries. His mother worked for Sughra Begum's family and, much like her employers, he subscribes to a feudal conception of domestic servitude whereby generations of domestic workers are expected to be 'obedient, grateful and submissive', in short, to behave like *namak halal*[8] servants (Mirza, 2016: 37): 'He strictly forbade Nuggo to speak to Begum Sahib about a day off. She'd always been kind to them, advancing wages ahead of time and letting them build their unsightly homes alongside the boundary wall. They owed her some loyalty for that' (Ahmad, 2014: 183). Sughra initially comes across as a not unkind employer; for instance, upon learning Nuggo has just given birth, she experiences pangs of empathy stemming from her own 'remembered pain surrounding a similar event thirty odd years ago' and makes arrangements for Nuggo to have two glasses of warm milk during her convalescence (2014: 175). But Sughra's kindness is inextricably bound up with the convenience of having a well-trained servant who spares her and her family the indignity of performing what are considered menial tasks. When, following the birth of her second child, Nuggo's trips home become more frequent, Sughra's benevolent attitude evaporates rapidly: 'If it hadn't been for the fact that she washed and ironed beautifully, that only Nuggo could remember which shirts belonged to whom and have everyone's clothes and shoes laid out ready for the morning just the way they liked them, Nuggo would have got the sack ages ago' (2014: 177).

Up until the last four pages of the short story, Nuggo is shown to lack the kind of self-confidence and faith in the legitimacy of the 'Sunday, Day Off campaign' that Raagni possesses. Moreover, Nuggo does not challenge her husband's acceptance of class hierarchies, even if she does find merit in Raagni's arguments: 'She was utterly frustrated with being at the heart of an insoluble controversy. She hadn't really considered herself at all, but the arguments on either side seemed both convincing and sound to her. She didn't know what to do' (2014: 183). Indeed, until Raagni points it out to her, the injustice of not being given a single day off from work does not occur to Nuggo. But instead of inviting us to see Raagni's and Nuggo's modes of resistance in oppositional terms, the text alerts us to how familial and not merely socio-economic conditions may determine the development of a woman's resistant subjectivity. Raagni and Nuggo share the same class and caste positioning, but their relationship with time is considerably different. The text foregrounds how resistance is intimately tied to time, not only because the act of resistance may itself be a demand for more private time, but also because resistance as an activity requires time and energy. Unlike Raagni, who is childless and separated from her husband, when not attending to her employers' demands, Nuggo is preoccupied with childrearing and housework in her own home. Although 'her education has been minimal', Raagni is shown to have the intellectual wherewithal and motivation, but also the time and energy to be involved in 'all sorts of activities', from 'matchmaking and fund-raising to sitting on committees and organising petitions', and she comes to wield considerable 'influence among the local groups' (2014: 180).

The text does not condone Nuggo's initial lack of political will, which manifests itself first in her inability to see that she is being exploited by her employer, and then in her extreme reluctance to demand a day off. But it does highlight how, for a woman like Nuggo, despite her recognition of the moral legitimacy of her demands, adopting an unequivocally oppositional stance may be particularly difficult, with constraints of time combining with serious emotional and financial pressures. The narrator draws our attention to the turmoil that Nuggo experiences while debating with herself whether or not to approach her employer. Even though Nuggo realises that the unremitting pressure of her job is precisely what Raagni's campaign aims to alleviate, her decision-making process itself is hampered by the relentless demands of her job and the 'duress of the quotidian' (Scott, 1985: 247):

> The unasked question simmered in her head all the time with a more personal immediacy than Samuel or Raagni could have imagined. It would pop up before her tantalizingly as she dragged the large merciless bundle of washing out of the linen bin and again rose before her as she bent her aching back to sweep up the rubbish in the backyard and yet again burst upon her consciousness as she faced the bottomless pit of the ironing basket. (Ahmad, 2014: 183–4)

Moreover, while the municipal sweepers succeed in securing more favourable working conditions and a holiday on Sunday through strike action, the unregulated nature of domestic service and the 'peculiar intimacy of the employer-employee relationship' (Ehrenreich, 2003: 93) that is a hallmark of domestic servitude do not afford Nuggo 'the luxury of open, organized, political activity' (Scott, 1985: xv). Nuggo's initial lack of political will also appears to be a product of pessimism, as indicated by the rhetorical question that she addresses to Raagni, which she then also proceeds to answer to drive home her feeling of powerlessness: 'D'you think it's possible for us poor people to change things? The world's not going to change that easily – just so I can visit you on Sundays. That's impossible' (Ahmad, 2014: 179). When prompted again by Raagni to speak to her employer, 'Nuggo had to confess sheepishly that she had not got round to it yet' (2014: 182). Nuggo's sheepishness can be seen as a sign of what she sees as her failure to live up to an ideal that Raagni embodies. But as Sara Ahmed explains, shame stemming from 'the failure to live up to an ideal is a way of taking up that ideal and confirming its necessity' (2014 [2004]: 106). Therefore, paradoxically, Nuggo's feelings of shame are a confirmation of her belief in the need for resistance.

However, it takes a stark clash, a few days later, between Nuggo's children's needs and her employers' unreasonable demands to ultimately cause the 'last lingering threads of courtesy and doubt' to snap in Nuggo's heart, making it suddenly clear to her 'what she had to do and why' (Ahmad, 2014: 185). While Nuggo is ironing clothes for Sughra's adult daughter Raabia one Sunday, her older son comes to the bungalow to let her know that her second born is crying, only to be 'shooed' off and spoken to peremptorily by Raabia (2014: 184). In that brief moment, the personal becomes irrevocably political for Nuggo: 'She looked Raabia squarely in the eyes as she handed her the dupatta she was ironing and said in measured tones, "I'm going now, Raabia Bibi. I won't be working on Sundays anymore. I will return to my duty tomorrow if Begum Sahib still wants me to work here"' (2014: 185).

'Class happens', according to E. P. Thompson, 'when some men [sic], as a result of common experiences (inherited or shared), feel and articulate the identity of their interests as between themselves, and as against other men [sic] whose interests are different from (and usually opposed to) theirs' (1963: 9–10). We see class 'happening' in this scene with Raabia's sharp dismissal of her children bringing home to Nuggo the chasm separating her own and her children's interests from those of her employers. The chasm becomes an even more gaping one when Sughra responds to Nuggo's assertion of her rights by threatening her family with eviction. Nuggo feels 'shamed and humiliated' by 'the sudden exposure of [her family's] vulnerability', but she refuses to comply with her husband's demand that she apologise to Sughra: '"I haven't done anything wrong", she said to Samuel over and over again' (Ahmad, 2014: 186). As Nuggo begins to make arrangements, with the help of Raagni, to move into a slum, Sughra sends Sarwari to inform her that she has decided to 'reconsider Nuggo's request for a day off' (2014: 186). Her husband encourages her to see Sughra's message as proof of her kindness, but Nuggo rejects this interpretation of Sughra's behaviour:

> Her eyes met Sarwari's in an attempt to confirm her own rebellious opinion on that subject, and found nothing but bland relief in her friend's face. But her face was laced with *defiance* as she *conceded* in a sharp voice, 'All right, then, Sarwari. Tell her, I'll return to work tomorrow.' (2014: 188; emphasis mine)

Rajeswari Sunder Rajan reminds us that '[r]esistance is not always a positivity; it may be no more than a negative agency, an absence of acquiescence in one's oppression' (1993b: 11). The spectre of homelessness destroys the façade of her employer's magnanimity, which, in the past, compelled Nuggo to 'obediently' follow her employers' orders; she is also able to see the contours of Samuel's false consciousness with far greater clarity than before (Ahmad, 2014: 184). While she succeeds in securing a day off for herself, Nuggo is aware of the ambiguous nature of this victory, as highlighted by the narrator's use of the verb 'concede' alongside the noun 'defiance' in the just-cited passage. Nuggo refuses to offer her husband a comforting nod of agreement, signalling her refusal to ideologically acquiesce to her own oppression, even if she realises that, given her family's financial precarity, she will have to resume serving a family who have no concern for her or her children's well-being and who will not hesitate from callously exposing them to the elements when their daily comforts are even slightly compromised. The direct speech attributed to Nuggo at the end of the story powerfully underscores her new, sophisticated understanding of class relations which aligns with Raagni's and that of other members of the Christian community; it also leaves open the need for further acts of defiance on Nuggo's part, not only in response to future conflicts with her employer, but also with her husband.

Transnational domestic servitude and duplicitous defiance

Koshy's 'Almost Valentine's Day' centres on the acts of defiance performed by Aruna who moves from New Delhi to Portland ostensibly to work for an immigrant Indian family as a domestic servant. The publication of Koshy's short story, together with earlier texts such as

Bharati Mukherjee's 1989 novel *Jasmine* and Sujatha Fernandes's 'A pocket full of stories' (2009), coincides with a 'resurgence of domestic service' in advanced capitalist countries from the late twentieth century onwards (Haskins and Lowrie, 2015: 9). Domestic paid labour in the US, as Mary Romero notes, is 'not only structured around gender but also is stratified by race and citizenship status, relegating the most vulnerable worker to the least favourable working conditions' (2016: 8); female immigrants of colour working as live-in domestic workers are often subjected to a wide range of abuses, including 'confiscation of personal documents, limited freedom of movement and ability to communicate with others, employers' threats of deportation, assault and battery, rape, servitude, torture, and trafficking' (Romero et al., 2016: 16). As Human Rights Watch reports, the US visa categories (A-3, G-5 and B-1) that apply to female domestic workers from the Global South themselves perpetuate 'the subordination of immigrant women of color as live-in domestic workers' (Romero, 2013: 193), as they entail limited state verification of employer compliance with the terms of the contract and are characterised by 'the Department of Labor's lack of involvement in the administration of these visas' (Human Rights Watch, 2001: n.p.).[9] Ethnographic studies on transnational domestic servitude tend to focus on white employers with '[e]mployers who are of colour rarely figur[ing] in the academic and popular literature on U.S. domestic servitude' (Ray and Qayum, 2009: 168). But, as the 2013 Sangeeta–Khobragade case dramatically demonstrated, the transnational domestic worker and employer's shared racial and gendered identity does not preclude the possibility of exploitation: Sangeeta, a domestic worker from India, exposed her mistress, Devyani Khobragade, an Indian diplomat based in New York, for paying her a wage that was far lower than what was stated on her A-3 visa form (and also lower than the minimum wage in the US), and for denying her access to her own passport.

In Koshy's short story, Meera and her husband Rahul commit another kind of visa fraud in bringing Aruna to the US: they lie about their relationship with Aruna, passing her off as a relative, rather than an employee, thereby circumventing the need to even appear to be conforming to US labour laws. Despite, in all probability, not paying her the minimum wage and despite taking her passport from Aruna, in some respects, Meera is a considerate employer, who expresses concern for Aruna's well-being: 'No need to start right away. Rest till you adjust to the time difference ... it's not possible to take everything in at once' (Koshy, 2014: 27–9). Indeed, Meera appears to consciously distance herself from certain discriminatory attitudes towards domestic help prevalent in India, notably the idea that servants are 'contaminated' and unfit to be touched. In fact, when Meera meets Aruna at the airport, she embraces her by way of greeting. Aruna is surprised by this physical contact and realises that the transnational setting has shifted some of the boundaries characterising the servant–employer relationship: '[S]hockingly, the woman had reached her arms around Aruna. Yes, Aruna thought, this is America. But this was a conclusion not without puzzlement' (2014: 28–9). Without suggesting that domestic service is a democratic profession in the US (as Bharati Mukherjee's 1988 novel *Jasmine* problematically does), Koshy's text reveals how it might be a less discriminatory practice than the culture of servitude in the Indian subcontinent which 'mimics prescriptions in orthodox Hinduism which are dictated by a profound anxiety about the ritual pollution of the upper castes by the lower castes' (Mirza, 2016: 35).[10] Unlike Nuggo's, Aruna's resistant subjectivity is not issue-based; instead Aruna is determined to resist her inherited class positioning and shed her servant skin: she has no intention of working as a domestic servant, whether in India or the US, whether for an Indian family or a white one, no matter how benevolent the employer.

If, as we saw above, Nuggo's act of defiance is ultimately an impulsive rather than a calculated move in response to Raabia's indifference to her children's needs, Aruna is driven by 'her own stubborn interests – above all self-interest',[11] and Koshy's short story exhibits a clear 'refusal to sentimentalize the subaltern' (Tickell, 2015: 157). Aruna arrives in Portland having resolved to play the role of the inefficient and insolent servant so that her employers, who paid for her visa and travel costs, would be compelled to release her of her bond and allow her to take up some other form of employment. Koshy has remarked in an interview that the protagonist of her short story is 'sneaky' and 'often baffling to [her] as a writer' (Mirza and Koshy, 2021: 176). While she does not resort to brutal violence against her employers like the chauffeur Balram does in Aravind Adiga's novel *The White Tiger* (2008), Aruna is more than capable of deception, manipulation and blackmail. She is, in many ways, an unlikeable character, embodying an unapologetically '[b]y any means necessary' approach to 'subaltern struggle', which includes disregarding the financial sacrifices that her mother, also a domestic servant, made for her (Mirza and Koshy, 2021: 177). Koshy's subtle characterisation of both Aruna and her employers invites ambivalence from the reader, making it difficult to arrive at an unequivocal conclusion about the moral tenor of Aruna's resistance and to fully come to grips with all her motivations. Aruna is ignorant in some matters and worldly-wise in others; she is all too aware, for instance, of the widespread sexual abuse of female domestic staff by male employers and suffers no illusions about the moral superiority of the middle and upper classes: 'The slightest creak of the house conjured images of Uncle slipping out of his bed and coming to her. These things happened, didn't they?' (Koshy, 2014: 26). Readerly response to Aruna as a character is further complicated by the reminders of her poverty punctuating the narrative in the form of the recurring image of the broken shoe that she tries in vain to repair.

Aruna not only refuses to carry out the work that she is expected to do, but also actively *creates* work for her employers, for instance, by leaving her own dirty dishes in the sink. She also starts taking the bus and exploring downtown Portland on her own, when she is expected to stay at her employers' home, minding their preteen daughter Seema. Aruna thus recasts the implicit terms of her employment and challenges conventional constructions of time and leisure for domestic workers, both in the Indian subcontinent and for immigrant women of colour in the Global North. As she informs her mother during one of their Skype conversations, 'Ma, tomorrow I am not returning home till late in the evening. Let's see how their precious Seema manages' (2014: 37). In stark contrast to Nuggo's days, Aruna's stint in her employers' home is marked by, first, defiant acts of omission, in other words, her wilful neglect of the household tasks she has been assigned to do, and second, by defiant acts of commission, which are meant to more openly provoke her employers' ire. Aruna is fully aware of the offensive and mutinous tenor of her demeanour. She refuses to prepare meals for the family, informing them, by way of explanation, that she is 'no good at cooking'; she also chooses to remain seated while her mistress Meera is standing, attempting to give her instructions

(2014: 40). As Ray and Qayum explain, the 'politics of sitting', or 'the question of where one's body may be placed' in India, lies at the heart of servant–employer relationships and is reflective of societal 'hierarchy, inequality and subordination/domination' (2009: 148–9). Therefore, her decision to remain seated in the presence of her mistress is far from a neutral act. Indeed, Aruna flouts not only the specific 'rules, at once, explicit and unspoken, that are meant to govern servant comportment in the space of the home' in the Indian subcontinent, but also, at times, the rules of etiquette across classes and cultures, for instance by swinging her feet up on the coffee table (2009: 148).

Bourdieu has argued that concealment and recourse to euphemisms are essential to maintaining the most 'elementary' forms of domination such as the master–servant relationship (1990: 129). Referring to domestic help as 'part of the family' in the Indian subcontinent often works to 'camouflage a disturbing reality' and render 'a profoundly unequal relationship relatively tolerable', not only for the mistress, but also for the maid (Mirza, 2016: 36). In the short story, however, Meera asks Aruna to refer to her as Mary (the name she has chosen to go by in the US), a request that Aruna wilfully ignores, persisting in calling her 'aunty'. Meera's rejection of this 'one of the family' discourse as well as her adoption of an 'American' name hints at her desire *not* to be seen as part of an ethnic labour enclave, which could throw into doubt her own narrative of integration within American society as an immigrant of colour. Aruna is quick to read and use to her own advantage Meera's feelings of insecurity and the impulse underpinning Meera's assimilationist desire; Aruna deploys the title of 'aunty' not to ingratiate herself to her employer or to alleviate her servant status but to provoke irritation and as yet another display of defiance: 'Aruna, who was practised at inflecting her 'Aunty's' [*sic*] with something not-respectful, mouthed the word to herself, "Aunty"' (Koshy, 2014: 28). (Aruna only agrees to call her mistress Mary towards the end of the text, once she concedes Aruna's demand to find her a job that does not involve domestic labour.)

The employers initially tolerate Aruna's defiant behaviour, but Meera's husband eventually resorts to physical force, a reaction, it is implied in the narrative, that Aruna aims to provoke by blandly insisting that she would like to work at Meera's workplace, instead of attending to housework: 'Uncle swooped from across the room and [took] her by the upper arm ... Aruna's arm felt wrenched from its socket. A part of her was elated' (2014: 41). Unlike the other protagonists considered in this chapter, in Aruna we have a subaltern figure who actively and indeed gleefully seeks a physical confrontation to achieve her goals; earlier in the text, she expresses regret that Meera's husband, who Aruna insists on calling Uncle, makes no attempt to have sex with her; here we see her 'lunging' and wrapping 'her arms tightly around Uncle's hips': 'Uncle pulled from her; she locked her fingers together and tightened her grip. She pulled him back to her. Aunty pulled Uncle from Aruna' (2014: 41). The repeated act of pushing and pulling concretises the class struggle between Aruna and her employers and also brings to the fore the strength of Aruna's resolve to secure her freedom. Aruna's physical response and 'braying' succeed in frightening her employers who begin to doubt her sanity and resolve to 'return her', suggesting that despite Meera's desire to be egalitarian, Meera and her family see Aruna as a commodity that can be acquired and then returned if found unsuitable (2014: 41). Aruna, however, has no intention of complying: 'I won't get on the plane. You'll see I won't get on the plane. They'll find out how you brought me here' (2014: 41). She is, of course, referring to the American authorities: Aruna knows that her employers have brought her over to the US under false pretences and risk facing prosecution for visa fraud. When Aruna threatens to expose them, Meera and her husband find her a job which entails 'driving a machine which cleaned a field-sized cement floor' in a warehouse (2014: 44).

Throughout the narrative, the underhandedness of Aruna's acts of defiance is juxtaposed against her philosophical reflections about the similarities between human beings, reflections which straddle the line between naivete and profundity and trouble our understanding of the individualistic nature of Aruna's approach to her own happiness. For instance, on one of her jaunts into the city centre by bus, she notices a man in Portland who reminds her of her former boyfriend Abhin in Delhi and causes her to wonder:

> if things are different here then how are they different ... You have to admit it's a funny thing for me to see people I know from there, bits of them, stuck to the people I see here. It makes me think, are the people back home walking around with some bits from here stuck to them. (2014: 42)

Having been given a job that does not involve domestic labour, in the closing paragraph, we see her expressing regret that her mother is unable to witness her success first hand, but then Aruna concludes that the woman who taught her to drive the cleaning machine at work is 'a little bit like her mother' (2014: 46). The similarities that she sees between the people that she encounters in Portland and those that she knew back home in Delhi could be seen as a coping mechanism which allows her to come to terms with (unrecognised) homesickness or perhaps as a cognitive strategy to assuage any guilt that she may be experiencing for failing to support her mother, but it could also suggest that Aruna sees humanity in collectivist terms and sees herself as connected to those around her, despite the morally dubious measures that she resorts to in order to escape domestic servitude.

Aruna's 'by all means necessary' approach is successful in securing her a job at a factory, which in sharp contrast to domestic service as a profession, comes with a well-defined job description and clearly specified work hours and wages. Aruna's triumph is evident in the closing paragraph, accentuated by her growing enjoyment of her new job: 'Aruna pushed her foot forcefully down on the speed pedal. The machine nearly bucked and she swiftly switched her foot to the brake pedal and laughed at the ease with which she controlled the machine' (2014: 46). In presenting us with this successful instance of resistance, the short story does not necessarily endorse Aruna's devious behaviour, but it also refuses to condemn it and to reduce Aruna to her, in many ways, reprehensible actions. Moreover, in showing how Aruna's new job is a low-paid one ($8.25 per hour) and how her supervisor at work has the 'same pinched face, the same look of sadness' as one of her female neighbours in Delhi, the short story refuses to equate Aruna's entry into the formal labour market in the US, despite her euphoria, with freedom, equality and unmitigated happiness (2014: 45); the text places itself, as Koshy has also noted, 'outside the mainstream narrative of the poor and huddled masses looking to the United States for their salvation'.[12]

The short stories examined in this chapter present us with female subaltern figures who are partly, if not wholly, successful in achieving goals as varied as better working conditions, freedom from particularly exploitative forms of labour, the right not to submit to an arranged marriage as well as the right to profess conventional desires and aspirations. As we have seen, they do not seek to dismantle deeply entrenched societal hierarchies nor to overturn prejudiced modes of thinking. But, brevity, a hallmark of the short story as a genre, allows a telescoping of short-term and spatially confined acts of defiance performed by individuals, so that their relevance to structural inequalities becomes difficult to ignore and their subversive power hard to deny. Ali Smith reminds us that the end of a short story 'is never an end, it's always some kind of middle or beginning' (Boddy and Smith, 2010: 68); indeed, the indeterminate ending of each of the four short stories raises as many questions as it answers, not only about interwoven inequities, but also about the forms that successful female resistance can and should assume.

Notes

1 In Buddhism, Seela's inherited religion, *karma* refers to the force produced by an individual's actions in one life that influences what happens to them in future lives; *sansara* or *samsara* is the cycle of birth, death and rebirth (*Cambridge Dictionary* [Online], 2022: n.p.).
2 Further information can be found at www.epilepsysociety.org.uk (Accessed: 21 March 2022). Bibi is never diagnosed with epilepsy in the text, but Lahiri in an interview refers to her as an 'epileptic' (Aguiar and Lahiri, 1999: 2).
3 According to Sarah Pinto, as '[a]n affliction involving unexplained fainting, fits, paralyses, and pains, hysteria has a long history in India, appearing, arguably, in the earliest Ayurvedic writing, appearing again in the Graeco-Islamic medical texts that arrived in the later medieval period, and arriving once again with Europeans. In nineteenth century medical journals, hysteria became a bellwether for the status of Indian medical knowledge and practice' (2016: 268).
4 Sarah Pinto, personal correspondence with the author (28 September 2021).
5 Given the prevailing association in India and Nepal of disability with bad luck, 'people with disabilities … are often discouraged from attending religious and wedding functions' (Devkota et al., 2019: 10).
6 Drawing on the timeline of the pregnancy and the uncharacteristic generosity that Haldar displays by leaving Bibi money before moving away, Fitz makes a fairly plausible case for Haldar being the man who fathered Bibi's child (2005: 130).
7 See Javed (2021: n.p.).

8 The term *namak halal* (Urdu/Hindi), meaning 'true to one's master's salt', evokes what are socially constructed as positive attributes of submissiveness and gratitude towards one's 'betters'.
9 See 'Hidden in the home: abuse of domestic workers with special visas in the United States' (2001). Available at www.hrw.org/report/2001/06/01/hidden-home/abuse-domestic-workers-special-visas-united-states (Accessed: 23 March 2022).
10 See also Ray and Qayum (2009: 153).
11 Mridula Koshy, personal correspondence with the author (1 May 2016).
12 Mridula Koshy, personal correspondence with the author (1 May 2016).

4

Queering resistance: *A Married Woman*, *Babyji* and *The Ministry of Utmost Happiness*

> Then the question is, who
> Is the man, who the girl,
> All sex-accessories being no
> Indication.
>
> – Kamala Das, 'The doubt', 1967

This chapter grapples with representations of queer characters in three novels by Indian writers, with the term 'queer' taken to refer to same-sex-desiring characters as well as intersex characters. I have opted to use the term 'queer' in this broad sense, not because, in the words of Iain Morland, 'intersex anatomies necessarily have queer desires', but because their bodies deviate from 'norms of embodiment' (2009: 289). The protagonists' experiences of non-normative gender, sexual and/or sexed identities unfold in the context of a series of interlinked social upheavals in India: the 1990 protests against the Mandal Commission, the demolition of the Babri Mosque in 1992 and the anti-Muslim riots that took place in the state of Gujarat in 2002. I will examine not only the tensions between collectivist action and individual freedom in the texts under consideration, but also how these tensions inflect our understanding of acts of resistance, whether queer or otherwise. As I will demonstrate, through their representations of anti-egalitarian forms of social movements orchestrated primarily by the privileged members of society, the novels invite us to unpack the politics of social activism and collectivist resistance which, instead of seeking to alleviate the plight of the downtrodden, may be rooted in intentional sociological shortsightedness and aimed at political aggrandisement. Indeed, representations of protests led by the powerful who often usurp the language of the dispossessed for political expediency are a potent reminder of the vulnerability of the idea of resistance to abuse and misappropriation. I explore the ways in which the portrayal of sexual and gendered wilfulness in these texts complicates the authors' portrayal of other minority identities and power imbalances based on caste, class and age in *Babyji*, and religion, specifically Islam, in Kapur's and Roy's novels.

Drawing on Medina's conception of the term *resistance*, I take queer resistance to mean '*contending with*, and not exclusively or fundamentally as *contending against*' heteropatriarchy and other intersecting 'forms of domination' and social power (2013: 16; italics in the original). Aravind Narrain and Gautam Bhan's reminder that queer struggle 'is not just a public movement for rights and legal change', but is also 'a map of how people navigate their most intimate geographies: their bodies, their desires, their families and their selves' is of particular relevance to my analysis (2005: 4). The chapter also engages with Sara Ahmed's work on the resistant potentialities of queer bodies and feelings in *Cultural Politics of Emotion* (2014 [2004]) and *The Promise of Happiness* (2010) and with Jasbir Puar's concept of 'queer assemblages' which 'deprivileges a binary opposition between queer and not-queer subjects, and, instead of retaining queerness exclusively as dissenting, resistant, and alternative (all of which queerness importantly is and does), it underscores contingency and complicity with dominant formations' (2005: 121–2).

Before I commence my analysis of the three novels, paying heed to Jacob Hale's 'Suggested rules for non-transsexuals writing about transsexuals, transsexuality, transsexualism, or trans ____' (2009), I would like to explicitly spell out my positioning as a heterosexual cisgender woman of colour. Both *A Married Woman* and *The Ministry of Utmost Happiness* are arguably non-identity-based writings, as their authors are also heterosexual cisgender women. To my knowledge, Dawesar has never spoken publicly about her sexual orientation, therefore it is difficult to surmise to what extent *Babyji* can be read as an example of literary self-identity work, but *Babyji* did win the 2005 Lambda Literary Award for Lesbian Fiction in 2005.[1] Echoing Aneeta Rajendran, the author of *(Un)familiar*

Femininities: Studies in Contemporary Lesbian South Asian Texts, the chapter eschews 'biographical sleuthing' and focuses primarily on the three literary works themselves, rather than on the authors' known or purported identities (2015: 6).

Babyji: queer resistance and social privilege

Anamika, the protagonist of *Babyji*, is an academically gifted schoolgirl who embarks on three same-sex relationships against the backdrop of the 1990 demonstrations in the Indian capital. These protests unfolded in response to the decision made by the Socially and Educationally Backward Classes Commission, headed by B. P. Mandal, to allocate 27 per cent of central government jobs and seats in educational institutions to the 'Other Backward Classes' or OBCs, comprising 'mainly lower-caste Hindu groups (non-Untouchable) and equivalent non-Hindu groups, identified on the basis of caste and class characteristics' (Bajpai, 2010: 676). As Arvind Rajagopal observes, members of the upper castes 'erupted in a storm of protest, and academics, university students, and the English language press, usually somewhere on the left in social issues, united in defense of the "meritocracy" they now declared was threatened' (2001: 192). Anamika enjoys a privileged position not only at her school, as its top student and Head Prefect, but also within Indian society at large as a member of the Brahmin caste. As I will demonstrate, Anamika's response to the Mandal Commission report is central to our understanding of her ambiguous resistant subjectivity.

In Anamika, we have a figure who is fairly unusual in the context of South Asian women's anglophone fiction: her queerness notwithstanding, she is the beneficiary of a profoundly hierarchical society, yet is shown to be almost constantly preoccupied with the idea of resistance and freedom. Moreover, she possesses tremendous sexual confidence, despite occasional moments of self-doubt. According to Rajendran, '[t]hat academic achievement enables sexual expression makes *Babyji* superficially at least a tremendous literary role model for those otherwise exposed only to pathological narratives of lesbianism within educational systems, where invariably pathologization is a concomitant of victimization' (2015: 81).

In addition to Anamika's scholastic talents, the irreverent tone of her first-person narrative and the pleasure that she derives from flouting social mores ensure that we as readers do not see her as a defenceless victim. At certain points, Anamika's language of resistance emerges primarily as teenage angst. While bemoaning having to follow her parents' rules (which entail, for instance, attending an engagement party with them), she melodramatically compares herself to at once 'a slave', 'a caged animal' and 'the citizens of authoritarian regimes', which rather than accentuate what she sees as her plight, highlights the petulance which is masquerading as great suffering, inviting us to not draw facile conclusions about Anamika's revolutionary spirit solely because she possesses same-sex desires (Dawesar, 2005: 103).

Moreover, despite the grievances that Anamika airs in the narrative, she is very much, in the words of Ahmed, a 'happily queer subject'; moreover, her rebelliousness and the 'trouble' that she causes 'turn on the axis of happiness' and centre on 'the relationship between the father and queer daughter' (2010: 118–19). Her father's conceptualisation of happiness is based on the institution of heterosexual marriage privileged by Hindu scriptures: 'But the stages of life prescribed in the ancient books answer our need for knowledge, for love, for doing good to others, and for renunciation' (Dawesar, 2005: 176). Anamika rejects this one-size-fits-all brand of happiness: 'You like tea, and I like coffee. I want to be a physicist, and Vidur wants to join the army. I don't want to get married, and mom did. How can the same formula make us all happy?' (2005: 176). Anamika's queerness foregrounds

> the idiosyncratic nature of happy object choices: different people are made happy by different things; we have a diversity of likes and dislikes, and includes marriage as one happy object choice among others. The inclusion of marriage as something that you might or might not like is picked up by the father, turning queer desire into a question that interrupts the flow of the conversation. (Ahmed, 2010: 119)

Anamika's happiness and her ability to disrupt the perpetuation of heteronormative expectations are certainly an integral part of her resistant subjectivity; as we will see below, they are also bound up in complex ways to her at times reactionary viewpoints.

Anamika is alert to the myriad social divisions that characterise her society, and she is also (partially) aware of her own complicity. As she notes early in the narrative:

> Indians, myself included, must immediately place everyone we meet ... There are categories for everything – educated or not, foreign car or not, brahmin or banya or what, English-speaking or not, meat-eating or not, if vegetarian then whether an eggitarian or strict, if strict then too strict to eat Western desserts with egg or not. All this in the case of women helps predict whether they might be led astray. In the case of men, whether they will misbehave with women given half a chance. (Dawesar, 2005: 5)

Anamika contests the hypocrisy underpinning the prevalent patriarchal norms that require women to be sexually chaste and clearly demarcate the spatial boundaries of their existence. Her loitering in Delhi does not take her as far away from so-called 'female', middle-class and heteronormative spaces, as that of Kari, the eponymous queer protagonist of Amruta Patil's graphic novel (2008). But Anamika's jaunts on her bike do take her to out-of-bounds spaces, such as the slum which serves as a source of domestic servants for the middle-class inhabitants of the adjoining neighbourhood, or the house of her older lover Tripta, in open defiance of the prescriptive 'unspoken assumption' in Indian society that 'a loitering woman is up to no good. She is either mad or bad or dangerous to society' (Phadke et al., 2011: vii). Anamika celebrates the subversive tenor of her sexuality and decides to 'avenge [her]self by holding hands and flirting with girls since Indian society was so holier-than-thou about having boyfriends', stating also that 'she had never wanted a boyfriend anyway' (Dawesar, 2005: 11).

Anamika's overtures to other women not only represent a rejection of the regulatory gendered mores of her society, but also work to interrupt the flow of the conversation, as Ahmed puts it, about transgressive behaviour for adolescents, which is imagined within the narrow confines of heterosexual activity. Anamika does not question the naturalness or the legitimacy of her proclivities, and her discussion of homo- and heterosexual desire in the same breath represents a dogged refusal to accept the societal othering of her longings. In the words of Cohen, Anamika's resistance comprises 'participation in cultural forms thought to be deviant' (2004: 39); it also appears to pay heed to Foucault's exhortation that 'the grips of power' should be resisted by 'bodies and pleasures' since he saw sexuality as being 'organized by power in its grip on bodies and their materiality, their forces, energies, sensations, and pleasures' (1978: 155–7). Her androgynous appearance, which, much like Kari, Anamika actively cultivates by keeping her hair short and dressing in what is conventionally deemed to be male clothing, forms part of this contestation of society's definitional tyrannies. As her lover Tripta's young son asks Anamika in bewilderment: 'Are you a Didi or a Bhaiyya?' (*didi* being the Hindi term for 'elder sister' and *bhaiyya* for 'elder brother') (Dawesar, 2005: 93). Anamika responds by saying, 'I am a Didi'. 'In the silence that follow[s]', she reflects on the restrictive nature of binary identities whether with respect to gender or age, but does not express a clear preference: 'A Didi who maybe really should have been a Bhaiyya. Or, rather, an Uncle. Nothing about my life was typical of a sixteen-year-old's ... It was impossible for me to be less of a Bhaiyya and to become a real *Didi*' (2005: 93; emphasis in the original).

Her affair with Rani, a lower-caste domestic servant, is her most obviously 'deviant' act. In fact, the title of the novel 'Babyji' is also the name by which Rani calls Anamika, with 'baby' referring to Anamika's position in the bourgeois familial hierarchy and the honorific 'ji' functioning as a marker of Anamika's superior class and caste positioning.[2] Though not a Dalit, Rani belongs to the *yadav* caste 'or milkman caste (associated with the Shudra varna)' (Freitag, 1992 [1989]: 122). Therefore, while Anamika and Rani's caste positionings may not be as polarised as Velutha and Ammu's in *The God of Small Things*, their erotic coming together remains a deeply transgressive act. It presents a challenge to both heteronormativity and to the rigid norms governing interaction between divergent castes and classes and necessitates a more opaque layer of secrecy and silence than do her other relationships. As Anamika tells us in no uncertain terms, the fact that she has 'consort[ed] with a person of much lower caste ... was something I could never tell anyone, not India, not Sheela, not Vidur, not my parents, not any future lover' (Dawesar, 2005: 123). Her relationship with Tripta, an older woman whom she names 'India', is also doubly transgressive by virtue of its queerness and the age difference that separates them. Age hierarchy is still a significant mode of social stratification in India, and one that Anamika is determined to defy: 'I hated the ageism of Delhi and its antediluvian norms, which required you to address anyone older as *Uncleji* or *Auntyji* and anyone younger with diminutives' (2005: 4). Her affair with Tripta whom she is expected to refer to as *Auntyji* dramatises the extent to which Anamika sees the female body as both an instrument and a site of resistance: 'All my life I'd been told to venerate elders ... Squeezing [her] rear violated every rule of veneration. It transformed her from an elder into a sexual being. It made me an adult' (2005: 25).

It is telling that all three of Anamika's relationships are marked by some form of inequality and power imbalance: her classmate Sheela is conventionally pretty with fair skin and a voluptuous figure, but Anamika does not see Sheela as her intellectual equal, describing her as 'relatively intelligent [but] lazy'; as we saw earlier, Rani's class and caste status is far lower than Anamika's, and Tripta is several years older than Anamika (2005: 31). In their examination of lesbian porn stories, Ann Russo and Lourdes Torres underscore the importance of evaluating the relationship between 'lesbian and gay sexual representations' and 'inequalities of race, class, and age'; the purpose of such an evaluation is not to downplay the power of queer eroticism or to make a case 'for and against censorship', but to 'create a critical discussion about social relations within our communities in the efforts to create a socially just society' (2002: 104–6). Without discounting the importance of such a reading, there is yet another way of assessing the intersecting transgressions that Anamika's romantic encounters encompass: for Anamika, the queerness of these relationships is not their most taboo-breaking aspect; instead, she is more aware of breaking social proscriptions pertaining to caste, class and age. Consequently, Anamika and the text as a whole refuse an othering of homosexual desire and instead present it as a given.

Anamika is also very aware that the expression of homosexual desire does not obviate the possibility of exploitation. When she forces herself upon her classmate Sheela, her desire is depicted as predatory and far from a liberatory force; her aggressive behaviour later fills her with guilt as she perceives her actions as that of 'a quasi rapist' and a 'bumbling sixteen-year-old with grand delusions about being a philanderer' (Dawesar, 2005: 211). This guilt about her sexual conduct intersects with communal shame as she recalls how, following Indira Gandhi's assassination in October 1984 by her Sikh guards, 'the state machinery, politicians, police and mobs, Hindus and Muslims, all joined hands to set fire to the Sikhs' and her 'feelings of shame at being Hindu in 1984' intermingle with her 'feelings of shame at having forced' herself on Sheela (2005: 217). While convincingly charting Anamika's sensitivity to her own and her religious community's abuse of power, the novel also complicates the progressive implications of her feelings of shame, which are shown to stem at least partly from Anamika's view of herself as a superior being. This sense of superiority is rooted not only in her intelligence but also, and more problematically, in her Brahmin identity. As we will see below, Anamika is ashamed of her behaviour partly because she believes that, as a member of the Brahmin caste, it *behoves* her to behave ethically, which has, perhaps, the unintended effect of recycling rather than challenging the myth of Brahmin superiority.

The narrative of lesbian desire as consistently and inherently resistant is further complicated by Anamika's conservative insistence on the separation of the public from the private, and of the erotic from the juridical. The direct and indirect speech attributed to Anamika is marked not only by an 'untenable but unchallenged foundation of caste privilege', but also by caste superiority (Rajendran, 2015: 81). She appears to believe that the Mandal Commission recommendations would result in the calcification, rather than the dissipation, of caste differences and perceives eroticism as the only means of challenging caste hierarchies: 'My Brahmin fluids had already mixed with her [Rani's] low caste ones. Mandal could stuff his list of schedules up his nose' (Dawesar, 2005: 145). When confronted by Sheela about her opposition to the Mandal Commission report, Anamika does not dismiss the 'atrocities committed' against the lowest castes in India, but insists 'the Mandal recommendations are perverse. If a lower caste guy gets admission on the basis of merit, he won't count in the reserved category … Reservations are for those who won't make it on merit' (2005: 126). As Gail Omvedt points out, in contemporary India, 'merit has become an ideology justifying continued upper caste monopoly ... It is as if upper-caste monopoly in high-level jobs were a result of genetically-coded ability to think and perform, while reservations were a "gift" presented – at the cost of slowing down efficiency' (2004: n.p.). Anamika's reliance on the concept of 'merit' to explain her opposition to affirmative action is meant to legitimise her essentially conservative and inegalitarian stance by endowing it with a patina not only of equality and social justice, but also of rationality.

Moreover, Anamika's reference without any trace of irony to her 'superior' genetic make-up as a Brahmin and to the idea of India as a monolithic entity makes her a deeply problematic figure of resistance: 'I wanted to sacrifice myself for the right thing, for justice, for *my pure brahmin genes*, and for India' (Dawesar, 2005: 253; emphasis mine). In her father's presence, she expresses disdain for the young Brahmin men reported to have set fire to themselves in protest against the Mandal Commission recommendations, deeming them as 'immature and reckless', because she feels that this is not the 'rational' way to challenge the recommendations; instead, she argues, 'they need to throw out the government' (2005: 170). However, later in the novel, while on holiday with India in Kausali, it becomes clear that she idolises those young Brahmin men and wishes to emulate their actions: 'The smell of kerosene and *young upper caste flesh* invaded villages where the reservation policy made no difference because there were no schools, no colleges, no drinking water. I wanted to make the same kind of *heroic* statement' (2005: 253; emphasis mine). Anamika appears to ignore the fact that the demonstrators are protesting against the recommendations not because they believe that a policy change would make no real difference in those parts of India that lack basic infrastructure, but because they fear that affirmative action would adversely affect their life chances. In fetishising 'upper caste flesh' and youth, Anamika seeks to endow the anti-egalitarian protests with dignity and to conveniently circumvent any discussion of the dilemma that centuries of structural injustices present to policy makers, despite presenting herself as the voice of reason. Heidi Nast's argument that 'white male homosexuality ... has structural opportunities others do not have, with the potential of some to become (in all their specificity) bastions of economic conservatism' (2002: 880) has a certain applicability here, in that Anamika's vocabulary of upper-caste, nationalist resistance ('sacrifice', 'justice', 'right thing') conceals a conservative ideology that is antagonistic towards policy making that could disrupt caste and class hierarchies.

Moreover, Anamika's understanding of cross-caste heterosexual relationships draws on 'images from Hindi art movies in which the upper caste brahmin falls in love with the lower caste servant and has passionate sex with her', effectively glossing over the systemic exploitation of Dalit women by upper-caste men (Dawesar, 2005: 12). The rape, stripping and parading of Dalit women, along with other forms of 'gendered humiliation', as Anupama Rao points out, reproduce upper-caste male privilege; this category of violence is 'particularly indecipherable as *caste* violence because it is normalized as upper-caste privilege and experienced as unspeakable form of intimate humiliation' (2009: 222; emphasis in the original). Anamika's recasting of herself as a Brahmin male, a symbol of privilege, is meant to heighten the forbidden tenor of her relationship with Rani and to accentuate its eroticism, but it problematically eclipses the lack of consent, humiliation and brutality that are often the defining features of Dalit women's encounters with upper-caste men.

Russo and Torres deem it 'problematic from a social justice perspective' to uncritically celebrate 'all lesbian, gay, and bisexual sexual expression simply on the grounds that it produces sexual pleasure' (2002: 104). While Anamika does foreground the transgressive power of homosexual desire across class, caste and age boundaries, she also dismisses, as we saw above, the possibility of change in the public sphere; moreover, although she is aware of the various power struggles that erotic desire can mirror and reproduce, her awareness of these complexities itself is intermittently self-reflexive, and her sexual and romantic fantasies are often imbued with patriarchal values. That said, if she appears to possess an arguably self-serving blind spot with respect to caste inequalities and inter-caste relations, Anamika displays a far keener awareness of her contradictory relationship with patriarchal modes of thinking. On the one hand, she yearns for the typically male privileges and expresses her desire to emulate the heroes in Hindi films who more often than not embody conventional forms of manhood. 'I wanted her to think of me as a mature, dependable, solid man. A Hindi film hero except with more intelligence, wisdom, and good sense, which those machos lacked' (Dawesar, 2005: 224). On the other hand, Anamika is conscious of how her romantic fantasies contradict the revulsion that she otherwise feels when faced with female submission and traditional gender roles in her own family:

> But I knew Rani would pick up after me. It was her way of showing love. Was this how women loved? Like slaves? Devotees? No wonder men took them for granted. My mother ran around cleaning up after my father. My aunt cleaned up after my uncle, my grandmother after my grandfather. On the one hand it outraged me. But on the other I found being a little prince suited me. When I grew up I'd have a big harem full of women. When I had a visitor, I'd be able to wave my hand and say, 'Oh! Don't worry, she'll do it', as I pointed to one of my brides. In turn I'd provide for them, give them gifts, and protect them. (2005: 132)

Furthermore, even as she is at pains to present herself as someone who rejects conventional modes of thinking which entail 'measur[ing] success by the same yardstick – car, house, electronic goods', and instead adores 'writers and scientists, intellectuals who could only be measured by the volume of gray matter in their brains', her avowed preoccupation with intellectual, rather than material, matters is undercut by Anamika's feelings of contempt for her father's colleagues, dressed as they are in 'cheaply made three-piece suits and flashy gold tiepins' (2005: 104). Displaying undeniable classism and a fairly conservative conceptualisation of success, she dismisses them for being 'low-level bureaucrats who hadn't done well enough on the civil service exams to make the grade for the foreign service or one of the more prestigious departments of the government. Water Works was as low as it got on the list' (2005: 104). Anamika's resistance, thus, at times acquires disturbing contours as we see her admiring power for power's sake, whether this power is of a bureaucratic or patriarchal nature, and exhibiting a conveniently parochial understanding of the implications of caste inequalities. As I demonstrate in the final section of this chapter, she also shows a fairly limited understanding of inequality in the United States, which further complicates her resistant subjectivity.

A Married Woman: religious fundamentalism and queerness

In Kapur's *A Married Woman*, the love affair between Astha, an unhappily married woman and mother of two, and Pipeelika, a young widow whose Muslim husband Aijaz was murdered by Hindu fundamentalists, takes place against the backdrop of the destruction of the Babri Mosque and the rise of anti-Muslim sentiment and violence in 1990s India. The reception of the novel's queer politics has been mixed: on the one hand, Kanika Batra considers it, alongside Shobha Dé's novel *Strange Obsession* (1992), an example of 'virulent or mildly homophobic representations of lesbians by Indian Women Writers' (2008: 254); on the other hand, Ruth Vanita finds in the novel a 'sympathetic portrayal' of lesbianism (2005: 254).

A Married Woman is punctuated by descriptions of anti-Muslim demonstrations as well as counter-demonstrations. It offers a trenchant critique of the Hindutva ideology propagated since the 1980s by the Bharatya Janata Party (BJP) which sees 'Islam and Muslims as an alien force which, through invasion and war, caused a seismic demographic shift to the detriment of the natural state of Hinduness in the subcontinent' (Waiker, 2018: 162). Taking the form of what Muthiah Alagappa refers to as 'militant social activism' (2004: 217), Hindutva ideology relies heavily on a language of righteous resistance; as the narrator of Kapur's novel observes:

> Waving saffron flags, Hinduism marched across the country in the following months, marched in time to film songs converted into bhajans, to Leaders trying to convince the masses that the glory of an ancient land could be resurrected by their united hands. Young men, show your manhood, rescue mother India from the influence of the Muslim invaders, whose long shadow falls over us even now. The wrongs of the past have to be righted. (2002: 184)

The novel charts the BJP-led procession (the Ratha Yatra) across the country to the site of the Babri Mosque[3] in a bid to shore up support from Hindu voters; in fact, this procession was in part a response to the Mandal Commission report as some members of the BJP thought the report 'was a plan to break up Hindu society' and, as Ramachandra Guha explains, the BJP found it to be politically expedient 'to shift the terms of political debate, away from Mandal and caste and back towards religion and the mandir/mosque question' (2007: 635).[4] According to Richard Davis, the tenor of the movement was deeply 'religious, allusive, militant, masculine, and anti-Muslim', leading to increased communal violence and the eventual destruction of the Babri Mosque in 1992 (1996: 42).

Astha and Pipeelika, who are both Hindu, are united in their opposition to religious extremism in the country, and it is not without significance that their first meeting takes place in Ayodhya (the site of the now-razed Babri Masjid) where Astha gives a speech on religious tolerance. Astha's queer awakening and her affair with Pipeelika bring in their wake a fundamental shift in her understanding of intimacy: the physical, emotional and spiritual communion that she experiences with Pipeelika ('skin on skin, mind on mind with nothing in between') is a far cry from her sexual relationship with her husband Hemant (Kapur, 2002: 303). Astha's caste is not specified in the novel, but she is clearly not a member of the lowest castes, and while she is married into a middle-class Hindu family, compared to Anamika, her enjoyment of the privileges that accompany those identity markers is limited. Her marriage to Hemant was an arranged one and he effectively robs her of her inheritance, usurps any money that she makes through her paintings and neglects her emotionally. Moreover, he is entirely insensitive to the plight of India's minorities, subscribing to a conveniently brutal eye-for-an-eye logic that deems that Muslims in India should suffer and their places of worship be destroyed, given that Hindus in Pakistan are treated with equal hostility, and their temples routinely desecrated. He derides Astha for her humanist sensibility, arrogantly signalling not only his lack of affinity with her ideals, but also his refusal to give serious consideration to her point of view: '"The fact that shrines are desecrated there, doesn't make it acceptable here. It's not a Muslim thing, it's a secular thing, a human thing." "It's a cowardly thing, a fool thing", he said mockingly' (2002: 130). Hemant is openly hostile to Astha's involvement in a play about the Babri Mosque directed by Aijaz, who would later become Pipeelika's husband, at the school where she teaches, and he seeks to deflate her enthusiasm by relying on well-worn patriarchal instructions: 'Keep to what you know best, the home, children, teaching. All this doesn't suit you' (2002: 116). These just-cited lines poignantly underscore Astha's sense of isolation within her marriage and bring to the fore the contrasting luminous beauty and camaraderie that characterise her bond with Pipeelika: 'After their first sexual encounter', we are told, 'Astha felt strange, making love to a woman took getting used to. And it also felt strange, making love to a friend instead of an adversary' (2002: 231). Pipeelika's marriage to Aijaz was a far happier one than Astha and Hemant's: Aijaz was an activist, using his street theatre group to address communal conflict, specifically the Babri Masjid-Ram Janam Bhoomi[5] controversy. Yet Pipeelika was unable to talk to him about her same-sex experiences, concluding that 'there were some things that could not be shared, no matter how understanding the other person' (2002: 130).

The course of Astha and Pipeelika's relationship, however, does not run smoothly either. The friction that develops between them stems primarily from their divergent conceptions of how queer lives can and should be lived. Pipeelika's is more clearly an activist sensibility: it is she who insists that Astha join her at a Gay and Lesbian Film Festival, Pipeelika again who asks her lover what is, in her eyes, a rhetorical question: 'We have to struggle for acceptance and the right to love as we feel. Don't you think so, Ant?' (2002: 237).[6] But Astha is unable to respond in the affirmative, feeling alienated from openly gay men and women that she sees on-screen as her sexual encounters with Pipeelika remain cloaked in lies, made possible only by the acceptance of homosociality in their culture.

Astha's queer resistance initially resides in the lies that she tells her husband allowing her to extricate herself from her duties as a housewife in order to spend time with her lover. These lies acquire a special significance since her husband is also deeply contemptuous of women's friendships, and never suspects Astha of having an affair with Pipeelika, seeing it as so unnatural as to be impossible. But Astha's duplicity does not challenge or shift the fundamental power imbalances that underpin her marriage. If Pipeelika is initially understanding of the constraints facing Astha as a wife in a conventional marriage, and in fact encourages Astha to resort to deception, she later becomes more exacting, insisting that Astha spend more time with her and cease lying about their relationship. Batra finds that in Pipeelika, Kapur has created a 'hypocritical lesbian activist', but perhaps Pipeelika's increasing assertiveness can be read as a shift in Pipeelika's own perception of herself as a lesbian (2008: 254). Having been in a loving relationship with her husband, Pipeelika begins to increasingly identify as a lesbian who quite simply wishes to come out. Her insistence (which causes Astha a considerable degree of discomfort) coincides with the changes that she undergoes as an activist. Having earlier worked for a non-governmental organisation that provided alternative education to slum children, the private and the public converge in her sensibility, and result in a change in her career path. She applies to a doctoral programme at an American university, intending to study 'the politics of communalism and how it is represented' (Kapur, 2002: 288). As part of her research, she visits the areas in India that were particularly affected by communal violence following the destruction of the Babri Mosque. Her desire to study this subject is sparked by 'what is happening around her' and by the possibility that it might help her come to terms with her husband's death (2002: 288). Both her identification as a lesbian and her new research interests are also a response to the realisation that she 'is not alone', and that her personal life and the 'outside' world are inextricably interlinked (2002: 288).

Astha's modes of queer resistance fall short of Pipeelika's vision of a fulfilling queer life, but the text invites us to see both as legitimate. In a scene towards the end of the novel, while anticipating her dissatisfaction with it, Astha describes to Pipeelika a recent dream of hers in which she is able to reconcile the various demands made on her by cordoning off her conflicting emotional needs:

> I have a fantasy, listen my love, and do not laugh ... I have a room, small but private, where my family pass before my eyes. It is very light, before me is a wall which divides the house, but I can see my children, that satisfies me, though to them I am invisible, that satisfies me too.
>
> This room will be our room, you with me, living in harmony. Our lives are separate, different things call to us, different demands are made on us, but always that solid base beneath us. (2002: 241)

It is significant that Astha described her vision as both a 'dream' and a 'fantasy', underscoring both its involuntariness *and* desirability for Astha. Unlike her lover who wishes to bridge the artificial public–private divide in her identity, Astha seeks to become even more firmly entrenched in her private self, which she is having to split repeatedly into compartments of diminishing sizes. While Pipeelika resists the forced invisibility foisted upon queer persons, Astha seeks refuge in that very invisibility, finding it difficult to conceive of a mode of parenting outside the confines of the traditional, heterosexual family even if it means resigning herself to a loveless existence:

> [F]or her the business of raising children had a set of dynamics that were the standard ones. That those dynamics did not include companionship and understanding was regrettable, but she had grown used to it. She saw herself as a bird pecking at a few leftover crumbs from the feast of life. (2002: 242)

However, as woefully inadequate as Pipeelika finds Astha's fantasy, it does represent a disruption of the home, and specifically, the conjugal home 'as a site of sanitized heterosexuality' (Gopinath, 2005: 176). Moreover, it is significant that in the weeks leading up to Pipeelika's departure for the US, to which I will return in the final section of this chapter, Astha's grief emerges as a protean, multifaceted force: she is overcome by an intense, almost frenzied desire to paint and, artistically, those weeks are the most prolific of her life. Astha's largest exhibition takes place a few days before Pipeelika's flight and features twenty canvases of which six are 'devoted to the Babri Masjid and different forms of protest, another six to various aspects of Pipee and herself ... four of her children, and two of men modelled on Hemant, one of her domestic servants' (Kapur, 2002: 302). As disguised as the paintings depicting Pipeelika and herself are, the exhibition is a queered political statement in which the various strands of her life come together and jostle for prominence, and suggest the sense of rupture and perplexity that Medina invokes in his conceptualisation of resistance. 'Basically my life' are the words in which Astha sums up the canvases (2002: 302). As she prepares her paintings for display, the narrator homes in on one of the canvases:

> The painting was an interior, two women sitting on a charpai. The patches of colour came from a red cushion, an open window, the white of a pillow on a bed, the bangles of one, the bag and chappals of the other thrown on the floor. The figures themselves were indistinct and shadowy, one had a drooping head, the other had her face turned away. The small canvas added to the sense of claustrophobia. (2002: 302)

The painting can be seen as a visual rendition of Astha's dream, discussed above. It is also reminiscent of the paintings *Two Women*

(1936), in which the two female figures are also not looking at one another (although the face of one of the female figures is fully visible), and *Woman on Charpai* (1940), both by the queer Indian artist Amrita Sher-Gil (1913–41). The two paintings by Sher-Gil feature women inhabiting confined domestic spaces, and the points of convergence between Sher-Gil's work and Astha's paintings suggest that Astha is tapping into a queer Indian genealogy.[7] The various 'feminine' accoutrements in Astha's painting (the bag, chappals and bangles) and the smallness of the canvas bring to the fore the limited space that Astha is able to allow her relationship with Pipeelika to occupy and the resultant unhappiness. But the presence of a shared charpai, a traditional woven bed, rather than a modern bed with a mattress (which is more likely to be found in contemporary, middle-class, urban homes), underscores both the sexual nature of their relationship and its timelessness. The demeanours that Astha lends the two female figures, with one figure's face turned away and the other with a drooping head, confound any attempts at identification on the part of the spectator. When her husband, who cannot imagine his wife having an affair with a woman, asks her if she and Pipeelika are the two women depicted in the painting, Astha responds categorically in the negative: '"Of course not", said Astha quickly. "They are imaginary. *You* can't see their faces. Could be anyone"' (2002: 302; emphasis mine). I would argue that Astha's use of the second person pronoun in this passage is strategic: it is ostensibly being used in its generic sense but can also be read as a deeply personal 'you', which functions as a critique of Hemant's inability to read Astha and Pipeelika's faces and the queer emotions that they exhibit. Moreover, her remark that the two women in the painting could be anyone suggests her desire to 'normalise', rather than reify, queerness and queer bodies.

The Ministry of Utmost Happiness: intersexuality, religion and resistance

As they are in Kapur's novel, unhappiness, queerness and resistance are closely linked in *Utmost Happiness*. One of the main characters peopling Roy's sprawling second novel is Aftab, who is born

Queering resistance

with intersex attributes but is assigned the male gender at birth. Aftab would later choose to call herself Anjum, a name used for both Muslim boys and girls. (The novel uses male pronouns when referring to Aftab/Anjum until she transitions; I have used the name Anjum in my discussion and have employed the pronouns 'she' and 'her' since Anjum identifies as female.)

Anjum's ambiguous genitalia at birth are a source of much distress for her Muslim parents, and in the ensuing years, her body is subjected to a series of surgical procedures and to a 'cultural project', led by her father, who is determined to inculcate 'conventional manliness' in Anjum by telling her 'stories about their warrior ancestors and their valour on the battlefield' (Roy, 2017: 17). A defining moment in her life occurs when as an adolescent she catches sight of Bombay Silk, 'a tall, slim-hipped woman wearing bright lipstick, gold high heels and a shiny, green satin kameez shalwar' (2017: 18). The narrator purposely does not specify whether Bombay Silk is a transgender or transsexual person, or indeed a transvestite, underscoring instead her heightened femininity and her distance from conventional womanhood and its constraints:

> He wanted to be her ...
> No ordinary woman would have been permitted to sashay down the streets of Shahjahanabad dressed like that. Ordinary women in Shahjahanabad wore burqas or at least covered their heads and every part of their body except their hands and feet. The woman Aftab followed could dress as she was dressed and walk the way she did only because she wasn't a woman. Whatever she was, Aftab wanted to be her. (2017: 18)

The repetition of the phrase 'he wanted to be her' underscores the power of this catalytic instance of recognition which enables Anjum to articulate a desire which is at once foundational *and* existential. While the articulation of her desire, as I discuss in greater detail below, does not keep at bay the spectre of identitary suffering and unhappiness, it does come with a sense of liberation. 'Not all desires lead to freedom', as John Berger observes in *Hold Everything Dear: Dispatches on Survival and Resistance*; instead, 'freedom is the experience of a desire being acknowledged, chosen and pursued' (2007: 2). And pursue her desire for femaleness is precisely what

Anjum does: she follows Bombay Silk to the dilapidated haveli named Khwabgah ('The House of Dreams') whose inhabitants are Hijras.[8] Anjum is initially 'shooed away' by the Hijras who do not wish to incur the wrath of her father (Roy, 2017: 21). But 'the admonition and punishment' that await her do little to diminish her resolve to be part of this community, and she strategically makes herself indispensable to its members who eventually allow her entry into the haveli:

> It was the only place in the world where he felt the air made way for him ... Over a period of a few months by running errands, by carrying their bags and musical instruments when the residents went on their city rounds, by massaging their tired feet at the end of a working day, Aftab eventually managed to insinuate himself into the Khwabgah. Finally the day dawned when he was allowed in. (2017: 21–2)

But this newfound happiness is soon blighted by the exigencies of her changing body, bringing home to her the relevance of the observations made by Nimmi, a Khawabgah resident, about gender dysphoria and unhappiness: 'The riot is *inside* us. The war is *inside* us. Indo-Pak is *inside* us. It will never settle down. It *can't*' (2017: 23; emphasis in the original). As she enters puberty, Anjum's 'body began to wage war' on her (2017: 24). The description of the masculinising changes that her body undergoes poignantly underscores how her body is both the enemy and a site of resistance for Anjum:

> He grew tall and muscular. And hairy ... He developed an Adam's apple that bobbed up and down. He longed to tear it out of his throat. Next came the unkindest betrayal of all – the thing that he could do nothing about. His voice broke ... He was repelled by it and scared himself each time he spoke. (2017: 24)

This radical change in her appearance, which causes her 'sweet, high voice' to be replaced by 'a deep powerful man's voice', severs her last tie to the 'real world' and she moves into the Khwabgah, becoming one of its occupants, instead of a mere visitor (2017: 24). This move costs Anjum her family or what Butler refers to as 'normative kinship configurations': her father disowns her and her mother can only bring herself to meet her at the shrine of a

Muslim saint (1994: 15). But with Anjum's new status as a resident of the Khwabgah comes the joy of being able to express herself through clothing and make-up. The narrator's meticulous cataloguing of Anjum's favourite clothes and accessories and the detailed description of her make-up routine bring to the fore the immense pleasure that she derives through this self-expression, reminding us of the pleasure that Arjie, the male protagonist of Shyam Selvadurai's novel *Funny Boy* (1994), derives from dressing up as a bride: 'The sequined, gossamer kurtas and pleated Patiala shalwars, shararas, ghararas, silver anklets, glass bangles and dangling earrings. She had her nose pierced and wore an elaborate, stone-studded nose-pin, outlined her eyes with kohl and blue eye shadow and gave herself a luscious, bow-shaped Madhubala[9] mouth of glossy-red lipstick' (Roy, 2017: 26).

Anjum eventually undergoes a series of gender reassignment surgeries that entails removing 'her male parts' and enhancing 'her existing vagina' (2017: 26). The surgeries, however, deprive her of the ability to experience sexual pleasure, since the vagina that her doctor constructs for her turns out to be 'a scam' (2017: 26). Roy's novel is at pains to highlight both Anjum's determination to visibly embody the gender that she identifies with and the exploitation by the medical profession to which it makes her vulnerable. Anjum is very much an outsider within the Hijra community in Delhi, even before she decides to leave Khawabgah, and even though she was at one time its most recognisable member for the outside, non-Hijra world. Much of Anjum's unhappiness lies in the apparent irreconcilability of her conventional and unconventional desires, which is reflected in her vocabulary which straddles convention and unconventionality; for instance, instead of the politically correct term Dalit, she deploys the pejorative term 'Chamar' when referring to the lowest castes (2017: 37). Unlike Saeeda, a younger trans person, who uses the terms 'cis-Man and FtoM and MtoF', Anjum mocks these important distinctions within the community which she dismissively refers to as 'trans-france' and doggedly prefers to use the less precise term Hijra (2017: 38). Like Bibi Haldar, the protagonist of Lahiri's short story, Anjum yearns to 'live like an ordinary person', 'to be a mother' and to not be relegated to the margins of societal constructions of womanhood (2017: 30). In inquiring whether 'ambitions such as these, on the part of someone like herself' were 'reasonable or unreasonable', the narrator points to the artificial legitimacy of gender-specific desires (2017: 30).

It is when she adopts Zainab, an abandoned child, that the pain of her gender dysphoria subsides: 'The warring factions inside Anjum felt silent. Her body felt like a generous host instead of a battlefield' (2017: 30). But Anjum's battle against her own body and its impulsions proves to be a lifelong one and eventually comes to be informed as much by her intersexuality as by the positioning of her Muslim body in an India that is becoming increasingly receptive to Hindutva ideology. During a visit to Ahmedabad with a friend, Anjum finds herself in the midst of the 2002 violent anti-Muslim riots that took place in the state of Gujarat. Hindu militant organisations including the Rashtriya Swayamsevak Sangh, Vishva Hindu Parishad and Bajrang Dal organised mass demonstrations in the aftermath of the Godhra massacre of the fifty-seven Hindu pilgrims and karsevaks returning from Ayodhya in February 2002. These protests set the stage for the pogroms of March and April that year, during which, as Pankaj Mishra notes, '[m]ore than 2,000 Muslims were murdered, and tens of thousands rendered homeless in carefully planned and coordinated attacks of unprecedented savagery' (2012: n.p.). Moreover, it is estimated that 'a minimum of 350 women must have been assaulted and raped' during the Gujarat pogrom (Khanna, 2008: 145).

Anjum's body is read by the Hindu extremists as Muslim, but also as neither male nor female: '*Ai Hai, Saali Randi Hijra!* Sister-fucking Whore Hijra. Sister-fucking Muslim Whore Hijra' (Roy, 2017: 62). While Anjum's recognisably male, Muslim friend is brutally murdered by a Hindu mob, Anjum is spared because of the superstitious belief that Hijras possess the divine ability to both bestow blessings and cast curses. Her intersex identity and her corresponding status as a talisman thus allow her to escape a violent death, but they also become a source of survival guilt. The hyphenated adjectives (un-killed, un-hurt) in the passage below highlight the fate to which Anjum's Muslim identity dooms her that day and the tragic exceptionalism that allows her to escape, but also binds her to the militants and their fortunes:

> They left her alive. Un-killed. Un-hurt. Neither folded nor unfolded. She alone. So that they might be blessed with good fortune.

Butchers' Luck.
That's all she was. And the longer she lived, the more good luck she brought them.
She tried to un-know the little detail as she rattled through her private fort. But she failed. (2017: 63)

Following the Gujarat riots, when Anjum expresses her desire to leave the Khwabgah and 'help the poor', it earns her the derision of her peers (2017: 56). Meher, a younger trans person, mockingly points out, 'which Poor would want to be helped by *us*', prompting others to giggle at 'the idea of intimidating poor people with offers of help' (2017: 56; emphasis in original). The intimidatory practices of the Hijra community constitute an integral part of their survival strategy: while begging in the streets, or performing at weddings or ceremonies marking the arrival of a newly born, Hijras deploy a series of performative acts, including loud hand clapping and the lifting of clothes to reveal their mutilated or absent genitalia. Such acts signal, as Gayatri Reddy has pointed out, both the refusal of the Hijra community to acquiesce to their social marginalisation and their resolve to 'proclaim their status publicly, acknowledging their stigma and playing on it' (2005: 137). Hijras are aware of how these acts 'label them' as Others (as also evident in the novel in Meher's meaningful use of the collective pronoun 'us'), but also enable them to 'threaten the public' and unsettle, however temporarily, the prevailing power balance (2005: 137).[10] By alerting us to these intimidatory tactics, the text refuses to cast Anjum or other Hijras as victims, but in charting Anjum's eventual departure from the Khwabgah, it also underscores Anjum's increasing dissatisfaction with a narrow understanding of herself based on her sexed identity and with a strict 'us versus them' dichotomy, no matter how liberatory and, indeed, necessary she had found it in her youth.

The narrator highlights the somewhat problematic privilege, alongside her subalternity, that marked Anjum's life at Khwabgah, especially once she became 'a sought-after lover' and 'Delhi's most famous Hijra', thereby shedding light on the complex contours of Hijra visibility and invisibility (Roy, 2017: 26–8). Even when embedded in drastically different notions of exceptionalism, the social meanings attached to Anjum's body as a Muslim Hijra by Hindu fundamentalists (as I discussed earlier) and by progressive artists and activists result in epistemic violence against her. If Anjum's encounter with Hindu fundamentalists reduced her identity to a negative adjectival presence (un-hurt, un-killed), necessarily defined in terms of the violence that would have visited her were hers not a visibly intersex body, the filmmakers, NGOs and foreign correspondents who were ostensibly interested in her story as an individual, too, sought to silence her and reduce her to a recognisable, legible text that would conveniently confirm rather than confound, their prejudices:

> In interviews Anjum would be encouraged to talk about the abuse and cruelty that her interlocutors assumed she had been subjected to by her conventional Muslim parents, siblings and neighbours before she left home … 'Others have horrible stories, the kind you people like to write about', she would say. 'Why not talk to them?' But of course newspapers didn't work that way. She was the chosen one. It had to be her, even if her story was slightly altered to suit readers' appetites and expectations. (2017: 26)

In the days preceding her departure from the Khwabgah, Anjum's resolve to burn all the mementoes of her international fame represents a rejection of the talismanic status of her intersex body and its distillation into a marketable, consumable product. By highlighting how the decision by foreign media outlets to spotlight certain Hijras is underpinned by commercial imperatives and the desire to perpetuate, rather than to lend nuance to, prevailing narratives about both India and intersex bodies, the novel offers a trenchant critique of the commodification of Hijra lives. Following the liberalisation of the Indian economy and its emergence as a nuclear power, the attention that foreign journalists once showered upon Anjum now comes to be directed at Saeeda, who acquires 'greater global currency' (Newport, 2018: 238).[11] Given Saeeda's ease with the English language and with Western clothing, she is seen to possess attributes more befitting the 'image of the New India – a nuclear power and an emerging destination for international finance' (Roy, 2017: 38). Therefore, Anjum's need to annihilate the tokens of her internationally celebrated past, which include 'three documentary films (about her)', 'two glossy coffee-table books of photographs (of her)' and 'an album of press clippings from foreign newspapers in more than thirteen languages … (about her)', represents a rebellion against the reification of her existence, 'a mad insurrection against a lifetime of spurious happiness' (2017: 57).

As we saw above, Anjum's identitary crises and resistances often unspool at a sartorial level. Upon her return from Gujarat, terrifyingly aware of the perils of being Muslim, especially a Muslim woman, in India, she extends her vestiary strategies to her adoptive daughter Zainab. Despite Zainab's vociferous protestations, she starts dressing her like a boy, opting for a Pathan suit to replace her 'frothy, puff-sleeved frocks and Made-in-China squeaking shoes with flashing heel-lights' (2017: 32). Anjum's aggressive parenting comes across as a subversive but also ambiguous negotiation of gender, queer and Muslim identities. A Pathan suit, which is 'a long shirt to the knees, worn over a loose-fitting *salwar*, or pajama' (Reddy, 2005: 245) brings to mind the Pathans who are historically from Afghanistan and who were a 'staple of the colonial homoerotic' (Cohen, 2002: 153). In choosing to cross-dress Zainab, Anjum queers her but does little to obscure her Muslim identity, since Pathans are predominantly Sunni Muslims; moreover, she insists on renaming her 'Mahdi'. (Mahdi in Islamic eschatology is a male messianic figure who will appear, alongside Jesus Christ, before the end of the world and rid it of evil.) Paradoxically, she also teaches Zainab the Gayatri Mantra, a Sanskrit chant, which would allow her to pass as Hindu. These imposed changes earn Anjum the ire of the other Khwabgah residents, who correctly read in Anjum's actions directed at Zainab a lack of consideration for Zainab's wishes: 'Forcing a little girl to live as a boy against her wishes, even for the sake of her own safety, is to incarcerate her, not liberate her' (Roy, 2017: 55). Anjum's gendered reimagining of her daughter can be read as part of the necropolitical resistance that Anjum enacts following her close encounter with brutality and death in Gujarat, to which Alex Tickell has drawn our attention (2018). The death of targeted individuals and groups, but also the death of society itself become the recurring motifs in her life, evident in her decision to leave the Khwabgah and set up home in a graveyard where many generations of her family are buried. In doing so, she reaffirms her Muslim identity and also poignantly and paradoxically brings to fruition the Hindu fundamentalists' violent dictate encapsulated in their slogan: '*Mussalman ka ek hi sthan! Qabristan ya Pakistan!* Only one place for the Mussalman! The Graveyard or Pakistan!'

(Roy, 2017: 62). Over time, Anjum converts the graveyard into a guesthouse by enclosing and building rooms around her relatives' graves. In the graveyard, she comes to inhabit a gendered existence which is more fluid and less obviously committed to femininity than her Khwabgah one. Foregoing her earlier flamboyant outfits in vibrant colours, she opts to wear Pathan suits in 'pale blue and powder pink', the two colours that function as conventional gender signifiers, particularly in childhood (2017: 66). If we take 'non-binary' as an 'umbrella term' for 'anyone who doesn't currently identify with the binary notion of being exclusively male or female', Anjum's use of both colours can perhaps be read as an indication of her desire to lead a non-binary life, even if she does not deploy this vocabulary in the narrative (Twist et al., 2020: 18).

Anjum's earlier intense preoccupation with forging a distinct gender identity is diluted by the emergence of a resistant subjectivity that is rooted in the ubiquity and inevitability of death and spawns a certain fearlessness in her. When she is questioned by municipal authorities for living illegally in the graveyard and is threatened with the demolition of the house that she has built there, she defiantly informs the officials that 'she was not living in the graveyard, she was dying in it – and for this she didn't need permission from the municipality because she had authorization from the Almighty Himself' (Roy, 2017: 67). Driven by the same fear that led the Hindu fundamentalists in Gujarat to spare Anjum, the officials retract their threats and Anjum compels them to choose instead 'the path of appeasement and petty extortion' (2017: 67). She emerges as a formidable negotiator and quite literally becomes involved in the business of death, as her new abode quickly develops into a funeral parlour, a paradoxical economic enterprise which is life-affirming because of its success and death-centred by its very nature. In renegotiating the line between life and death in the graveyard, thus Anjum also redefines the meaning of resignation and defiance.

Movement and queer resistance

In this concluding section, I assess what the three novels reveal about the relationship between queer resistance and space. Tellingly, all three texts signal a departure of sorts for queer characters: it is the physical departure of Pipeelika and Anamika from India for the US in *A Married Woman* and *Babyji* respectively. In Roy's novel, Anjum enacts a double departure: first from her familial home situated in what the Hijras refer to as 'Duniya', which is Urdu for the world, or 'what most ordinary people thought of as the real world', for the Khwabgah, and then, from the Khwabgah for an even more markedly liminal social space: a graveyard (Roy, 2017: 24).

Tickell has noted that the graveyard in Roy's novel 'is a space of both literal and figurative exclusion: a zone where those who are not accepted or welcomed in wider society can find a kind of sanctuary' (2018: 109). Indeed, I argue that Anjum's 'necropolitics', to deploy Tickell's terminology, should be read as a distinctly exclusion-centred resistance, with death being the ultimate form of exclusion. The graveyard becomes a 'hub for Hijras who, for one reason or another, had fallen out of, or had been expelled from, the tightly administered grid of Hijra Gharanas' (Roy, 2017: 68).[12] Anjum's illegally constructed house thus becomes a safe haven for groups and individuals who find themselves relegated to the margins of society and who constitute the 'Other of the Other', including Tilo as we saw in Chapter 2 (Žižek, 1996: 136). Anjum's departure from the Khwabgah and her setting up of another kind of house of dreams suggests a broadening of the meaning of exclusion for her, and one that is not solely based on gender, sexual or sexed identity. As Roy has observed in an interview, Anjum is not meant to be 'a signifier' and is instead only 'a character, like many other characters in the book, very unique, very much herself' (*Democracy Now!*, 2017: n.p.). Roy goes on to specify that the novel is 'not a sort of social history of the trans community' (2017: n.p.). In setting up home in a graveyard, Anjum exchanges one form of otherness for an entire spectrum of otherness. Her funeral parlour's clients are united only by their shared dismissal by the 'real world', a world that is defined by hierarchies and exacts conformity: 'The one clear criterion was that Jannat Funeral Services would only bury those whom the graveyards and imams of the Duniya rejected' (Roy, 2017: 81). Indeed, Anjum's politics of inclusionary exclusion blurs also the line separating humans and animals, with Anjum's mother buried in the same plot of land as Bismillah, a former Hijra, and Zainab's goat. In this exclusionary social space Anjum forms a community comprising out-of-favour Hijras, but also Dalits, illicitly adopted little girls and supporters of Kashmir's independence from India.

If, before her departure from the Khwabgah, her daughter Zainab had declared 'Mummy's never happy', the novel's denouement does not allow us to read Anjum (simply) as an unhappy queer (2017: 57). Her desire to mother a child finds fulfilment in Udaya Jebeen and she finally achieves a sense of belonging that eluded her in both her familial home and the Khwabgah. In the final pages of the novel, as Anjum takes little Udaya Jebeen out for a walk in the city, she looks back at Jannat Guest House 'with a sense of contentment and accomplishment' (2017: 438). The optimistic note on which Roy's novel ends, telling the reader that 'things would turn out all right in the end. They would, because they had to. Because Miss Udaya Jebeen, was come', keeps Anjum entrenched in the world of death, but with a clear stake in the future in the shape of Udaya, the child of a Maoist activist (2017: 438). It is significant that the closing paragraphs chart Anjum and Udaya's midnight stroll into the city and their safe return to the graveyard, suggesting also that 'Duniya', the real world, and the inhabitants of Jannat Guest House, may come to converse with each other after all, that the spatial boundary may become blurred, allowing movement and spillages in both directions.

I discussed the significance of Anamika's transgressive loitering in the city of Delhi earlier in the chapter; Anamika's first-person narrative is also punctuated by references to her yearning for a much bigger spatial displacement which would take her to the United States. This desire is concretised in the form of Anamika's visit, towards the end of the novel, to the offices of the United States Educational Foundation in India to speak to a counsellor about her plans to apply to American universities. The counsellor informs her that 'she is the best candidate from Delhi' with the 'best extracurricular activities' to have 'walked through the door this year' and encourages her to apply to Ivy League universities (Dawesar, 2005: 354). Anamika's initial response to the counsellor's praise is one of embarrassment: 'I smiled sheepishly. I could suddenly think of no extracurriculars except Sheela and India and Rani. I felt hot in the face' (2005: 354). But this awkwardness then gives way to self-assurance; as she catches sight of Harvard University's motto 'Veritas' ('truth') on the back cover of its brochure, she adapts it to reflect her confidence in her intellect: '"Meritas", I thought to myself' (2005: 354). Ahmed acknowledges how at one level the novel's 'investment in the freedom to be happy for queers corresponds with conventional class desires for upward mobility, in which the good life is associated with getting up and getting out', but she also alerts us to how in this closing scene queerness 'gets in the way' with Anamika's corporeal response – the hot face and sheepish smile triggered by the memory of her same-sex encounters – allowing 'the body to intrude with another kind of desire' (2010: 120). This queer desire then complicates Anamika's focus on a conservative and predictable variety of success. Indeed, queerness in Dawesar's novel troubles the distinction between the ambition of material success and transnational movement in the direction of the 'First World' and a struggle of a distinctly existential nature, which Ahmed describes as 'the freedom to breathe' (2010: 120).

But perhaps *because* the two become blurred, Anamika cannot (yet) see how limited and distorted her understanding of identity politics in the US really is. The two gay American men, both white, whom she encounters at an upscale bakery located in the diplomatic enclave in Delhi remain for Anamika, as Rajendran puts it, '[t]he final image of freedom', making America, in sharp contrast to India, synonymous with inclusiveness and non-normative desires and identities (2015: 81). As I have demonstrated elsewhere in my discussion of Kamila Shamsie's *Salt and Saffron* (2000), literary representations of cross-class romantic relationships set in the Indian subcontinent which locate the 'happy ending' necessarily off-stage and in more economically advanced countries run the risk of glossing over the inequities that beset those societies (Mirza, 2016). In a not dissimilar vein, Anamika's notion of (queer) freedom which she equates with her much-anticipated journey to the US, or with transnational spaces within India, elides any recognition of the prevailing homophobia in the US or of the challenges of inhabiting a queer identity as a woman of colour, or indeed the persistent, if not growing, class inequalities that give the lie to the idea of the American Dream resting as it does on the 'concept of class fluidity' even though study after study has repeatedly shown upward mobility in the US to be a myth (Samuel, 2012: 7).[13]

Long before Pipeelika leaves for the US to pursue a doctoral degree, geographical displacement is shown to play a key role in her relationship with Astha. As we saw earlier, their first meeting takes place in Ayodhya, hundreds of miles away from Astha's marital home in Delhi. Then, a few months into the relationship, Astha and Pipeelika embark on a three-week trip around India, on the heels of the Ekta Yatra, the so-called National Integration or Unity Procession, that took place during the months of December 1991 and January 1992. Led by the BJP leader Murli Manohar Joshi, the procession started from Kanyakumari and ended in Kashmir, concluding with the hoisting of the Indian flag at Lal Chowk in Srinagar (in the presence of Narendra Modi, the current Indian Prime Minister). The Ekta Yatra was ostensibly aimed at dousing 'the flames of separatism and fundamentalist terrorism – fanned, aided and abetted by Pakistan' (Bhushan and Katyal, 2002: 13), but it actually sought to bolster Hindu nationalist sentiments and to mark Kashmir 'as a Hindu territory' (Sökefeld, 2012: 104). This trip together is at once the longest span of time that they spend together as a couple and also the beginning of the end of their relationship, as it allows Pipeelika to begin carrying out field research on communal violence which would feed into her doctoral dissertation. Like Anamika, Pipeelika's desired transnational displacement is a manifestation of her educational aspirations and is certainly constructed as an intellectually liberatory move. But, given the subject matter of Pipeelika's proposed PhD, her move to the US also comes with the possibility of her acquiring a keener understanding of her own country and its politics. Moreover, Pipeelika's departure for the US coincides with Astha's geographical immobility, both in terms of national and domestic frontiers. Not only does Astha stay behind in India, but she also chooses to remain with her husband, children and parents-in-law in her marital home. But, as Oliver Ross has argued, 'the opposition of the "foreign", politicized gay/lesbian, and the "indigenous", apolitical same-sex desiring subject emerges as a rudimentary fallacy' in Kapur's novel (2016: 160). Astha *is* an unhappy queer, but unlike what we see in Dawesar's novel, the queer figure's departure for the US in *A Married Woman* is not equated with freedom and political liberation, or indeed, with a rejection of India. Equally, Astha's decision to stay in India, despite the sadness that it spawns, is not presented as being synonymous with creative stagnation, or with an acceptance of the political status quo. Ahmed has argued that '[t]he ethical and political question for queer subjects might ... not be *whether* to grieve but *how* to grieve' and that '[q]ueer feelings may embrace a sense of discomfort, a lack of ease with the available scripts for living and loving, along with an excitement in the face of the uncertainty of where this discomfort may take us' (2014 [2004]: 155–61; emphasis in the original). The final three short sentences of Kapur's novel – 'Her mind, heart and body felt numb. It continued like this for days. She felt stretched thin, thin across the globe' – are not suggestive of excitement and instead underscore Astha's pain stemming from her inability to find a script for living with Pipeelika (Kapur, 2002: 307). However, the temporal marker which tells us that Astha remained in such a state 'for days' hints at the eventuality of this numbness receding and giving way to other forms of queer living and loving which would remain intertwined with her artistic creations (2002: 307). Astha's desire to challenge the rise of communal hatred in her country through her art is a product as much of her humanist values and queer grief as it of her geographical *immobility*, which keeps her anchored in India:

> As her brush moved carefully over the canvas, her hand grew sure, her back straightened, she sat firmer on her stool, her gaze became more concentrated, her mind more focused. A calmness settled over her, tenuous, fragile, but calmness nevertheless. She thought of her name. Faith in herself. It was all she had. (2002: 299)

Movement across the canvas, rather than across and away from heterosexual domestic or national spaces, then, emerges as Astha's preferred avenue for expressing her dissident desires and for registering, perhaps more to herself than to others, her presence as an individual.

In juxtaposing the depiction of queer lives against instances of collective politics in contemporary Indian history which sought to deepen, rather than alleviate, power imbalances, the three novels not only shatter the public–private binary but also trouble the divide between queer resistance and forms of dissent that are not ostensibly connected to sexed identity or sexual orientation. The three texts compel us to see queer resistance as a necessarily polyvalent phenomenon, encompassing acts which are self-consciously subversive and others that are undeniably conservative; some forceful, others far less so. Ahmed reminds us that it is for 'very good reasons that queer theory has been defined not only as anti-heteronormative, but as anti-normative'; it is only fitting then that these literary representations of queer resistance should invite uneasiness and interrogation, and should resist normative scripts of contestation and defiance (2014 [2004]: 149).

Notes

1 The Lambda Literary Foundation is a Los Angeles–based LGBTQ+ organisation.
2 The suffix 'ji' or 'jee' in Punjabi, Urdu and Hindi functions as a sign of respect.
3 The Babri Masjid was a sixteenth-century mosque, the site of which many Hindus believe to be the birthplace of the Hindu deity Rama.
4 'Mandir' means temple in Hindi and Urdu, while a 'masjid' is a mosque.
5 Janam Bhoomi (Hindi): birthplace.
6 After being punishable by law for almost 150 years under Section 377 of the Indian Penal Code, homosexuality in India was decriminalised by the Delhi High Court in 2009; however, the decision was overturned four years later by the Supreme Court. Finally, on 6 September 2018, consensual gay sex was legalised by India's Supreme Court.
7 As Ruth Vanita and Saleem Kidwai observe, Sher-Gil's 'letters reveal her lesbian involvements' (2001 [2000]: 199).
8 According to Reddy (2005: 2), 'for the most part, hijras are phenotypic men who wear female clothing and, ideally, renounce sexual desire and practice by undergoing a sacrificial emasculation – that is, an excision of the penis and testicles – dedicated to the goddess Bedhraj Mata'.
9 Madhubala (1933–69) was a famous Bollywood actress.
10 Commenting on the significance of Hijras exposing their genitalia, Reddy notes that it 'signals a paradoxical inversion of power in favour of hijras, both by exposing the mutilation of the body and by implicitly incorporating a potential curse, as if to say, "By exposing myself to you, I curse you with such a fate"' (2005: 139).
11 Previously a semi-planned, semi-socialist economy, in response to a debt and foreign exchange crisis in 1991, India opened up to international trade and finance and adopted economic policies prescribed by the World Bank and the International Monetary Fund as part of their

Structural Adjustment programmes. India officially became a nuclear power in 1998.
12 The word 'gharana', as Rekha Pande explains, 'comes from the Hindi word *ghar* which means house, and the term refers to shelter, safety and belongingness', as well as to familial ties (2018: 218).
13 See, for example, Mark Robert Rank et al.'s *Poorly Understood: What America Gets Wrong About Poverty* (2021).

5

Troubled resistance, troubling resistance: *Homework*, *The Namesake* and *A Disobedient Girl*

> These tarnished rays, this night-smudged light – This is not that Dawn for which, ravished with freedom, we had set out in sheer longing, so sure that somewhere in its desert the sky harbored a final haven for the stars, and we would find it. […]
>
> Friends, come away from this false light. Come, we must search for that promised Dawn.
>
> – Faiz Ahmed Faiz, 'The dawn of freedom (August 1947)', translated by Agha Shahid Ali, 1996

This chapter focuses on the depiction of troubling and troubled, or what I also refer to as distorted, acts of resistance. Uday Chandra reminds us that 'the *failure of resistance* ought to be differentiated from the *failure to resist*' (2015: 565; emphasis in the original). I seek to differentiate distorted resistance from both the failure of resistance and the failure to resist, and I address some of the ways in which contemporary South Asian women's fiction grapples with acts of contestation which trouble our understanding of resistance as a progressive, emancipatory, strategic or even 'necessary response to intolerable circumstances' (Flynn, 2001: 17).

Of course, as mentioned in the Introduction, the unequivocally positive meaning attributed to certain resistant practices has been questioned by several postcolonial scholars, who have highlighted the limitations of nationalist modes of resistance and have challenged the triumphant tenor of discussions of anti-colonial resistance in view of the problems that continue to blight most postcolonial societies. The Introduction also invoked how feminist writings can embody a distorted form of resistance if they are insufficiently attentive to forces of oppression other than patriarchy or to the ways in which patriarchal oppression coalesces with other coordinates of subjugation. Moreover, in her essay 'A phoenix called resistance', Jasbir Jain underscores the susceptibility of the idea and practice of resistance to distortion, given that it is 'in constant danger of freezing into a fundamentalist position'; she finds a 'very fine dividing line between resistance and fundamentalism, between an oppositional stance and a hardened orthodoxy' (2007: 172–6). Resistance can also become a deeply problematic practice when it entails the use of physical force, presenting a serious 'ethico-political bind' (Butler, 2020). If Gandhian thought rejects political violence wholesale as a legitimate and effective form of resistance, as discussed in Chapter 2, Arundhati Roy, amongst others, has been concerned with how violence may be the only means by which disenfranchised groups can fight the grotesque injustices of the status quo, while also recognising how violence inevitably perverts any social movement and is particularly inimical to women. Indeed, considerable scholarship exists on the complex politics underpinning violent militancy and ideological extremism, the most obviously distorted forms that resistance can assume, as explored in novels by South Asian women writers such as Monica Ali's *Brick Lane* (2003), Kiran Desai's *The Inheritance of Loss* (2006), Anam's *The Good Muslim* (2011), Nayomi Munaweera's *Island of a Thousand Mirrors* (2012), Shamsie's *Home Fire* (2017) and Fatima Bhutto's *The Runaways* (2020).[1] This chapter, however, examines three novels which present us with figures of defiance who neither embrace a hardened orthodoxy nor resort to armed violence to contest the status quo, yet their acts of resistance speak to their troubled and troubling relationships with the idea of resistance.

The characters that I analyse below are an unnamed middle-aged Indian male immigrant in Australia in *Homework*, who agitates, often comically, for Goa's liberation following its takeover by India; Moushumi, a young Bengali-American woman in *The Namesake*, whose ostensibly transgressive academic, linguistic and amorous trajectories confound the line between self-defeating and constructive defiance; and, finally, Latha in *A Disobedient Girl*, for whom the erotic emerges as the primary source and form of agentic behaviour. An examination of these three figures will allow us to both broaden and deepen our understanding of what might constitute 'bad' and 'good' resistance and how the two might intersect with each other.

Home, homeland and irrelevant resistance

When Peres da Costa's *Homework*, a magic realist novel set in 1980s suburban Sydney, opens, the child narrator Mina's father is shown to have been protesting for over two decades against the Indian state's annexation of Goa in 1961.[2] As Peres da Costa has mentioned in a recent interview, the novel satirises 'the political relevance' of this event in Indian history for Mina's family (Lahiri-Roy and Peres da Costa, 2021: 98). By extension, I argue that the novel provides us with a compelling representation of *irrelevant* resistance; as we will see below, Mina's father's 'contentious politics' entails deploying many of the well-worn tactics of civil disobedience, but it is his primary political goal – Goa's liberation from India – that make his resistance both immaterial and baffling (Tilly and Tarrow, 2006).

His political agitation takes place alongside an increasingly desperate domestic crisis: his wife, Dolores, appears to suffer from manic depression, a condition that becomes heightened after she undergoes a hysterectomy. It is Dolores's often vocalised desire to die, her 'impenetrable, inconsolable grief', as well as her fits of frenetic activity and indifference towards her family, which occasionally slip into outright animosity, that frighten Mina; they often also reduce Mina's father to tears, and he retreats into the basement of the familial home (Peres da Costa, 1999: 176). His hopelessness and despair at his wife's deteriorating mental health and her bouts of hostility are juxtaposed against his unrealistically optimistic acts of resistance aimed at securing Goa's liberation from India, despite almost twenty-five years having elapsed since the event and despite there being no evidence of any support for this cause either within India or in the Goan diaspora. The author has noted that in *Homework*, she has tried to show 'how the double and triple yokes of colonialism, such as we find among Goans and Indians of the diaspora(s), can give rise to contradictions and crises of identity, even psychopathologies' (Lahiri-Roy and Peres da Costa, 2021: 98). Mina's father's reference to India's takeover of the state as an 'invasion' elides the status of Goa as a former European colony and echoes the language used in the Portuguese imperial centre to describe the incident (Peres da Costa, 1999: 156).[3] Of course, as Pamila Gupta has also pointed out, Portuguese India's integration into independent India took place in a distinctly 'anti-Gandhian manner' (2011: 330), with the then Prime Minister Jawaharlal Nehru using military force to effect the takeover, but there was very little resistance to it by the Goan population, a historical fact which is reflected in Peres da Costa's novel: 'Now, when I was ten, some twenty-five years after Nehru had occupied Goa with no resistance save those few boys from Bambolim College flicking rubber bands in the direction of the advancing Indian army ... Dad was still devising a plan to conquer his homeland' (Peres da Costa, 1999: 155).

Mina's father restores an old printing press and proceeds to write, edit and publish a triannual periodical on Goan liberation; he uses every opportunity to draw attention to this manufactured Goan cause, giving rise to a number of humorous episodes in a progressively bleak novel. For instance, he takes his three children to Canberra to stand for hours in the forecourt of the Federal Parliament, holding up a placard bearing the legend 'Free Goa'; later that day 'at the sitting of the House of Representatives', he proceeds to address his plea to the Prime Minister from the public gallery: 'And Goa, what is to be done with Goa?' (1999: 155). To cite another example, during a visit with his children to Old Sydney Town,[4] when he gets stuck in a mock guillotine and the subsequent rescue operation attracts the attention of the local television channels, Mina's father uses this as an opportunity to apprise Australian viewers of his beloved cause: '"Free Goa, *Goa libre*, Free Goa, *Goa libre!*" he suddenly chanted, beaming at the eight million potential viewers who may have seen him on commercial news that night' (1999: 170). His propagandist activities as a migrant in Australia, thousands of miles away from his homeland, bring to mind Benedict Anderson's discussion of 'long-distance nationalism'; according to Anderson, a long-distant nationalist:

> rarely pays taxes in the country in which he [*sic*] does his politics; he is not answerable to its judicial system ... he need not fear prison, torture, or death, nor need his immediate family. But, well and safely

positioned in the First World, he can send money and guns, circulate propaganda, and build intercontinental computer information circuits, all of which can have incalculable consequences in the zones of their ultimate destinations. (1998: 74)

But if Mina's father as a middle-class migrant is indeed well and safely positioned in Australia and if he does actively produce and circulate anti-Indian propaganda, there is much that separates him from the long-distance nationalist in Anderson's discussion. Perhaps most significantly, despite his admiration of armed insurgent groups, his acts of subversion remain unambiguously nonviolent in nature. Also, none of Mina's father's activities have any consequences in Goa or for Goans, whether diasporic or otherwise, given that a post-1961 Goan liberation movement never existed. Moreover, Anderson's work focuses on nationalist mobilisation amongst transnational groups, whereas Mina's father acts alone. He draws strength from far more recognisable insurgent movements; as Mina informs us, 'it wasn't just the Sikhs from whom he took his lead'; he also 'borrowed anthems from the Tamil Tigers of Elam, the Inkatha Freedom Fighters', and 'the Basques and the Sinn Fein were separatists whose aspirations and minor histories my father reconstituted into a private education' (Peres da Costa, 1999: 155). He relies on (other) political struggles around the globe to provide him with a vocabulary to articulate his own politics and thus to lend legitimacy or, more accurately, a presence to the Goan cause. Moreover, his insistence on bequeathing a muddled legacy of resistance to his Australian-born children appears to stem in part from his need to create a community of transnational Goan activists, which would in turn allay the loneliness of his struggle. Such is his preoccupation with the cause that the first words that Mina utters as a baby are '*Free Goa!*' (1999: 152; emphasis in the original). The young Mina, who shares a far stronger bond with her father than she does with her mother, is sometimes bewildered by but mostly admiring of her father's politics. However, his strategies of contestation also occasionally become a source of consternation for her; she recalls, for example, how during a school assembly, when she and her classmates were asked to present a flag of their countries of origin, he forbade her from brandishing the Indian flag with its 'evocative spinning wheel bound by amber and green familiar to Miss

Anderson', compelling her instead to hold up 'to the bored student body the unusual specimen of a Lusitanian flag', which caused a 'great deal of controversy' at the school and Mina 'much heartache' (1999: 156). Mina's father seems oblivious to how his denunciation of the Indian government at times becomes tantamount to foisting a Portuguese identity upon his offspring, in stark contradiction to his condemnation of European imperialism: '"Where are you from?" To this question he had drummed into me to answer, "Goa"; should I be further interrogated – worse, should I be accused of pedantry – I was to explain that since Goa was illegally confiscated by the Indian state, my allegiance was technically not Indian but Portuguese' (1999: 156).

His catechistic indoctrination of his children in the just cited passage also gives the lie to his broader criticism of social institutions, particularly of schools, which he dismisses as instruments of control, forming part of the 'ideological apparatus of the state' (1999: 152). Indeed, on several occasions, the text invites us to see his actions as an example of defiance for defiance's sake. He appears to have a penchant for struggles aiming to overturn irrevocable political decisions and reverse irreversible events. As a nineteen-year-old, for instance, he challenged a political treaty that was signed hundreds of years ago. He filed a claim in the World Court of the United Nations, 'attempting to upturn that pact by which the Iberian empires had – four hundred years before – divided the world between themselves along the border of Brazil: the Treaty of Tordesillas' and, as Mina informs us, 'even now, miles away in Sydney, Australia, we were still receiving documents in the mail signed in the hand of the Secretary General, detailing the technical problems involved in settling this arduous case' (1999: 162).

Of course, the ethical *impulse* underpinning his activism is entirely defensible, since his petition to the World Court is a contestation of European imperialism, but it is the timing of his actions which renders his Goan activism moot. As evident from the following passage, Mina's father often adopts an oppositional stance for the performative dividends that it yields:

> he sympathised dearly with the extremist subordination of the Sikh nationalist struggle and often remarked that a fight for a separate state in the Punjab was a struggle only second to his agenda to free

Goa. When he was feeling particularly ineffectual in his political conscious, he would wrap a tea towel turban-style around his head and brandish a kitchen knife in his hand as if it were a scared kris. (1999: 153–4)

In her essay 'Is transgression transgressive?', Elizabeth Wilson acknowledges the emancipatory potential of defiant behaviour; in particular, transgressive acts allow us to 'insist that we are there, that we exist, and to place a distance between ourselves and the dominant culture' (1993: 117). But she argues that unless transgressive action is accompanied by a preoccupation with 'how things could be different', transgression and the related concepts of 'dissidence, subversion and resistance' become synonymous with 'mere posturing' (1993: 113–16). Mina's father's nationalist politics is devoid of any discussion of how things would be different for Goans were Goa to become liberated from India. Moreover, his borrowing of the emblems of the Sikh armed insurgency, in an attempt to elevate his solitary protest politics to a collective movement that rouses extreme, indeed violent passions, far from having the intended effect, works only to underscore the emptiness of his struggle. But our understanding of Mina's father's troubling relationship with resistance is complicated by his oftentimes unerringly accurate commentary on colonial history, specifically Australia's brutal oppression of aboriginal peoples. If he problematically insists on schooling Mina in what he sees as the 'superiority of [her] "Goan Soul"', he also painstakingly explains to her that 'the history of the very land on which [they] were living was founded in blood' and that the poverty of the aboriginal peoples 'was due not to lack of enterprise or laziness or godlessness at all, but because these people didn't have the meanness of spirit to go to the continent of Africa and turn the bodies of many Africans into fast money' (Peres da Costa, 1999: 156–61). Even more tellingly, Mina's father works for the Department of Immigration and Ethnic Affairs and spends his working hours counselling refugees and immigrants: 'He often told us of the Indo-Chinese refugees whose lives were held in his own tender but somewhat clumsy hands. They were locked in cold suburban detention centres. Like animals or murderers. Sometimes, I knew, he'd be advocating on their behalf for weeks, for months. Clemency was never certain' (1999: 125).

Therefore, while his nationalist politics *is* marked by mere posturing and unrealistic claims, his professional activities are steeped in humility and pragmatism, geared towards helping the dispossessed and the bureaucratically beleaguered. Upon meeting two Vietnamese migrants who are compelled to take up underpaid jobs for which they are vastly overqualified while they await their bridging visas, Mina's father immediately offers his help in speeding up 'the processing of their applications' (1999: 170). His work as a counsellor thus shows that he is more than capable of making 'transformation' rather than 'transgression' his watchword, as Wilson advocates (1993: 116). It is worth noting that Peres da Costa's choice of magic realism, a self-consciously paradoxical narrative mode, is particularly effective in accentuating the contradictory manifestations of Mina's father's oppositional politics. Magic realism, as Stephen Slemon points out, 'is an oxymoron, one that suggests a binary opposition between the representational code of realism and that, roughly, of fantasy' (1995 [1988]: 409). Mina's father's acts of resistance are characterised by both a deeply realistic understanding of power relations and a fantastical optimism. As Mina notes, his happiness is 'indexed to what seemed aeons of defeat; he was an enthusiast who held his head in his hands a great deal' (Peres da Costa, 1999: 229). His enthusiastic agitation for his homeland Goa, his activist support of refugees and immigrants in Australia and his utter despair at the crisis unfolding in his own home point to the complex sedimentation of the divergent, but ultimately interlinked, registers of his resistant subjectivity.

His nationalism, misplaced as it is, both geographically and temporally, lends him a paradoxically stable identity of a dissident as his homelife crumbles around him. Mina invokes in vivid detail 'the scent of decay' and the devastation wrought by her mother's and then her father's withdrawal from the familial home, with 'roaches scurr[ying] from unwashed dish pans and maggots crawl[ing] out of griddles encrusted with rancid ghee' (1999: 185–232). Dolores takes to disappearing for hours at a time and stealing birds' nests, and Mina's father, in an act not unlike that of the proverbial ostrich burying its head in the sand, vanishes into the nether regions of the house where, despite having no knowledge of the intricacies of electric circuits, he obsessively sets about rewiring the house. Mina observes with considerable alarm as her mother frantically hoards and even steals everyday provisions which are in plentiful supply and packs them in suitcases with no journey in view (1999: 123). Shown to be helpless before the sight of an ever-increasing number of suitcases, Mina's father is reduced to frustration, which he occasionally voices: '"This is madness!" he said, now striking his fists on the table. "Plain madness. What do you want to do, live like a refugee?"' (1999: 125). His use of the term 'refugee' suggests that his wife's behaviour has thrown into doubt, and indeed shattered, the sense of belonging that the family might have begun to feel in their host country. The term 'refugee' also evokes forced movement and transience and highlights the fracturing of the familial home as well as the family as a unit. Given that his day job consists of working with refugees and other groups with precarious immigration status, the suitcases appear to carry a particularly haunting quality for him and fuel his Goan nationalism.

Building on Avtar Brah's (1996: 16) work on diasporic identities, Anne-Marie Fortier describes 'homing desire', which Brah distinguishes from the 'desire for a "homeland"', as a desire 'to feel at home'; this desire is 'achieved by physically or symbolically (re)constituting spaces which provide some kind of ontological security in the context of migration' (Fortier, 2003: 115). If Mina's father's Goan nationalism may seem to be an expression of his 'desire for a "homeland"', I argue it can also be read as a sort of homing desire, which stems not only from his family's migration to Australia, but also from the breakdown of familial life in Sydney. This homing desire for Mina's father is tied in with and reinforced by a *resisting* desire, a desire to challenge authority and contest established norms. His protest politics in Sydney help him to maintain a link, however tenuous, with his youth in Goa where he first began dabbling in activism. Moreover, his reconstitution of the garage as the headquarters of his one-man Goan liberation movement and the politicisation of the family (through his comparison of Dolores with the autocratic Indian Prime Minister Indira Gandhi) suggests that he may be trying to achieve a modicum of ontological comfort, an *at-homeness* through the performance of political resistance. His conflictual relationship with his wife becomes sublimated into their divergent opinions about the Indian Prime Minister, with Mina's father gleefully celebrating her assassination by her Sikh guards and her mother, who wears a picture of Indira Gandhi around her neck, 'weeping for the end of dynasty' (Peres da Costa, 1999: 157). Her father's stylised resistant stance also seeps into Mina's consciousness, as she describes the rift in her parents' marriage in a language befitting an armed rebellion. She notes that her father performed 'many acts of insurgency by way of fortune rather than tactical intent. He fled on a few occasions, all the times when ambushed by this aforementioned woman – my mother. His revolution was slow' (1999: 151). Mina's political vocabulary, inspired by her father's lexicon, paradoxically also works as a cognitive strategy aimed at rendering a painful familial conflict slightly more distant, and therefore more palatable. Mina, too, comes across as a troubling figure of defiance as she imagines the disintegration of the familial home as a physical partition, akin to the Partition of India. In the closing pages of the novel, she disturbingly resorts to 'Gandhian models of self-sacrifice', including self-starvation, in a vain attempt to stave off the demise of her relationship with her mother and the destruction of the family as a whole:

> It is now that I envisioned the tragic vanity of my sacrifice; that the house had been, was going to be partitioned regardless of the extent of my suffrage; that a nation had to be born even if it meant it was swaddled in blood, if the fruit of the mother had to be ripped right apart ... For those who are seeded and nestled in the womb, only for these whom we intimately loved, are we quite willing to have ourselves a massacre. (1999: 246)

The novel ends with the accidental death of Mina's parents in a fire resulting from her father's ill-informed tinkering with electric circuits. The novel's magic realist ending sees Mina's mother transform into a 'glorious phoenixlike' bird and rise from the burning house, while the firefighters categorically rule out the possibility of rescuing her father; he is 'literally buried beneath the structure' (1999: 257). The two concluding paragraphs read like a eulogy, as Mina declares her father to be the one 'whom she loved most in the world', lovingly recalling his 'somewhat clumsy hands that had bathed [her] infant form and that had held [her] face away from the gaping canyon on [her] mother's elusive misery' (1999: 258–9).

If Sissy Helff interprets Mina's parents' death as an event signalling a break from Mina's 'Indian heritage', which may well allow the young girl to start 'creating a space to negotiate and invent an Australian self' (2013: 116), I would contend instead that the poignant terms in which Mina remembers her father, her disturbing joy at the destruction unfolding before her and her refusal to say 'I did not love my mother' are an indication of the extent to which she had absorbed her father's essentially humane, if confused, politics (Peres da Costa, 1999: 259). In the concluding paragraph, her thoughts move away from the specifics of her own pain to alight on the trauma marking the lives of all human beings. She declares that 'on and on each of us arrives and advances, flying with her face forever gazing at the sometimes hideous and occasionally divine shapes of the history from whose thigh she sadly slides' (1999: 259). In these closing lines, we can detect traces of her father's contradictory oppositional sensibility, marked as it was by an unwarranted enthusiasm, an ineffable feeling of defeat, a warm solidarity with the dispossessed as well as a sense of the present being inseparable from the past.

Gender, transnationality and (anti-)normativity

In this section, I focus on Moushumi's character in *The Namesake*, who, unlike Mina's father, is a second-generation Indian immigrant in the Global North. I will be invoking Gogol, the novel's protagonist, only tangentially here; in doing so, I do not wish to elide the ambiguous nature of his acts of rebellion, but rather to elucidate what I see as Moushumi's more complex resistant subjectivity. Gogol's acts of defiance, which include his decision in his late teens to formally change his name to Nikhil against his parents' wishes and his adoration of his white girlfriend Maxine's lifestyle accompanied by his temporary rejection of his own family, intersect with Moushumi's in that both characters attempt to turn their backs on their families at several points in their lives. However, Moushumi's oppositional stance is more multi-layered than Gogol's not only because of its longer lifespan, but also because it often manifests itself inconsistently, linked either directly or indirectly to her gendered identity. While Gogol's parents are disappointed by his choice of white girlfriends, as we will see below, he is spared the kind of familial pressure that comes to bear on Moushumi from a very young age. Furthermore, following his father's sudden death around the halfway mark of the novel, Gogol ceases to push back against familial expectations and familial intimacy, which had previously appeared oppressive to him, and he no longer wishes to 'get away' from all that he had spent his childhood and early adulthood wanting to escape (Lahiri, 2003: 182). Moushumi's actions, on the other hand, invite us to consider the meaning of resistance both within an intergenerational and intercultural/interethnic framework and independently of it, by alerting us to the paradoxical ontological functions that a gendered oppositional stance can perform.

In my analysis of Moushumi's acts of rebellion, I am not seeking to reinforce the necessity of a 'return to roots' narrative that would deem the wholesale or even partial acceptance of one's parents' culture of origin or one's parents' values as an indisputable social good; nor am I endorsing a cult of authenticity which is suspicious of divergences from cultural traditions and norms, as implied by the 'ponderous and overused acronym ABCD' (American-born confused desis) for second-generation South Asian Americans, with the idea of the 'homeland' being wielded against them, suggesting that they are 'culturally inadequate and unfinished' (Prashad, 2001: 131). In a similar vein, I am aware that a critical examination of Moushumi's extramarital affair runs the risk of echoing prescriptive patriarchal discourses that are designed to curtail women's expression of their sexuality. But what I do wish to establish in this section is a link between Moushumi's various acts of transgression, both those that appear to be geared towards self-fulfilment and others far less so, and to demonstrate how they alert us to Moushumi's inconsistent relationship with the idea of resistance, which, on several occasions, causes her to trade one kind of conformity for another.

Certainly, many of Moushumi's actions and *re*actions represent a feminist rejection of an oppressive familial 'happiness script' (Ahmed, 2010: 59) that she was expected to follow and social arrangements that she was required to embrace 'from early childhood' (Lahiri, 2003: 213). As she recounts to Gogol, Moushumi had been relentlessly 'admonished not to marry an American'; from five years of age, her relatives cross-examined her on her choice of attire for her future wedding – 'red sari or a white gown' – a leading multiple-choice question which was designed to leave no doubt in young Moushumi's mind that she was required to opt for the former (2003: 213).[5] At twelve years of age, she solemnised her growing unease with her family's expectations by making a 'pact' with two other Bengali girls 'never to marry a Bengali man' (2003: 213). Pushing back against the 'ideology of women as the primary bearers of cultural continuity and tradition', Moushumi refused to participate in her parents' schemes to find her a Bengali husband, and declined to speak to her father's young colleagues whom he brought home to introduce to her (Jackson, 2014: 114). She recoiled from conversations focusing on her future wedding, 'the menu and the different colors of sari she would wear for the different ceremonies', objecting to the implication that it 'were a fixed certainty in her life' (Lahiri, 2003: 213).

When she gets married to Gogol, she once again asserts her independence by refusing to take his last name; given how acutely aware Gogol is of the significance of names in his own life, his secret disappointment at Moushumi's decision to keep her family name reveals not only a masculinist streak in him but also a lack of sensitivity. Alongside the traditional vows in Sanskrit uttered in public on her wedding day, Moushumi makes a promise to herself that 'she'd never grow fully dependent on her husband' (2003: 247). In particular, she is determined to avoid the state of helpless dependence that her mother, a 'perfectly intelligent' woman, came to assume when she moved to the US with Moushumi's father: 'For even after thirty-two years abroad, in England and now in America, her mother does not know how to drive, does not have a job, does not know the difference between a checking and a savings account' (2003: 247). The occasional meals that Moushumi, once married, insists on eating alone at restaurants are a strategy aimed at ensuring that her sense of self does not whittle down to her marital status or more broadly, to a joint identity. These meals serve to reassure her that she exists as an individual and is 'capable of being on her own' (2003: 247). Moushumi's academic trajectory, too, represents a constructive form of subversion. (I discuss the broader implications of her Francophilia later in the section.) Like many Indian immigrants in the United States, Moushumi's parents favour careers in what are referred to as STEM areas, i.e. the fields of science, technology, engineering and mathematics. Indian immigrants are often perceived to be a 'model minority' in the US and 'education and success' in the sciences have become an important part of 'navigating identity' for the diasporic community (Thakore, 2016: 12).[6] If she refuses to comply with her parents' demand that she should pursue a career in chemistry, like her father before her, she does not reject academia or the narrative of academic success indiscriminately. Without telling her parents, she majors not only in chemistry as they had insisted, but also in French, immersing herself in French culture. She comes to excel in her chosen field, publishing 'articles on French feminist theory in prestigious academic journals' even before she completes her PhD (Lahiri, 2003: 246).

But these undeniably constructive decisions are juxtaposed with acts of defiance that disrupt, rather than nurture, Moushumi's quest for personal fulfilment and greater agency as a woman. Her submission during her teenage years to many of her mother's demands continues to haunt her as an adult, long after those expectations have either receded or vanished entirely: 'She regrets her obedience, her long, unstyled hair, her piano lessons and lace-collared shirts' (2003: 214). Moushumi's transgressive behaviour as an adult, at times, comes across as a compensatory tactic, meant to redress and make amends to herself for her docility as an adolescent. Indeed, Moushumi constructs a happiness script that *stipulates* certain forms of anti-normative behaviour on her part, which has the effect of not only eclipsing normative behaviour that is actively inimical to her happiness, but also of shearing some of her rebellious acts of their emancipatory tenor. For instance, if we see Moushumi, much like Gogol until his father's death, rebelling against parental dictates, her friendship with Astrid and Daniel, a white couple of Moushumi's age, emerges disturbingly like a parent–child relationship, with Moushumi's devotion to them exhibiting filial overtones. Moreover, it is Daniel who introduces her to Graham, a white American, to whom she will go on to become engaged, echoing the arranged marriage scenarios orchestrated by her own parents that she is so determined to flee. It is in Astrid and Daniel's house that Moushumi seeks refuge and stays for two months when her relationship with

Graham collapses; she also embraces Astrid and Daniel's 'brand of life' and consumerist ethos, obediently following their 'unquestionable stream of advice about quotidian things', such as which shops to patronise while buying meat and bread, which sheets to use for her bed and which style of coffee maker to welcome into her home (2003: 136).[7]

Upon graduating, 'deaf to [her parents'] protests', Moushumi moves to France; in sharp contrast to her celibacy in the US, she has a string of sexual escapades in Paris which suggests a newfound self-confidence (2003: 215). But, as Moushumi acknowledges 'in retrospect', it was her 'sudden lack of inhibition' rather than the men themselves that had 'intoxicated her' (2003: 215). In the passage where she describes her sex life in France to Gogol, she foregrounds the men's desire for her and their methods of seduction, rather than the joy or pleasure that Moushumi may have derived from these interactions:

> [A]fter years of being convinced she would never have a lover she began to fall effortlessly into affairs … with no hesitation at all, she allowed men to seduce her in cafés, in parks … she allowed the men to buy her drinks, dinner, later take her in taxis to their apartments, in neighbourhoods she had not discovered on her own … They were a bit excessive, she tells Gogol with a roll of her eyes, the type to lavish her with perfume and jewels. (2003: 215)

The verbal phrases deployed in this passage – 'began to fall', 'allowed men to seduce her', 'allowed the men to buy her drinks' and 'lavish her with perfume and jewels' – suggest a passivity and lack of agency on Moushumi's part, despite the superficially taboo nature of her sexual encounters, entailing as they did having sex with 'one man after lunch, another after dinner', with some of the men 'being married, far older, fathers to children in secondary school' (2003: 215). These interactions, as uninhibited and taboo-breaking as Moushumi perceives them to be, replicate masculinist constructions of heterosexual desire, marked by a power imbalance between Moushumi and the men who are both considerably older and wealthier than her.

If at a fairly young age, she contests her ethnic community's endogamous expectations, her casual sexual encounters in France notwithstanding, Moushumi is oblivious to the extent to which the expectation of coupledom, particularly for women, permeates mainstream American culture. As Ahmed points out:

> The happy stories for girls remain based on fairy-tale formulas: life, marriage, and reproduction, or death (of one kind or another) and misery. Maybe there are compromises; maybe there is a diversification of styles of feminine accomplishment; maybe heterosexuality can now be done in more ways than one; but the investments remain rather precise. (2016: 49)

If Moushumi resists her parents' schemes to get her married within her community for many years, she simultaneously internalises mainstream American 'happy stories for girls', which are no less prescriptive. Through Lahiri's use of indirect discourse, we learn that, all the while contesting her parents' demands, Moushumi feels ashamed of her single status as a woman: 'The shameful truth was that she was not involved, was in fact desperately lonely' (Lahiri, 2003: 213). Later, following the end of her engagement with Graham, she 'swallow[s] half a bottle of pills', is 'forced to drink charcoal in an emergency room' and 'stop[s] going to school' (2003: 217). Moushumi is seized with a debilitating panic when she finds herself single and 'all her friends married'; in fact, she sees her failed relationship with Graham as her 'disgrace', which Gogol eventually 'obliterate[s]' by marrying her (2003: 249). Her choice of words implies a disturbing acceptance of her own worth being defined in terms of the presence of a man in her life, which underpins as much conventional Bengali values as it does mainstream values in the United States. In fact, Moushumi's suicide attempt perhaps says less about the strength of her feelings for her erstwhile fiancé and more about the immense pain she experiences because of her '"failure" to achieve heterosexual happiness' (Ahmed, 2010: 245).

Moushumi's decision to marry Gogol, too, is reflective of her muddied relationship with the notions of defiance and compliance. Tamara Bhalla contends that 'from the start, Gogol and Moushumi's relationship is founded on a shared desire to remedy their cultural displacement by being together' (2016: 116). I would argue instead that while Gogol, having recently lost his father whom he had ignored in favour of his white girlfriend and her family, is certainly driven by a desire to make cultural amends, Moushumi is not. Her determination from a very young age not to marry a

Bengali, paradoxically, comes to acquire the weight of a prescriptive injunction. Her breach of this injunction, first by agreeing to meet Gogol at her mother's behest and then by commencing a romantic relationship with him, lends the romance a subversive complexion despite the relationship's progression being perfectly aligned with both her and Gogol's parents' desires. Precisely because Gogol, given his Bengali roots and close connection to her own family, 'was not who she saw herself ending up with', her romance with him 'had felt forbidden' to Moushumi, 'wildly transgressive, a breach of her own instinctive will' (Lahiri, 2003: 250). As she had appeared to be while conducting short-term affairs in Paris, Moushumi seems detached from the proceedings, propelled forward less by her own desires than by the legitimacy that her romance with Gogol attains in her eyes by virtue of its violation of a self-created taboo. The power of the taboo soon wears off, however, following which she no longer sees Gogol as a transgressive choice, only as an unwanted reminder of 'the life she had resisted and struggled so mightily to leave behind' (2003: 250).

Indeed, the marriage quickly begins to lose its shine for both Moushumi and Gogol, as they discover traits in each other that they dislike, but it is ultimately Gogol's discovery of Moushumi's affair which ends the marriage.[8] For Robin E. Field, the dissolution of their marriage signifies that Moushumi and Gogol have discarded 'any cultural prerogatives about the permanence of marriage … in favor of divorce', which is, by implication, a more liberating, individualistic decision than the marriage itself (2004: 173). In a similar vein, Karen M. Cardozo sees the affair as an emancipatory act, arguing that through her extramarital affair and departure for France following her divorce, Moushumi '[v]ot[es] with her feet', choosing 'originality over origins' (2012: 20). By contrast, I read Moushumi's affair as a self-defeating form of resistance against familial and cultural expectations, but not necessarily because the man she chooses to have an affair with is white, suggesting that Moushumi sees 'whiteness universalized through the gender of the male subject' as a 'signifier of freedom of choice and escape from tradition' (Bhalla, 2016: 118). Instead, I find the affair a disempowering act of defiance primarily because it prevents Moushumi from asserting her independence and ending an unhappy marriage. The unflattering terms in which her lover Dimitri is described, as seen through Moushumi's eyes (a 'balding, unemployed middle-aged man, who is enabling her to wreck her marriage') makes it difficult to argue that either Moushumi or the narrator sees the affair as an original or liberatory experience (Lahiri, 2003: 266). Moreover, it is no coincidence that she first met Dimitri as a teenage girl and thus at a time she was deeply anxious about her desirability to men. The affair can then also be seen as a misplaced tactic deployed to keep doubts and insecurities, both old and new, at bay. Indeed, Moushumi resorts to adultery, an ostensibly transgressive act, to ward off having to end her marriage, which would be a far more resounding assertion of her independence than a secret affair with a man for whom she harbours no real desire. As Moushumi acknowledges, 'the affair causes her to feel strangely at peace, the complication of it calming her, structuring her day'; the marriage only ends when she accidentally mentions Dimitri in a conversation with Gogol and then has no choice but to own up to the relationship (2003: 266).

Finally, I return to the contradictory role that Francophilia plays in Moushumi's life. Françoise Král interprets Moushumi's adoption of a third language as a failed strategy of empowerment, arguing that it 'cannot make up for the void left by the denial of her cultural heritage and that the empowering phase is soon followed by the bitter realization that the new language cannot allow her to reach a stage of ontological plenitude' (2009: 141). By contrast, I argue that Moushumi's love of French culture is not accompanied by a rejection of her Bengali heritage; her wedding ceremony, after all, is a traditional one; moreover, she takes her American fiancé to Calcutta to meet her extended family and it is Graham's disparaging remarks about 'her family's heritage' that lead Moushumi to end the engagement (Lahiri, 2003: 217). Moreover, as we saw above, Moushumi's interest in French literature and culture leads to an intellectually fulfilling professional life, one that she was unlikely to have had if she had succumbed to parental pressure and become a chemist and, in that respect, it does represent 'a willful denial of social arrangements meant to reproduce the future as a copy of the present' (Song, 2013: 173). That said, while my interpretation of it diverges from Král's, I do find Moushumi's Francophilia troubling. If Moushumi began actively cultivating her interest in 'a third language, a third culture' for the stark contrast that it presented to all 'things American and Indian' and the 'refuge' that it offered her, this interest ultimately becomes fetishistic which hinders her attainment of ontological plenitude, although this is by no means the only obstacle standing in the way of her empowerment, as my discussion of her uneven resistant impulses demonstrates (Lahiri, 2003: 214). Her need to assume a unitary French identity fuels her ontological insecurities, with her refusing to let Gogol photograph her on their visit to Paris, lest she be mistaken for a 'tourist' in the city (2003: 234). The reverence in which she holds French culture is also reminiscent of the blind loyalty she displays towards her friends Astrid and Daniel's choices as consumers.

The shift to Gogol's mother Ashima's and then Gogol's perspective in the closing chapter of the novel provides no insight into Moushumi's life following her divorce, only that she decides to move back to France; this suggests that she puts an end to her affair with Dimitri and does not allow herself to unravel the way she did following the breakdown of her relationship with Graham. But the abruptness of this exit, both in narratological and geographical terms, precludes the emergence of a neat resistant subjectivity, foregrounding instead how Moushumi's transgressive and compliant tendencies continue to jostle within her for prominence.

Class, gender and erotic resistance

Of the three characters examined in this chapter, Latha in *A Disobedient Girl* is most unequivocally a subaltern, subordinated within Sri Lankan society because of her gender and class as well as her status as an orphan, and, in the first half of the novel, her age. After being abandoned by her mother Biso at a convent, she is brought into an upper-class home by Mr Vithanage.[9] He is shown to be an essentially well-meaning but timid man who bows before his domineering wife in most matters, and does not intervene when she makes Latha perform domestic labour long before she has entered her teens. This section engages in detail with the disquieting implications of Latha's erotic resistance: her attempts to use her sex appeal and desirability in the eyes of men to contest the socio-economic and affective status quo. As Alice Walker warns us, '[w]omen have to be extremely careful about choosing something that they consider an act of defiance that can really be used to further their enslavement' (Wajid, 2006: n.p.). I demonstrate below that while the novel does not condemn Latha's socially transgressive expression of her sexuality and desire, it does alert us to the limitations of women's erotic power when deployed in heterosexual relationships marked by both gender and class inequities.

The first paragraph of the novel establishes the eleven-year-old Latha's wilfulness through her refusal to see herself as a member of the serving class and her unwavering belief that she deserves much more in material terms than what she is entitled to as a servant, the stolen cakes of soap serving as a symbol not only for her appreciation of fine things, but also her awareness of her own physical beauty and her desire to nurture it:

> She loved fine things and she had no doubt that she deserved them. That is why it had not felt like stealing when she'd helped herself to one of the oval cakes in the cabinet underneath the bathroom sink in the main house. Every day, at 3:30 pm, she cleaned her face, feet, underarms, and hands at the well, using one of the cakes of Lux, which, despite having escaped, undetected, with thieving, not daring to smell like flowers all day long, she reserved for this ritual.
> (Freeman, 2011 [2009]: 3)

In ironically remarking that 'servants by definition are not supposed to be beautiful. It's not their prerogative', the narrator of Suniti Namjoshi's *Goja* decries the self-serving bourgeois discourse in the Indian sub-continent that deems beauty as a natural concomitant of class superiority, and by extension, the lack of physical attractiveness as a hallmark of poverty (2000: 9). Latha, however, even at eleven years of age, successfully resists internalising these prevailing class ideologies. Her fastidious cleanliness also challenges stereotypes about domestic workers who are seen to 'represent the dirt, disease, and "rubbish" of a disorderly outside world that employers commonly associate with the lower class and that pointedly contrast with the ideal cleanliness, order, and hygiene of their own homes' (Dickey, 2000: 462). In fact, the narrative, told from Latha's perspective, foregrounds not only her superior looks and hygiene but also her superior intellect compared to Mr Vithanage's daughter Thara, who is the same age as Latha: 'Her math was better than Thara's, her social studies and science were better than Thara's too, and she didn't even get extra tuition like Thara did. Even her handwriting curving with perfect ispili and pāpili, was better than Thara's' (Freeman, 2011 [2009]: 46). Inspired by her school principal, a Marxist, as young as she is, Latha is determined 'to be better than she was' in material terms, even if that meant 'gett[ing] "it wrong" and get[ting] in trouble' (2011 [2009]: 5).

Sri Lanka, as Sudesh Mukhopadhyay and Sunita Chugh note, 'is the only country in South Asia which constitutionally guarantees free and compulsory education for all children' (2012: 267).[10] In June 2020, the minimum working age in Sri Lanka was raised from fourteen to sixteen years; given that the narrative is set during the Sri Lankan civil war and therefore under the old law, the Vithanages are undeniably guilty of extracting labour from a child, robbing her of the leisure, play and opportunities to learn that their own daughter Thara is expected to enjoy as a matter of course. Despite her talent for scholastic pursuits, Latha is not allowed to continue her education beyond the minimum state-stipulated level. What is more, Mrs Vithanage withholds Latha's salary, effectively blurring the line between slave labour and domestic service. In particular, when, at fifteen years of age, having already performed 'ten years of paid work' and not received any wages, Latha asks Mrs Vithange for some of her own money to buy a pair of sandals, Mrs Vithanage rejects her request, claiming that the money is 'safer in the bank' and patronisingly instructing Latha not to 'waste [her] money' (Freeman, 2011 [2009]: 43). Mr Vithanage advocates only 'mildly' and 'disinterestedly' on Latha's behalf, and does not act to redress the injustice of his wife's decision (2011 [2009]: 43–4). Having had nothing but hand-me-downs to wear all her young life, Latha comes to see footwear, above all else, as a marker of class identity. Her resolve to escape her class subalternity manifests itself in her determination to buy a pair of new sandals to replace her second-hand ones, which are both old and ill-fitting: 'Everything else she could, by careful dressing, by pinning and tucking of hand-me-downs, contrive to present as her own, made-especially-for-her attire. But real brand-new footwear was different; it was what set the blessed apart from the unspared' (2011 [2009]: 44). The broader injustice that Mrs Vithanange's refusal implies – denying Latha access to her own money – is not lost on Latha. She resents having to explain to Mrs Vithanage why she needs the money: 'it wasn't about what she had but about what she wanted and should be allowed to buy with her own money!' (2011 [2009]: 43–4). Latha is able to recognise that the language of benevolence and the maternal tone that Mrs Vithanage deploys to reject her request are meant to petrify, rather than alleviate, her servant status and to keep her 'in the limbo of childlike dependency' (Ray and Qayum, 2009: 96). Mrs Vithanage reads Latha's legitimate request as insolence, born of Latha's access to education, and subsequently resolves to put an end to Latha's schooling so as to transform her into a 'proper servant', one who is resigned to be a domestic worker and does not harbour any ambitions, no matter how small (Freeman, 2011 [2009]: 46).

It is against this backdrop of material, scholastic and emotional deprivation that Latha enacts her erotic resistance. In stark contrast to her previous minor defiances, consisting of stealing household items like soap, powdered milk and mango chutney to enliven her drab existence and render it marginally more tolerable, the sexual becomes a means for her to cause a far more dramatic disruption in her employers' lives. She decides to avenge herself by seducing Ajith, Thara's upper-class boyfriend, despite being in love with Ajith's friend Gehan and despite considering Thara a friend. Latha's erotic defiance is an example of what Elizabeth Flynn has described as 'reactive resistance', which is a 'spontaneous and emotional reaction that may have multiple and conflicting motivations and effects' (2001: 18). Latha's resistance is aimed at punishing Mrs Vithanage's for denying her not only her wages, but also the possibility of a future that does not involve domestic servitude. In seducing her upper-class friend's boyfriend, her primary motivation is to puncture Mrs Vithanage's class complacency and arrogance which allows her to treat Thara and Latha, two fifteen-year-old girls, so differently, and this in spite of Latha's talents and outstanding scholastic performance: 'the only things Thara had that were better than Latha's were her clothes and her fancy boyfriend. And even Latha's fancy boyfriend looked at her, Latha, in *that* way. Proper servant? Ha!' (Freeman, 2011 [2009]: 47; emphasis in the original).

Francesca Seagal has noted that Latha 'is a tough and frequently unsympathetic heroine' (2010: n.p.). The pain that Latha's erotic resistance causes Thara and Gehan does make her a figure who is not always easy to like, suggesting a refusal on Freeman's part to romanticise the subaltern, much like Koshy's refusal to idealise the lower-class protagonist of her short story 'Almost Valentine's Day', as we saw in Chapter 3. But Latha's decision to seduce Ajith underscores, above all, the extent to which her age, socio-economic positioning and the total absence of familial support limit the kinds of resistance that she can enact. Moreover, the ease with which Latha decides to use her own body to exact revenge on Mrs Vithanage serves as a disturbing reminder of her familiarity, despite her young age, with predatory masculine desire. Latha knows that she will succeed easily in seducing Ajith

> the way fifteen-year-old girls know these things, even those who have never had the need to put their theories to the test because there were always enough men in their worlds to let them know in subtle and not so subtle ways that they would be proved right if they did have the chance to do it. (Freeman, 2011 [2009]: 47)

With no money and no hope of being able to continue her education, Latha is unable to see any other way of contesting the status quo than through sex. She delights in being able to remain emotionally detached while being sexually intimate with Ajith, 'letting her body feel pleasure, peak and release without ever giving up her heart, her mind constantly on the other boy, Gehan' (2011 [2009]: 89). In fact, consciously glossing over the pain that she causes Gehan, Latha perceives the erotic as a form of class warfare and sees it as means to avenge not only herself, but also Gehan who belongs to a lower class and a lower caste than do both Ajith and Thara: 'Hadn't she avenged them both, herself and Gehan, for that neglect by the people closest to them?' (2011 [2009]: 89).

The seduction episode in Freeman's novel is reminiscent of Wajida Tabassum's Urdu short story 'Utran' ('Cast-offs'; 2013 [1975]) in which Chamki, the young daughter of a servant, who has had to wear Shahzadi Pasha's cast-offs all her life and has been the target of Pasha's cruel mockery, takes her revenge by seducing Pasha's bridegroom the night before their wedding. In doing so, she is seeking to invert the prevailing socio-economic logic which makes Chamki the perennial recipient of second-hand personal items and to reduce Pasha's husband to a 'cast-off' article, so that, for once, it is her mistress who is being passed down something which Chamki first enjoyed: '"Pasha, all my life I took your cast-offs. But today, you too …" she started laughing wildly. "All your life … you will use mine …!" She could not control her laughter' (2013 [1975]: 115). But if Chamki's erotic resistance is aimed at punishing her tormentor, Latha's act of defiance is misdirected in that it affects Mrs Vithanage only circuitously; it is Thara who suffers the most from Ajith's withdrawal of affection, without knowing what or who triggered it. While Latha becomes 'an addiction for Ajith', Thara 'wilt[s] and wane[s]' and eventually fails her school leaving exams (Freeman, 2011 [2009]: 47).

While Latha experiences a modicum of satisfaction in watching how Thara's failure 'crushe[s]' Mrs Vithanage, she is aware that her act of defiance does little to alleviate the 'miserable drudgery' of her existence, now 'that she could not see Gehan', had to 'steal Thara's textbooks and read them in secret to stop herself from losing her mind' and was still unable to buy a pair of new sandals (2011 [2009]: 47). Later Latha feels a 'momentary flash of glee at the horror in Mrs Vithanage's voice' when she discovers that an upper-class boy living in Colombo 7 has impregnated Latha; Latha also takes 'pride in her defiance, and in the absence of a single tear' when her mistress yanks 'her out of the storeroom by her hair, her hands and body shaking with rage' and asks her 'what she had been thinking to repay their kindness with whoring' (2011 [2009]: 50). Latha delights in the 'shame' and 'inconvenience' her illicit pregnancy causes Mrs Vithanage with its potential to tarnish the family's reputation; moreover, the upper-class identity of Latha's lover is an unwelcome reminder for Mrs Vithanage of the permeability of class boundaries and that Colombo 7, an affluent neighbourhood, is 'just as crass and vile as the worst of slums' (2011 [2009]: 50). But if Tabassum's short story ends with Chamki's triumphant laughter, following a fleeting sense of victory, Latha has to face the consequences, both physical and otherwise, of her bodily resistance.[11] Ajith offers no help to her and Latha is sent away to the same convent, where unbeknownst to her, she was abandoned by her mother as a child. Once she gives birth, the child is promptly taken away from her, never to be seen again and leaving her incapable of speech for months. Two years later, unable to imagine any other life for herself, in response to a letter from Thara sent before her wedding, Latha returns to Colombo to work as a domestic servant in her friend's marital home, learning only belatedly that Thara's husband is none other than Gehan.[12]

During the course of the narrative, Latha becomes pregnant no fewer than three times, on each occasion by a man who enjoys a far higher class positioning than her, and on each occasion she is abandoned by her lover. Latha's second pregnancy results from an affair with Daniel, an American living in Colombo, who compels her to have an abortion and then refuses to see her again, and the third and final is a consequence of an affair with Gehan; he, too, disassociates himself from Latha upon learning about the pregnancy. In an interview, Freeman argued that Latha's relatability as a female character stems from the fact that 'most women adapt and respond to the predicaments in which they find themselves by design or chance, many of which are circumscribed by the way the men in their worlds hold power' (My Friend Amy, 2009: n.p.). But while Freeman's depiction of Latha's multiple pregnancies certainly works to foreground exploitative male behaviour, it also necessitates endowing Latha with a passivity and short-sightedness which contradicts, if not belies, her education, intelligence and ambition highlighted in the earlier chapters. Upon her return from the convent after giving birth to her first child, even after Mr Vithanage finally gives her the money that is owed to her and she is able to open a bank account, Latha chooses to remain a servant, and that too, in the house of her childhood sweetheart. Later, in a fit of rage, she spits at and slaps Gehan's mother when the latter refers to her as 'the little bitch' and, in a bid to demean Thara's family, insinuates that either Mr Vithanage impregnated Latha or that she was the product of an illicit liaison that he had 'with some other woman up in the estates' (Freeman, 2011 [2009]: 164).[13] Even after this episode, instead of seeking employment elsewhere, she initiates a relationship with Daniel as a means to 'forget that she was still a servant and, worse, that she was still Gehan's servant' (2011 [2009]: 200–1). She later commences an affair with Gehan in Thara's house, despite having witnessed him beating his wife and whipping the young houseboy Podian; she romanticises both him and their relationship and experiences 'a secret thrill ... wrapped as it was in the danger of being found out, and she had to admit it, the insolence of carrying on this way right under Thara's nose' (2011 [2009]: 300). Latha's eroticism, then, is not the kind Audre Lorde invokes in her seminal essay 'The uses of the erotic: the erotic as power' arguing that, as women, '[o]ur erotic knowledge empowers us, becomes a lens through which we scrutinize all aspects of our existence, forcing us to evaluate those aspects honestly in terms of their relative meaning within our lives' (2007 [1978]: 90). Instead, Latha's erotic acts entail separating 'the erotic demand from most vital areas' of her life 'other than sex'; it becomes a weapon of obfuscation, rather than a conduit for greater clarity and greater scrutiny of patriarchal and class-based oppression (2011 [2009]: 88).

It is only in the closing chapter, after Gehan's final rejection, that Latha begins to question her deep-seated beliefs, not only about the superiority of men, but also about the ability of heterosexual romance to shatter class divides. She finally realises that she had counted on the upper-class men in her life to be strong and decisive, and that Gehan 'was not a strong man; he had never been one ... all she knew were men who had used her or permitted her to use them' (Freeman, 2011 [2009]: 348–9). Latha is compelled to recognise the extent to which her erotic resistance curtailed rather than nurtured her agency as a lower-class woman:

> All the years she had thought she was in control, she had been fooling herself. She had been exactly what they had wanted her to be: a servant. Serving them. Serving herself to them, something they packed along with other necessities, like rice and salt and dhal. There to trim the beginnings and endings of their days, there to embellish their lies, there to blame their half-truths on. Present every waking moment to wash them of guilt and innocence. (2011 [2009]: 370)

Flynn has observed that the distinction between 'reactive' and 'strategic' resistance, where the latter refers to 'planned and positive action in opposition to oppression', can often become blurred (2001: 18). As she prepares to leave Gehan and Thara's house, Latha's actions in the closing chapter become 'deliberate' and measured; even her destructive acts are performed consciously and purposefully (Freeman, 2011 [2009]: 369). Latha reveals to Gehan and Thara's family details of Thara's affair with Ajith and then proceeds to smash Thara and Gehan's wedding crockery to bring home to them her disdain for their marital bond, which they seek to hypocritically uphold following Latha's revelation of her relationship with Gehan. The sari which Latha sets on fire is the one Thara had lent her and which had reignited Gehan's sexual interest in her, its burning embers symbolising the destruction of the illusions that Latha had continued to harbour about cross-class friendship and heterosexual love. She packs her belongings slowly and meticulously, making sure to take all her bank documents with her. Her final act of resistance consists of withholding information about her plans so as to no longer 'serv[e] herself' to her class Others: she lies to Mr Vithanage about intending to return to the convent and erases the last link between them by letting the piece of paper with his name and telephone number slip away (2011 [2009]: 370).

This departure is different from her other departures, in that she now has both 'a destination' and an 'intention'; Latha is determined to no longer abdicate control over her life or her body (2011 [2009]: 369). It is she, and not the Vithanages or her former lover, who decides that she will proceed with the pregnancy and form her own family consisting of the houseboy Podian, her friend Leela and her unborn child.[14] As she informs Podian on the train: '"We are going up-country to get Leelakka, then we will come back south … I know how to live in the city. I have money. I will take care of you … we will be a proper family", she said. "I will see to that"' (2011 [2009]: 372). Even if they leave unclear whether or not Latha has come to re-envision heterosexual erotic and romantic relationships across class in the light of her previous encounters with men, the short, staccato sentences coupled with her repetitive use of the first-person pronoun in the just-cited passage powerfully underscore the dramatic shift in her understanding of her own agency. The closing lines bring to the fore her conscious reconfiguration of kinship ties and her newfound faith in her own ability not only to survive but also to help others like her who are marginalised because of their class or gender, or indeed both.

By spotlighting irrelevant, ill-thought-through, short-sighted and contradictory acts of defiance, the texts examined in this chapter trouble the positive connotations of resistance as a concept and complicate the empowering potential of transgressive decisions. But, by also underscoring the pressing affective, intellectual and/or material needs that may be articulated through these distorted acts of resistance and by showing us how the three characters' subversive choices are intimately bound up with their pursuit of freedom, independence and indeed meaning in their lives, the three novels compel

Troubled resistance, troubling resistance 177

us to acknowledge the often-fuzzy distinction between 'good' and 'bad' resistance. Paradoxically, then, they reinforce rather than undermine the importance of adopting an oppositional stance in the face of oppressive discourses and practices.

Notes

1 See, for instance, essays and articles by Debjani Banerjee (2020), Thilini N. K. Meegaswatta (2019), Birte Heidemann (2019 [2017]) and Claire Chambers and Susan Watkins (2015); monographs exploring the relationship between gender, violence and resistance include V. G. Julie Rajan's *Women Suicide Bombers: Narratives of Violence* (2011) and Nimmi Gowrinathan's *Radicalizing Her: Why Women Choose Violence* (2021).
2 Peres da Costa's representation of Mina's 'feelers', a pair of magical antennae growing out of her head, can be contrasted with her realistic depiction of the psychological trauma that Mina and her father experience as Dolores's mental health continues to deteriorate.
3 See Alito Siqueira (2002: 213).
4 Old Sydney Town, an open-air museum and theme park where scenes from Australia's past were enacted, was opened in 1975 and shut down in 2003.
5 For Moushumi's parents the stigma of interracial dating dissipates only when she is in her late twenties and thus 'old enough' for it to no longer matter that her partner was not Bengali, as long as a wedding was on the horizon (Lahiri, 2003: 216). By that time, 'enough of their friends' children had married Americans, had produced pale, dark-haired, half-American children, and none it was as terrible as they had feared' (2003: 216).
6 As Rupam Saran warns us, the model minority stereotype vis-à-vis the Indian diasporic community neglects to take into account the fact that the successful members of the immigrant community often belong to the higher castes in India and have therefore effectively carried with them centuries of caste privilege, notably its concomitant 'sociocultural educational hierarchy' (2015: 70).
7 This section of the novel, narrated from Gogol's point of view, indicates his exasperation at Moushumi's blind devotion to her friends' lifestyle choices; yet he is oblivious to how similar Moushumi's behaviour is to his own earlier admiration of Maxine's lifestyle.
8 Gogol views Moushumi's smoking with growing disgust and Moushumi is disappointed to learn that Gogol's 'architect mind for detail fails

when it comes to everyday things' (Lahiri, 2003: 248). For example, he does not bother to hide the receipt for the shawl he bought as a gift for Moushumi on their first, and what would also be their last, wedding anniversary.

9 Vithanage meets Biso on a train while she is escaping an abusive marriage with her three children. Her two oldest children are kidnapped by two white male foreigners, following which she commits suicide by setting herself on fire. Before leaving her at the convent, Biso instructs four-year-old Latha to tell the nuns that she is an orphan and to give them Vithanage's contact information in the hope that he would provide some financial support. Latha has no recollection of her original family, until Vithanage reveals the truth about her childhood, as he knows it, in the final chapter of the novel.
10 Bangladesh, Bhutan, India, Nepal and Pakistan only provide a partial guarantee for the right to education. See Mukhopadhyay and Chugh, 2012.
11 The Vithanages conceal the truth from Thara, blaming their driver, another servant, for Latha's pregnancy and dismissing him. But they are unable to prevent 'everybody' from assuming that Mr Vithanage 'was the one who had done it' (Freeman, 2011 [2009]: 51).
12 Theirs is an unhappy marriage and, riddled with guilt, Latha effects Thara's reunion with Ajith. The two commence an affair, with Latha taking charge of raising Thara's daughters.
13 Thara's mother and Gehan's parents are convinced that their child has married down: Thara because of Gehan's relatively low-class, low-caste positioning, and Gehan because of Thara's family's tarnished reputation, stemming from the prevailing assumption that Mr Vithanage impregnated Latha, a servant.
14 Latha befriends a young woman called Leela during her stay at the convent following her affair with Ajith; Leela is an orphan who also became pregnant while working as a domestic servant and while she was still a child herself.

6

Writing as resistance? *A Golden Age*, *The Good Muslim* and *The Gypsy Goddess*

> 'In any case, if the poet's wife did complete the poem – and I do not agree for more than one moment that she did – why did she not say so, and claim the credit for it?'
>
> 'Perhaps it would have cost her more than her life was worth to say so', said the questioner. 'So she let Lord Krishna take the credit.'
>
> – Yasmine Gooneratne, 'Masterpiece', 2002

The Sri Lankan-Australian writer Yasmine Gooneratne's short story 'Masterpiece' (2002) serves as a powerful reminder of the extent to which, for women, the acts of writing and of taking ownership of their writing have historically been fraught with unpleasant social and interpersonal implications, lending the works an intrinsically subversive tenor. But in *Real and Imagined Women: Gender, Culture and Postcolonialism*, Rajeswari Sunder Rajan alerts us to the perils of what can perhaps be referred to as resistance sleuthing, that is, the insistence on detecting subversive and dissident strands in writings by women. As briefly invoked in the Introduction, Sunder Rajan makes a case for recognising that women's writing is 'not always resistant'; moreover, she underscores the need to historicise 'scrupulously' the conformism characterising women's literary production (1993b: 4). While Sunder Rajan's scholarly intervention concerns feminist *readings* of women's writings, I argue that it also invites us to unpack the complex politics underpinning the portrayal in women's fiction of the figure of the writer and of the act of writing itself.

I analyse Anam's characterisation of Maya in the novels *A Golden Age* and *The Good Muslim*, which are set against the liberation war of Bangladesh in 1971 and the political turmoil of the 1970s and 1980s. I also examine the role of the author-narrator in *The Gypsy Goddess*, a retelling of the 1968 massacre of striking Dalit peasants in the village of Kilvenmani in Tamil Nadu. I evaluate the sociopolitical import and the meanings assigned to the acts of writing, publishing and reading in the three works in order to better come to grips with the complex relationship not only between writing and social hierarchies, but also between writing and other forms of (gendered) resistance, including political violence.

Dissenting lives, dissenting stories: *A Golden Age* and *The Good Muslim*

Maya's resistance to the status quo through writing is briefly invoked in *A Golden Age*, the first book of Anam's Bengal trilogy. However, it is in the following novel *The Good Muslim*, which is narrated primarily from Maya's point of view, that the relationship between the written word and Maya's protest politics is delineated in greater detail. Set in Bangladesh, or what was known as East Bengal after the Partition of India and then as East Pakistan until 1971, the two historical novels chart the resistance mounted by East Pakistanis under the leadership of Sheikh Mujibur Rahman against the economic, political, linguistic and military hegemony of West Pakistan, itself a former British colony, which now 'ruled the eastern wing of the country like a colony' (Anam, 2012 [2007]: 34).[1] Anam's depiction in *The Good Muslim* of the clash that develops between Maya's unyielding secularism and her brother Sohail's religious extremism, which causes Sohail to neglect his young son Zaid, has drawn considerable critical attention; in particular, Claire Chambers (2015) and Saumya Lal (2019) have analysed the dangers of the hardened ideological worldviews that the two siblings come to assume following the independence of Bangladesh. While this clash between the two siblings is certainly relevant to my analysis, my main aim in this section is to evaluate what Maya's activities as a female writer reveal about the complex politics of anti- and 'postcolonial'/post-Independence resistance.

Writing as resistance? 181

In *A Golden Age*, Maya is shown to be a medical student at Dhaka University who is strongly committed to an independent Bangladesh but experiences frustration at her ineligibility, on the basis of her gender, to join the guerrilla resistance. We first detect Maya's need to be physically involved in the freedom movement in her disappointment at not being present on campus on the night that Dhaka University is attacked by the Pakistani army, with tanks climbing over the barricades and bullets being fired at the students. She feels 'sidelined', wanting some visible 'mark, some sign that the thing had happened to her. A bruise on the cheek' (Anam, 2012 [2007]: 73). Later, when Sohail and other young men become engaged in armed resistance in response to the genocide perpetrated by the Pakistani army, even though she continues to participate in demonstrations, chanting her discontentment and uttering 'strong words', Maya does not see her mode of resistance as being as valuable as the armed struggle unfurling in the countryside far away from Dhaka in the months leading up to the liberation of Bangladesh in December 1971:

> She behaved as though no one had told her that once the war began there would be nothing for her to do but wait. No one had told her that she would only be allowed to imagine it from a distance. No one had told her how lonely, how hot, how tiresome, the days would be. (2012 [2007]: 88)

At the same time, the dissenting words that she utters during demonstrations and that she then writes while drafting press statements for the liberation forces become intimately bound up with her body and acquire a combative physicality. Her mother Rehana notices the way in which the 'throaty chants' intoned by Maya in the street and her contestatory ideas had 'changed her physically: suddenly the angles of her face had moved, sharpened, so that she was no longer young, or even pretty' (2012 [2007]: 78). When Shona, the familial home, is transformed into the city headquarters of the resistance movement, Maya spends 'long hours' helping the freedom fighters write press releases: 'They found her an old typewriter, and she could be seen hunched over it hungrily, scowling at the letters, hitting the keys hard with her two forefingers. Sounds like a machine gun, Sohail said' (2012 [2007]: 105).

Anam's representation of Maya in the act of writing in *A Golden Age* lends further nuance to our understanding of what Butler terms 'aggressive nonviolence' (2020: 21). Underlining the need for aggressively pursuing nonviolent forms of resistance and drawing on Mahatma Gandhi's notion of satyagraha or 'soul force', Butler contends that while this force cannot simply be reduced to 'physical strength', it does take 'an embodied form' and comprises 'gestures and modes of non-action, ways … of using the solidity of the body and its proprioceptive object field to block or derail a further exercise of violence'; for instance, when 'bodies form a human barrier' during a demonstration (2020: 21–2). But, as the just-cited passage of the novel suggests, Maya's belligerent body language and gestures at Shona while writing oppositional texts – the scowl on her face, the forceful striking of the typewriter keys, her voracious handling of the machine and the threatening, machine-gun-like sounds that her typing produces – constitute a form of aggressive, embodied nonviolence that is *not* predicated on the physical presence of the enemy in the immediate space in which the writing is taking place. Indeed, the passage powerfully illustrates both the physicality of writing and the physically transformative effect that the defiant words that she writes can have on the resistant writer. This overlap between the physical and the intellectual foreshadows how Maya's dissident writings will become inseparable from her other resistant acts. Following the brutal rape and murder by Pakistani soldiers of her best friend Sharmeen, Maya travels to Calcutta where she continues writing press statements and articles, drawing attention to the atrocities committed by the Pakistani forces; she also volunteers in refugee camps in the city, providing medical supplies and care to refugees crossing the border to flee the Pakistani army.[2] The act of writing is also central to Maya's activism in *The Good Muslim*; her post-Independence articles are 'deliberate engagements with recuperation' and a reflection of Maya's desire to set 'the story "straight"' but here, as I demonstrate below, her writing intersects in less seamless ways with her other dissident selves and compels both her and us as readers to reconsider the meaning of erasure and recuperation of difficult personal and national stories (Wisker, 2010: 28).

The narrative in *The Good Muslim* is split into two timeframes: one focusing on the two years following the liberation of Bangladesh and the growing ideological distance between Maya and Sohail, and the second, a decade later, at a time when Bangladesh is being ruled by the military dictator Hussain Muhammad Ershad and Maya has returned to the familial home in 1980s Dhaka, having gone into exile in the countryside following her brother's embrace of a hardline version of Islam. Except for the affectedly chatty letters that she and her mother send each other, comprising 'elaborate pleasantries, long passages about the weather, telling each other everything and nothing', Maya does not write at all during her time in the countryside (Anam, 2012 [2011]: 16). She spends her exilic years working as a 'lady doctor', delivering rural and tribal women's babies, 'stitch[ing] their wounds afterwards and teach[ing] them about birth control' (2012 [2011]: 11). Prior to this, in line with the prevailing government policy, she performed abortions for *birangonas* in Dhaka. Women raped by the Pakistani army during the war were given the title of *birangona* (meaning 'war heroine') by Sheikh Mujibur Rahman's government to spare them from being 'socially ostracized' in a society where women's sexuality is seen as a repository of male honour and its desecration is considered a matter of great shame for the victim's family and community (Mookherjee, 2015a: 7). The new Bangladeshi government 'also set up various rehabilitation programs and centers for the women in 1972, organized marriages for them, and helped them enter the labor market' (2015a: 7). While recognising that the government's attempt to destigmatise and valorise the raped women as war heroines 'remains almost unparalleled' in history, Nayanika Mookherjee explains how offering the pregnant rape victims the alternative of 'either abortion ... or international adoption of the babies', the state was also seeking to '[purify]' the women and '[expunge]' their babies 'physiologically and geographically' which was effectively an attempt to 'gain visible control over the sexual and reproductive functions of birangonas' and 'to restore national honor' (2015a: 7–144). As we will see below, Maya's role in the implementation of Rehman's policy sits uncomfortably with her recuperative activities as a writer in 1980s Bangladesh and with her feminism, since the abortion policy robs the raped women of agency over their own bodies.

On her return to Dhaka, following a chance meeting with Aditi, a female journalist working for an anti-establishment newspaper called *Rise Bangladesh!*, Maya is drawn back into the world of dissident writing. As Maya browses through an issue of the publication, she notices an article 'about the Dictator's wealth, another exposing corruption in the army. It ended with a tirade on the changes that were being made to the constitution'; it is in the offices of *Rise Bangladesh!* that for the first time since returning to Dhaka, 'she fe[els] a ripple of belonging' (Anam, 2012 [2011]: 87). She explains to the editor Shafaat that she wishes to write about 'what's *really* going on out there' in the countryside, signalling the recuperative impulse underpinning her renewed desire to write (2012 [2011]: 88; emphasis mine). Maya is determined not to separate her post-Independence country's story from that of the oppression experienced by Bangladeshi women. The first article that she writes, 'five hundred words on the true story of the countryside', is the 'true story' of a pregnant female villager Nazia who, when prompted by Maya and in breach of the prevailing norms dictating where pregnant women should and should not bathe, had gone for a swim in a pond on the hottest day of the year (2012 [2011]: 87). Nazia was given a lashing for this transgression and Maya, in the face of intimidation by the men in the village and upon receiving news of Sohail's wife's death, decides to return to Dhaka. Maya decides that 'Nazia's story, her daring to swim in the pond and the lashes with which she paid for such bravery, would be chronicled. It would be there in black and white; people would read it and they would know that their freedom was as thin as the skin around Nazia's ankles' (2012 [2011]: 106).

While speaking to Shafaat during their first meeting, Maya describes her future piece as a 'sort of memoir', but it is also an example of overtly value-driven journalism and its various manifestations (2012 [2011]: 88). These include advocacy journalism, which 'speaks or pleads on behalf of another, giving the other a face and a voice' (Careless, 2000: n.p.), a '*journalism of attachment* ... which cares as well as knows ... that will not stand neutrally between good and evil, right and wrong, the victim and the oppressor' (Bell, 1998: 16; emphasis in the original) and what Ibrahim Seaga Shaw refers to as human rights journalism, contending that journalists 'have the moral responsibility – as duty bearers – to educate the public, increase awareness in its members of their rights and monitor, investigate and report all human rights violations' (2012: 2).[3]

The impulse driving Maya's writing and chronicling of Nazia's story also appears to be aligned with that of the Subaltern Studies theorists seeking to recover 'the voices and histories of the subalterns excluded from elite-centred historiographies (whether colonial or national)' (Mirza, 2016: xix). She is dismayed, for example, to see that Shaheed Minar, a national monument (commemorating the lives lost during the Bengali Language Movement demonstrations of 1952), which was destroyed by the Pakistani Army, was subsequently 'rebuilt, taller and wider'; Maya wishes the Bangladeshi government 'had left it broken, because now, shiny and freshly painted, it bore no signs of the struggle' (Anam, 2012 [2011]: 44). But if the Subaltern Studies theorists have been primarily preoccupied with historical subaltern silences, Maya's writings are explicitly aimed at bringing about social change and shifting elite-centred understandings of her country's present and its extremely brutal recent past. While Maya's first piece of writing grapples with Nazia's story and gendered oppression, to which I return below, her subsequent columns address other abuses of power and are marked by a determination to reject the rural/urban and the human/environmental divide. In her columns, she attacks 'the Dictator, the clergy, the Jamaat Party, Ghulam Azam, Nizami';[4] she also writes about the exploitation of the Hill Tribes, the Garo and the Chakma, and makes an impassioned case for safeguarding indigenous knowledge and healing practices:

> Ask yourself, citizen, have you ever met a tribal? Ever sat next to one at school? Ever known anyone who knows anyone who has a tribal for a friend? I thought not.
>
> They know the medicine of the forest. Plants that you soak and paste over a wound. They chew the leaf and smear it over your cut. There is a treasure, they say, in every inch of this land.
>
> In exchange, we raze their villages, and let the army rape their women. We take their forests and smoke them out of their villages. This is no kind of freedom. (2012 [2011]: 156–211)

As the just-cited passage illustrates, eschewing 'distance and detachment' or what Martin Bell refers to as 'bystanders' journalism', Maya adopts a combative, confrontational tone and deploys a range of literary techniques (negative statements, rhetorical questions and the use of the first-person collective pronoun) in her columns, which are unashamedly aimed at jolting privileged urban readers out of their pernicious indifference and spurring them into action (1998: 15). In particular, the repeated use of the first-person collective pronoun is suggestive of Maya's desire to acknowledge her own class and geographical privilege and to bring home to the readers the need for collectivist action.

But, perhaps because of Maya's far closer personal connection to the story, the resistant politics of her first column proves to be more problematic: this piece of writing is meant to lend a voice to Nazia, Maya's class Other, and to compel the privileged sections of society to revisit their understanding of freedom in post-Independence Bangladesh. Since Nazia is a member of the rural poor who do not have access to the kind of progressive familial upbringing and formal education that Maya enjoyed growing up in Dhaka and Karachi, Maya's writings about Nazia, despite the salutary intentions underlying them, are fraught with the perils of 're-presentation' about which Spivak has warned us, alerting us to how it can itself become an exercise of power (1988: 275). In fact, even before Maya writes about Nazia, by encouraging her 'to break a taboo against pregnant women bathing in the communal pond', Maya 'indirectly causes the Rajshahi villager Nazia to be severely beaten by local menfolk' (Chambers, 2015: 143). Maya's quick dismissal of Nazia's doubts about the wisdom of swimming in the pond suggests a certain arrogance on Maya's part and a misplaced confidence in her own ability to change mindsets: when she encourages Nazia to join her for a swim, Maya is convinced that since she has been 'lecturing' the villagers 'for years … about science and superstition and their rights', no one in the village puts stock any more in age-old superstitious prescriptions (Anam, 2012 [2011]: 18). The consequences of Maya's defiance of oppressive patriarchal taboos, while unpleasant, are far less severe than they are for Nazia; equipped with a medical degree and the option to return to her middle-class home in the city, despite her estranged relationship with her family, Maya is much freer than Nazia is to challenge misogynistic practices. Since they share the same gender, Maya presumes that Nazia also shares her desire to openly contest patriarchal prescriptions and is unable to grasp that, after having been publicly shamed and physically punished for her transgression, Nazia might be yearning for acceptance by her own community, rather than seeking to incur its further displeasure. When Maya visits Nazia in the village hospital after the lashing, she is eagerly looking forward to the day when, with Nazia's wounds healed, she and Nazia would 'begin to resist'

(2012 [2011]: 24). But, instead of welcoming Maya's presence, Nazia pleads with her to leave her alone: 'But Nazia said no and her black foot said no and Maya realised she would have to leave the wound open, leave the village with her protests still urgent, still angry' (2012 [2011]: 24).

Her preoccupation with subalternity, particularly gendered subalternity, notwithstanding, some of Maya's actions reveal a dangerous naivete about the material consequences of her attempts to help Nazia and a limited understanding of how her actions may imperil the lives of the very people whose suffering she is trying to alleviate. While she does try to conceal Nazia's identity in her column using an anagram of Nazia's name, 'Aizan', as well as by adopting an albeit thinly disguised pseudonym, S. M. Haque, Maya makes no attempt to obtain Nazia's permission to disseminate her story. The piece draws the ire of conservative groups in Nazia's village, with the Khatib of the local mosque sending a letter to Shafaat, clearly indicating that Maya's attempt to camouflage Nazia's and her own identity was unsuccessful. The readers are left in the dark about the exact contents of the letter since that passage is narrated from Maya's perspective and, apart from sardonically noting that the Khatib appears to be an 'upstanding fellow', Shafaat does not supply any further details about the letter to her (2012 [2011]: 155). Although Maya does enquire if the letter is 'threatening', not out of concern 'for herself, only for the people for the people of the village, for Nazia', instead of probing Shafaat and making an effort to find out if her column has had deleterious consequences for Nazia, Maya allows herself to be reassured by his vague response with disturbing alacrity (2012 [2011]: 155). Like Maya, Shafaat lives and works in Dhaka and appears to have no means of confirming Nazia's safety with any certainty. Yet Maya does not give further thought to Nazia, resolving instead to continue writing: 'He told her not to worry. Static through the receiver as he blew smoke out of the corner of his mouth. All right, then. She would keep on writing' (2012 [2011]: 156).

In using the story of an individual she personally knows and cares for, Maya can bring herself to only partially anonymise the incident as it is precisely its personal nature that helps her to humanise the suffering of women in Bangladeshi villages and perhaps to more convincingly puncture the narrative of freedom which the privileged members of Bangladeshi society find it convenient to uphold. But, in doing so, Maya also runs the risk of reinforcing Nazia's subalternity and her already precarious position in her village. In emphasising how gender 'intersects with other social relations such as class and race, such that women's experiences of power and disempowerment are divergent', Sara Ahmed argues that '[f]eminists positions that are committed to women as a collective (a structure of social alliance) must accept their status as partial interventions, as limited by the personal/social economies that shape them' (1996: 75). While Maya's writing represents a resistant practice aimed at recasting the meaning of freedom in an Independent Bangladesh, the feminist impulse driving her writerly endeavours becomes compromised by Maya's limited recognition of the divergent material conditions that define Nazia's and her own life as well as by her lack of acknowledgement of how a woman's freedom to resist is itself intimately bound up with her class and geographical positioning.

As we saw above in my discussion of Maya's first column, her desire to bear witness to subaltern struggles and to foreground subaltern stories is an effort not devoid of ethical dilemmas. Moreover, Maya's dedication to the recuperation of subaltern stories is neither uniform nor consistent. Lal notes that 'in contrast to her insistence on hearing the particularities of Sohail's war trauma, Maya does not mind eliding the details of Piya's story' (2019: 11). Indeed, when she first meets her, Maya does not allow Piya, a *birangona*, to articulate and share her unique experiences of wartime rape and pregnancy: Maya 'knew exactly what had happened to Piya. No explanation was necessary' (Anam, 2012 [2011]: 70). Maya's elision of Piya's story contrasts sharply not only with her insistence that Sohail talk about his wartime experiences, as Lal points out, but also with her determination to shatter the silence surrounding female subaltern stories through her writing.[5] Mookherjee's work alerts us to the construction of 'a public culture of "knowing"' in Bangladesh with respect to the *birangonas*, predicated on a 'homogeneous understanding of gendered victimhood' and on the assumption that 'wartime rape is experienced in the same way by all victims' (2015a: 6). As suggested by the use of indirect discourse in the passage from the novel cited earlier, possibly fearing the discomfort that accompanies cognitive dissonance, Maya prefers for Piya's story to remain untold so that she can more easily conflate it with what Lal refers to as the 'generic meta-narrative of the *birangona*' (2019: 11). I invoked above the abortions that Maya carries out for wartime rape victims at the government's behest; Maya's role in the implementation of this policy, designed to expel 'the seed of [the] enemy' from the body of the nation, too, constitutes an erasure of the *birangonas* as individual women capable of disparate responses (Anam, 2012 [2011]: 244). But because Sheikh Mujibur Rahman did not 'want the children of war', Maya, who is not a wartime rape victim herself, attempts to convince herself, although not always successfully, that such an erasure is in the best interests of the *birangonas* (2012 [2011]: 142).[6] As she tells her mother in an attempt to dispel Rehana's reservations about the abortion policy: 'Isn't it better, Ma, to erase all traces of what happened to them? That way they can start to forget' (2012 [2011]: 142).

The disjuncture between what is deemed worthy of being chronicled and what remains unrecorded or is actively forgotten, and the power imbalances inherent in these distinctions come home to Maya towards the end of the novel when she is arrested following the publication of a column in which she refers to the ruling dictator as a war criminal. The publication of this piece which, unlike her other columns, Maya signs using her real name, coincides with her attempt to rescue her nephew Zaid from the ultra-orthodox school to which Sohail sends him and where she has reason to believe Zaid is being subjected to sexual abuse. This rescue operation is a tragic failure with Zaid dying by accidental drowning. The religious extremist groups and the country's dictator find a convenient common enemy in Maya and conspire to have her punished; after spending several days in jail, she learns that she could be facing charges of either slander or treason. But what truly dismays Maya is the knowledge she has been imprisoned, not for 'kidnapping [her] nephew' as she had believed, but because of her anti-establishment writings: 'She buries her face in her hands. They had not come for her because of Zaid. No one had cared about that little boy' (2012 [2011]: 285). Shafaat, too, is arrested following the publication of the article, but unlike Maya, he is delighted at this outcome, since 'being arrested is exactly what Shafaat has always wanted. He's a hero. She's done him a favour' (2012 [2011]: 285). Maya's lawyer also informs her that 'the public is on [her] side' and that a protest march is being organised for her and Shafaat. Zaid's disappearance, however, draws neither the attention of the authorities nor of the press: he remains as neglected in death as he was while alive, his story being eclipsed by power plays on a national level, underlining the hierarchies and exclusionary imperatives underpinning even explicitly dissident writings, their publication and dissemination. Moreover, the news of Shafaat's delight at being arrested dilutes any satisfaction that Maya may have felt at her role in drawing the public's attention to the dictator's and the religious right's abuses of power. Shafaat's gleeful eagerness to be arrested suggests an appetite for personal glory, rather than a genuine commitment to social justice. Even before her arrest, Maya begins to recoil from the 'sordid' and exploitative gender dynamics that ensure the smooth running of *Rise Bangladesh!* as an anti-establishment organisation (2012 [2011]: 224). The young female journalists are compelled to 'sugar' Shafaat, the older male editor, which sometimes entails quite literally plying him with sweets and by assuming a subservient role in the office, tolerating his innuendos and invasive questions about their personal lives and serving him regular cups of tea in order to convince him to publish a story that is important to them (2012 [2011]: 224).

The epilogue of the novel is a fictional re-enactment of the Gono Adalat, the symbolic trial of Ghulam Azam, the politically reinstated collaborator and leader of the Jamaat-e-Islami, held by the Nirmul Committee in 1992. It does not tell us if Maya is still a writer, but it is a section that is explicitly concerned with the act of testifying and bearing witness.[7] Amongst those called to the witness box during the trial in the novel is Piya. It is suggested that Piya's presence at the trial is at least in part a result of Maya's encouragement; but if Maya has been instrumental in bringing Piya to the trial, it is Piya who, having chosen to give birth to her war baby, tells her own story. Piya recounts how she and a neighbour's daughter were captured and tortured by the Pakistani army; how they were gang-raped and how she survived, but the neighbour's daughter did not. In casting Maya in this closing scene in the role of a listener, rather than a chronicler, of a subaltern woman's story, the novel does not dismiss the importance of writing as a resistant practice.[8] But by foregrounding a subaltern speech act in the final pages, the narrator ensures that the readers do not lose sight of the power imbalances and hierarchies characterising anti-establishment writings seeking to lend a voice to the subaltern. It is worth noting that three *birangonas* were present at the actual Gono Adalat, but, unlike Piya in the novel, they did not speak, since 'their very presence was deemed as testimony against Gholam Azam' (Mookherjee, 2015a: 39). Anam's decision to replace the real-life *birangonas*' visual testimony with the fictional Piya's oral testimony is arguably an exercise of poetic licence meant to recognise that while the three *birangonas* may not have spoken at the Gono Adalat, *birangonas* have not uniformly remained silent about their wartime experiences and oral testimonies of *birangonas* do exist.[9]

In *A Golden Age*, we see a preteen Maya introduce herself to her classmates in the following words: 'My name is Shehrezade Haque Maya. I was named after a famous storyteller'; later in the novel, just before she leaves for Calcutta to volunteer in the refugee camps and to write press releases for the liberation movement, by way of bidding her farewell, her mother urges her to 'write some good stories' (Anam, 2012 [2007]: 47–130). Despite the long hiatus from her typewriter coinciding with her stay in the countryside, Maya does write many stories during the course of the two novels, and when *The Good Muslim* draws to a close, despite her newfound scepticism about the role of dissident writings and the gendered hierarchy underpinning their publication, she has not lost her love of the written word. This is evidenced by her continued regret that she will never again be able to share the joys of reading with her brother, for whom the Quran has become the only book worthy of being read and revered. But the tensions between Maya's various acts of resistance and her various dissident selves, both writerly and otherwise, which the second novel of the trilogy underscores, are both a result and an indication of her country's brutal and tragic history in general and of her countrywomen's varied and multifaceted struggles in particular.

Narration, anger and resistance: *The Gypsy Goddess*

If I noted the combativeness of Maya's writings in the previous section, refusing to be decorous and well-behaved, the female author-narrator of *The Gypsy Goddess*, with her frequent displays of sarcasm, her use of abusive language and her confrontational tone while addressing the reader, is even angrier. Also, within the text itself, the narrator of *The Gypsy Goddess* constantly interrogates the very point of her endeavours as a writer. This non-linear, polyphonic novel is interspersed with fictionalised documents, such as a letter from the Paddy Producers' Association to the Chief Minister of Madras and a Communist Party of India (Marxist) pamphlet; it also features a fictitious question and answer session with the author and asides about the author's relationship with her mother, all the while interrogating the validity of the novel as a genre to tell the story of 'Tamil Nadu's worst massacre of Dalits to date' (Kandasamy, 2014a: 277).[10]

The massacre took place in the village of Kilvenmani on 25 December 1968: forty-four women, men and children, belonging to Dalit agricultural families who were on strike following the murder of a communist leader, were burned alive by rowdies in the pay of the local feudal landlords. In focusing on the Kilvenmani atrocity, Kandasamy is careful not to present it as an isolated event or to equate Dalit existence with oppression. The narration is woven in with a detailed, if fragmented, account of the daily acts of injustice and violence committed against the Dalit labourers in Kilvenmani both before and after the massacre, as well as with descriptions of the myriad forms of resistance that the Dalit community enacted and continues to enact in the face of this oppression. The shifting temporal frames coupled with the author's liberal use of metafictional asides preclude a categorisation of this novel as historical fiction and they serve as a searing reminder of the extent to which the oppression experienced by the Dalit community in Kilvenmani is far from a thing of the past. As Filippo Menozzi points out, the text 'does not allow the story of Kilvenmani to be safely locked in the past: 1968 is closely tied up with the present of the narration and the future' (2020: 85). *The Gypsy Goddess* is not merely an attempt at recuperating an important episode in the history of Dalit resistance; it also serves to underscore the continuing relevance of this episode.

In this section, I focus on the novelist-narrator's efforts to bring to the fore the significance of anger in protest politics by imbuing the writing style with anger, effectively echoing the anger of the Dalit peasants in general and of the female peasants in particular who were subjected to horrendous acts of casteist sexual violence.

Moreover, I demonstrate that Kandasamy is keen to draw our attention not only to 'failures of the genre of the novel', which preoccupy many of her asides, but also more broadly, to the complex relationship between Dalit protest politics and the written word (in English) (Gajarawala, 2020: 45). Given the conflation of the narrator and author in this novel, much more so than elsewhere in this book, my analysis draws heavily on interviews with the author and her other non-fictional writings, including the acknowledgements section of *The Gypsy Goddess*, where Kandasamy addresses her own identity and/or the process and politics of writing. In the acknowledgements section, without resorting to irony, Kandasamy evokes the challenges of grappling with this gruesome event in post-Independence Indian history. Kandasamy confesses that she was 'too shy' to take up the 'challenge' of writing a history of the massacre, suggesting that a novelistic retelling of the event, though by no means easy, was a less daunting project (2014a: 277). Yet the extensive research that Kandasamy carried out, including the interviews with the surviving villagers, is an integral part of the novel; as the narrator tells us:

> Sitting here in Canterbury,[11] with video footage of the village ready to run continuously for five solid days, and with four diaries bristling with notes, I shall surmise and theorize, assume and presume, speculate and conflate and extrapolate every detail revealed by my field research in order to make it fit into the narrative mode of my novel. (2014a: 100)

The novel consciously blurs the line between fiction and non-fiction, a blurring which is reinforced by Kandasamy's decision to muddle the distinction between narrator and author.

In the Introduction, I noted the predominance within Dalit literature of life-writings and works of fiction in Indian languages other than English; I also briefly invoked the political import of the English language in Dalit creative lives. As the Dalit poet Chandramohan Sathyanathan has recently observed: 'Indian writers in English tend to be nearly exclusively from the upper castes and poets of my background and socio-political leanings tend to be a rarity on the contemporary Indian English poetry scene'; his observation can be extended to other literary genres including memoirs and fiction (2021: n.p.). Given the arguable status of *The Gypsy Goddess* as part of the 'emergent dalit segment of Indian writing in English' and the author-narrator's preoccupation with language as an identity marker, a more detailed discussion about the relationship between Dalit identity, the English language and Dalit literary production is in order here (Wiemann, 2017: 135). The English language, or more precisely, the Dalit community's limited access to the language is both a measure of the community's marginalisation within India as well as a weapon to keep the Dalits marginalised. According to the Dalit scholar Kancha Illiah Shepherd, for the

> vast numbers of Indians who are outside the English-speaking milieu – food producers, such as the Shudra, Dalits and Adivasis, who work in the fields ... their local languages – Hindi, Tamil, Telugu, Malayalam, Bengali, Marathi, Gujarathi or tribal languages and so on – are the medium of instruction in schools and colleges ... A small number of English-educated Indians, in this globalised world, have taken the lead in every sphere of life. The rural masses cannot catch up with the globalised, English-educated Indian ruling and business classes unless they too acquire that language, right from their time in school. (2020: n.p.)

In Kandasamy's novel, when the peasants seek justice in a court of law, the English language is the medium in which the perpetrators of the massacre and the judges collude with each other to obfuscate facts and to keep the subalterns subordinate. 'We marvelled at the words that came out of their mouths, always English, always in a steady tone, like a thresher at work ... Their English could shoot like darts, it could curl and coil around itself' (Kandasamy, 2014a: 248). The novel thus underscores the importance of Dalits having access to the English language, the language of various forms of power, including judicial power in India.

In view of the prevailing alignment of creative expression in English with upper-caste identity, Kandasamy's self-identification as a Dalit and her choice of the English language to express herself arguably make *The Gypsy Goddess* and her other works innately resistant texts. But it is important to note here that Kandasamy has consciously problematised her Dalit positioning; in a 2011 interview, she remarked that she had embraced Dalithood as an identity, since '[p]eople will force that label on you so you might as well make the most of it' (Stancati, 2011: n.p.). In a lengthy Facebook post a few years later she specified that she belongs to a 'mixed-caste, intercaste' background and that she does not wish to 'identify [herself] with any caste' in keeping with Ambedkar's 'dream of the annihilation of caste' (Kandasamy, 2014b: n.p.). In the same post, she explains her 'self-referential usage of the word Dalit' in terms of her intention to locate herself 'outside the spectrum of the caste order' and to 'problematize that someone with such a mixed-caste heritage cannot claim to belong to any caste in particular' (2014b: n.p.). She also recognises that the cultural capital to which she had access growing up sets her apart from the Dalits who appear in her novel; in her own words, her mother is a 'world-renowned mathematician' and her father 'a Tamil scholar of repute' (2014b: n.p.). At the same time, Kandasamy has underscored how personal a project the writing of *The Gypsy Goddess* was for her. Kandasamy's father's Andi Pandaram caste identity[12] and his position at the 'receiving end of the caste system' have shaped her writerly concerns (2014b: n.p.): 'I wanted to tell a story which for me was something that identified me with my roots in Tanjore (a city in the southern Indian state of Tamil Nadu) and help me understand why a person like my father would so desperately want to escape from there' (London School of Economics, 2014: n.p.).

Kandasamy has also acknowledged how she has come to see herself 'as an Indian writer in English as opposed to anything else' and has argued that '[i]f you are educated in a certain medium and you come from a certain class, it makes sense to write in English while making that kind of noise' (2014b: n.p.). In writing in English about the massacre and in charting the struggles of the Kilvenmani Dalit peasants, Kandasamy is not claiming to have had the same experiences of caste violence and oppression as the Dalits depicted in the novel; she is also not attempting to speak on behalf of the Dalits. Kandasamy instead draws attention to the distance between the Kilvenmani Dalits' resistant practices and her own and, in an authorial aside, she recognises the very limits of story-telling when grappling with the oppression experienced by the Dalit community in Kilvenmani, and the women more specifically: 'The atrocities committed by the policemen against the women labourers are so savage that they cannot even be written down' (2014a: 95). Kandasamy explains that *The Gypsy Goddess* is not meant to giv[e] voice to the voiceless. That sounds like you are a Messiah or a Mahatma. It's about me getting inspired by their militancy, by understanding that they have been standing up to the system without any of the safety nets we take for granted. I look at them and ask, What am I doing? Why am I not fighting? They are giving me courage. (Kidd, 2014: n.p.)

These comments, which Kandasamy made during an interview, contrast sharply with Maya's belief in *The Good Muslim* in her ability to speak and act judiciously on behalf of her class Others, but, paradoxically, are also reminiscent of Maya's valorisation of militant resistance in *A Golden Age*.

Kandasamy's anglophone novel both lends itself to *and* resists being read as a work of Dalit identity-based writing and this underlying tension helps Kandasamy to unpack the multifaceted nature of Dalit identity and Dalit resistance. If the caste–class nexus is an important vector of oppression and resistance in the novel, Kandasamy's preoccupation with the specific forms of violence directed against Dalit women and the women's acts of resistance bestow a distinctly Dalit feminist sensibility upon the novel. As the narrator explains, Gopalakrishnan Naidu, the leader of the Paddy Producers Association and the man behind the Kilvenmani massacre, 'was a woe to women in five villages … People kept a tally of the women he had raped, the virgins he had ordered to be sent to him, the girls who were never seen again' (Kandasamy, 2014a: 142). The novel contests not only prevailing classist and casteist worldviews, but also mainstream Indian feminism which elides the 'triply burdened' positioning of Dalit women, stemming from their gender, caste and class identities (Arya and Rathore, 2020: 7). As Sunaina Arya and Aakash Singh Rathore explain:

> The neglect of *Dalit* in the Indian discourse on gender is deeply problematic because Dalit women occupy subordinate positions in most organised production of feminist knowledge … Indian feminist discourse, which ought to bring gender-justice to *all* Indian women, at least in theory, has suppressed the caste question to such an extent that 'feminism' itself has been seen as a modality of subjugating women from Dalit communities. (2020: 2; emphasis in the original)

If sexual violence in the domestic arena has been a major concern for mainstream Indian feminists, violence, especially sexual violence, against Dalit women 'is disproportionately public rather than domestic because working as labourers is peculiar to Dalit women's living' (2020: 8–9). Amongst the acts of violence 'traditionally reserved for Dalit women' are: 'extreme filthy verbal abuse and sexual epithets, naked parading, dismemberment, … pulling out of teeth, tongue and nails, and violence including murder after proclaiming witch-craft' (Manorama, 2006: n.p.). In the fourth section of Part 2, entitled 'Seasons of violence', *The Gypsy Goddess* homes in on Dalit women and underscores how central resistance is to their identity. This part of the novel reads both like a litany of the injustices suffered by Dalit women and an anthem celebrating their resilience and refusal to accept their lot. The use of repetition, with the phrase 'when women take to protest' functioning as a refrain, the varying length of the sentences coupled with a matter-of-fact tone and a simple vocabulary lend this section a poetic quality, allowing the narrator to pay tribute to the protesting women and their courage, while also accentuating the everydayness of their struggle (Kandasamy, 2014a: 75). Moreover, this interlude focusing on Dalit protest politics invites an understanding of Dalit women's protests both as part of Dalit communist politics at large as well as something quite distinct:

> Sometimes their demands are related to women alone, like when they demanded daily wages instead of the weekly wage for women … Most of the time, they fight for everybody … The jails are full of fighting Madonnas. They are not afraid. They are not afraid of arrests. They are not afraid of hurt. (2014a: 75)

While highlighting the indignities and violence that Dalit women are subjected to, the narrator also refuses to romanticise the figure of the protesting female Dalit and she does so primarily through her focus on the women's words and their language. She underscores the ire of Dalit women in the form of a rhetorical question which leaves no doubt as to the legitimacy of this anger: 'How not to expect anger from women whose friendliest banter involves swearing to cut off each other's cunts?' (2014a: 78). The violence that is implicit in the women's 'friendliest banter' in the novel is reminiscent of the Dalit writer Urmila Pawar's recollections in *The Weave of My Life* of the women of her childhood, with their 'fiery expletives' and 'choicest abuses' as they travelled great distances to sell their wares in a market, the loads they carried 'heavy enough to break their necks' (2009 [2008]: 1–9). Kandasamy also charts the myriad ways in which Dalit women's anger translates into targeted political action:

> When women take to protest, there is no looking back. This time it is the tractors. This time it is a Polydol death. This time it is a disappearance. This time it is a strike for higher wages. This time it is the demand for punishment for a rapist – the issues came and went and came again … Once they smashed pots to protest their poor wages. Once, when the Paddy Producers Association put up its yellow flag in their village, they hauled it down, set fire to it and broke the flagpost. Once they went to the fields to harvest in the middle of the night, saying that they alone would harvest the crops they sowed, and that the landlords had no business deploying outside labour. (2014a: 75)

The narrator-novelist renders the Dalit women's angry actions (the smashing of pots, the burning of the Paddy Producers Association's flag and the breaking of the flagpost) and the 'choicest abuses' that they scream in front of 'every job-stealing tractor' inseparable from their specific demands for more humane working conditions and their broader calls for justice to be served for the violence, both sexual and otherwise, to which their community is systematically subjected (2014a: 75).

If the women are protesting against various forms of violence, the narrator highlights how their loud protests lead to further violence: the landlords punish the 'shrill-voiced women by stripping them almost naked and tying them to trees and whipping them in front of the whole village' and the police punish them 'by making them kneel and walk a few miles on their knees until they have no choice' (2014a: 76). Kandasamy's depiction of the protesting women in the novel draws attention to how the Dalit women's 'vulnerability' and their 'precarious position' in Indian society, as evident in their exposure to 'dispossession, poverty, insecurity, and harm', compels them to mount various forms of public resistance and how their physical vulnerability and precarity is 'further enhanced' by these acts of public resistance; it also demonstrates how this multi-layered vulnerability is 'a potentially effective mobilizing force in political mobilizations' (Butler, 2016: 14). But I argue that the novel compels us to broaden our definition of the concepts of 'vulnerability' and 'precarity' to necessarily include the concomitant feelings of anger harboured by the vulnerable, in this case Dalit women, so as to better understand why vulnerability can be such a powerful mobilising force. As the narrator tells us, despite the corporeal punishment the women receive at the hands of the landlords and the police for protesting against the status quo, 'these blows do not break them. They are bold beyond the bruised skin and the bleeding knee' (Kandasamy, 2014a: 76). The narrator-novelist consciously mirrors the Dalit women's 'shrill-voiced' anger in her asides, directing her fury at the feudal landlords as well as the readers of the novel of whose ability to take concrete action in support of the Dalit struggle she is deeply sceptical. Indeed, Kandasamy's novel's engagement with anger or what Barbara Tomlinson (1996) refers to as 'textual vehemence' manifests itself in two main ways: first, the writing itself is belligerent, and second, much of the narrative is focused on the relationship between Dalit protest politics and Dalit anger (2016). *The Gypsy Goddess* echoes Arundhati Roy's defence of the political necessity of anger rooted in facts:

> Anger is based on reason. They're not two different things. I feel it's very important to defend that. To defend the space for feelings, for emotions, for passion ... I'm a writer. I have a point of view. I have feelings about the things I write about – and I'm going to express them. (2008a: 98)

The author-narrator's angry tone and 'gimmicky asides' in *The Gypsy Goddess* are accompanied by dates and figures, in short, recognisable, impossible-to-ignore facts (Sawhney, 2014: n.p.). Kandasamy also deploys expletives liberally in the text: she refers to the architects of the Kilvenmani massacre as 'feudal bastards' and accuses the readers of being 'lazy' and of living 'amoral lives' (2014a: 22–71). Kandasamy decries dispassionate forms of writing, in particular, the police and medical reports that were drafted in the wake of the massacre, where the horrors of Dalit oppression were obscured by a commitment to recording 'neutral' data. The police, as one of the survivors tells the narrator, 'are meticulous in their observations', and 'their reports talk about gunshot wounds sustained by coconut trees'; similarly, the forensic pathologist prepares a carefully 'tabulated report of the pellets she finds in [their] bodies ... She tabulates the other gunshot wounds too. Name, number of wounds, location' (2014a: 222). In offering a critique of these writings, Kandasamy highlights how official report writing reflects and perpetuates the prevailing power imbalances, but she is also keen not to elide the significance of facts and figures and of accurate record keeping. In fact, the narrator insists on repeatedly correcting the official count of the dead which stood 'at forty-two (plus two, silent)' and which glossed over the murder of two babies (2014a: 188, 218, 230, 246, 247). We also witness a conversation between the narrator and Ramalingam, a Dalit man who lives on 'the same street where the tragedy took place' and who urges the narrator to 'write this all down and put in the papers and tell the truth to the whole world. Let everyone read about what happened here and let them burn with anger', an exhortation that underscores the importance of relaying facts to a wide readership, but in a way that provokes anger and, by implication, action (2014a: 182).

Alongside satirising seemingly objective record-keeping and the postcolonial readership with its 'craving for unintelligibility' which arguably serves as an excuse for political inaction, *The Gypsy Goddess* offers a more wide-ranging meditation on the relationship between subalternity and the written word (Kandasamy, 2014a: 70). For instance, the novel alerts us to how the agreements that the landlords sign, promising to adhere to a fairer wage structure, are not worth the paper they are written on and instead serve to silence the Dalit peasants. Class and caste power is accompanied and in turn reinforced by the ability to disregard written agreements and break promises with impunity. As the villages tell the narrator, the landlords 'know that words on paper have a life only on the page. They know nothing can bind them. They know these words don't belong to anybody. They know that words are stillness, meant to arrest hostile action. They treat paper no more preciously than pubic hair' (2014a: 224). Echoing Audre Lorde, who reminds us that '[a]nger is loaded with information and energy', the novel is as erudite and extensively researched as it is unrelentingly furious, allowing Kandasamy to uphold both the rationality as well as the legitimacy of subaltern anger (2019 [1984]: 60). Also, and again like Lorde, the author-narrator is not seeking to present anger as an unproblematic emotion, or as a necessarily productive or even a sufficient response to injustice. She alerts us to how in the months and years following the massacre 'anger prevents Kilvenmani from disorienting itself … anger keeps the people together, provides them with a reason to leave, pushes them into action', but by making us privy to the fears about her community harboured by Maayi (whom I discuss below), the narrator also brings to the fore the danger of this rage turning 'inwards' and 'eat[ing] up' the community (Kandasamy, 2014a: 202). As Lorde notes, while invoking the significance of anger in the lives of women of colour in the United States, 'we have had to learn to orchestrate those furies so that they do not tear us apart' (2019 [1984]: 61). In addition to fighting societal injustice, the Kilvenmani survivors are burdened with an internal struggle to ensure their anger does not engulf them and incapacitate them as political agents.

It is telling that even if she does not 'dwell on character, interiority, or affect' in this novel as Toral Jatin Gajarawala has observed, the one character that the author ensures has a distinct presence in the narrative is Maayi, who is based on the elderly women that Kandasamy interviewed while researching the book (2020: 45). Kandasamy has noted that this was a deliberate choice since old women 'are largely ignored in fiction because they are not sexualisable' (Taylor, 2018: n.p.). In creating Maayi, an 'old woman who held the village together after the massacre and helped people deal with their PTSD', the author pushes back against this pernicious literary tendency (2018: n.p.). Moreover, the woman's age and the attendant imperviousness to sexualisation is of particular significance in the context of hegemonic constructions of Dalit women; it effectively represents a rejection of 'brahmanical sexualization of dalit women's bodies as a result of which dalit women, considered inherently impure and lustful, often remain confined to certain kinds of jobs that perpetuate their sexualization' (Pan, 2021: 205).[13] The narrator also tells us that Maayi 'never cried' in front of the journalists who came to Kilvenmani in search of a moving story, intending to exploit her exoticness ('she without a blouse, she with the long dangling earlobes, she with tattoos all over her arms') for commercial ends (Kandasamy, 2014a: 211). Maayi refuses to share the village's stories with the self-serving reporters: 'Those stories are her village's wounds of shame, they cannot be displayed to passing spectators' (2014a: 211). In greater detail than *The Good Muslim*, Kandasamy's novel charts the exploitation that accompanies seemingly engaged journalism. With ferocious contempt, Kandasamy delineates how journalists, ostensibly seeking to foreground subaltern stories, are often only interested in such stories as long as they subscribe to a predetermined formula that sells: 'She never cried so they listened to her and asked her more questions with the hope that she would start weeping and they could go back with a story of how strong women crumbled. She never cried in front of them' (2014a: 204). Kandasamy's novel thus highlights how Dalit women's often physical resistance against oppressive caste, class and gender hierarchies is accompanied by a resistance against and a refusal to participate in the production of easily digestible narratives that cast them as victims.

The epilogue, written in the second person, introduces a deliberate temporal obfuscation and is addressed to the implied reader of the novel who is shown to travel to Kilvenmani in the year 1980, twelve years after the massacre and over thirty years before the publication and hence the act of reading *The Gypsy Goddess*. Kandasamy inserts the reader into the text and turns this reader into a character who visits Kilvenmani, meets Maayi, learns about the murder of Gopalakrishnan and also witnesses the ensuing celebrations. Through the heavy-handed use of second-person narration and the ultimate revelation of this time-travelling reader as a journalist who is attempting to write an 'anniversary special' story, the novel accentuates its earlier indictment of exploitative readerly and writerly practices (2014a: 271). The second-person pronoun and the introduction of temporal inconsistencies emphasise the distance between the reader and the narrator, with the latter coming to assume a diminished presence in the epilogue; they also starkly bring home to us the distance between the reader and the Kilvenmani peasants, even as the reader/journalist joins them 'as they rejoice in their revenge' following Gopalakrishnan's murder (2014a: 273).[14] The author-narrator's diminished role in the epilogue, where the news of Gopalakrishnan's death and the resulting celebrations are relayed via the reader/journalist, coincides with a certain linearity, with the repeated reference to Gopalakrishnan's death as 'the end' (2014a: 273). The closing sentences read: '*Mudivu kandachu*. It has been completed. We have seen the end' (2014a: 273). They underline Kandasamy's understanding of how, having suffered appalling abuse and loss and having been failed by the judicial system as well as the media, for the long-suffering and long-resisting people of Kilvenmani, while important, the telling, listening and writing of stories could not suffice and only rebellion in the form of violent revenge was able to provide some semblance of closure.

By their very existence, the three novels can be seen as an affirmation of the subversive power of (fiction) writing, focusing as they do on stories that run counter to hegemonic narratives, whether national or feminist or indeed both. But these literary works also alert us, implicitly in the case of Anam's novels and far more loudly and stridently in the case of Kandasamy's text, to the limitations of reading and writing as resistant practices. They demonstrate how intimately bound up the written word is not only with hierarchies of class, caste and gender, but also with a complex constellation of human flaws and weaknesses, including laziness, greed, arrogance and a thirst for personal glory, making it as much a tool of oppression as of liberation.

Notes

1 This quasi-colonial rule was steeped in ethnocentrism and accompanied by 'a demeaning attitude towards Bengali culture and the Bengali population' (Zakaria, 2019: n.p.). In March 1971, the Pakistan Army launched a brutal military operation named Operation Searchlight to quell the rise of pro-independence nationalism in the region, with the resulting deaths estimated to have been 'between 300,000 and 3 million people, with hundreds of thousands of women raped' (2019: n.p.).
2 An estimated ten million people are believed to have left East Pakistan for India between April and December 1971, making it the 'largest single displacement of refugees in the second half of the century' (UNHCR, 2000: 59). '[T]he vast majority' of these refugees 'returned within a year to what became the independent state of Bangladesh' (2000: 59).
3 These kinds of journalism contrast with what Morris Janowitz refers to as the 'gatekeeper' approach to journalism, with its emphasis on 'the search for objectivity and the sharp separation of reporting fact from disseminating opinion' (1978: 343). While not dismissing the importance of 'fairness' and a 'scrupulous attention to the facts', increasingly, journalists themselves have come to see the ideal of objectivity in the field as an 'illusion and a shibboleth' (Bell, 1998: 16). See also Robert A. Hackett and Yuezhi Zhao's *Sustaining Democracy? Journalism and the Politics of Objectivity* (1998).
4 Ghulam Azam was a member of the extremist Jamaat-e-Islami political party, which collaborated with the West Pakistani army; Motiur Rahman Nizami was the leader of Al Badr Bahini, the paramilitary force of the West Pakistani army.

5 Maya's resistant subjectivity is marked by another kind of erasure, that of Islamic teachings and practices, since she comes to see Islam in an unequivocally negative light and as an ideology used to justify all manner of abuses of power. See also Chambers (2015).
6 We learn later that, in deference to Piya's wishes, Maya did not in fact proceed with the abortion.
7 Jahanara Imam (1929–94), author of the wartime diary *Ekatterer Dinguli* (*The Days of Seventy-One*; 1986), campaigned for war crimes trials following the end of the liberation war in Bangladesh and formed the Ghatak-Dalal Nirmul Committee (Committee to Exterminate the Killers and Collaborators).
8 In *The Bones of Grace* (2016), the concluding book of Anam's Bengal trilogy, set around thirty years after the end of *The Good Muslim*, we see Maya travelling all over Bangladesh, gathering the testimonies of *birangonas* and collecting information that would help legal efforts to put war criminals on trial.
9 Notably, Nilima Ibrahim's *Ami Birangona Bolchi* (*This Is the War Heroine Speaking*; 1994–95) provides 'personalised accounts of sexual violence against seven women with whom Ibrahim had been in close contact with [sic] when she worked in the Women's Rehabilitation Centre in 1972' (Mookherjee, 2015b: n.p.).
10 See Herrero (2019 [2017]) and Menozzi (2020) for detailed explorations of Kandasamy's use of postmodernist metafictional techniques in the novel. Gajarawala's essay sheds valuable light on Kandasamy's deployment of an 'excessive' form of story-telling (2020: 49–51).
11 As Kandasamy mentions in the acknowledgements, she completed the first draft of the novel while she was a Charles Wallace India Trust Fellow at the University of Kent in 2011 (2014a: 276).
12 Andi Pandaram, as Kandasamy explains in her Facebook post, is a 'Dalit community from Kerala and Tamil Naidu' (2014b: n.p.).
13 As the Dalit activist Ruth Manorama points out, 'the Devadasi system of temple prostitution is the most extreme form of exploitation of Dalit women' (2006: n.p.). This age-old practice forces young Dalit women to provide sexual services to priests and patrons.
14 Overriding the Nagapattinam district court judgement which sentenced Gopalakrishnan Naidu to ten years of imprisonment in 1970, the Madras High Court acquitted him in 1975. Naidu was waylaid and murdered by a group of people in 1980.

Epilogue: resisting idealising resistance

'The revolution has already happened! What more revolution do you want?'
'Yes, it's been a real revolution!' The Sikh, still attempting to stand steadily, said complacently, "Twas indeed a revolution.'
'Was there a revolution?' Pandey pointedly asked Nayyar.
'Revolution?' Nayyar asked Puri in turn, 'Was it a revolution?'
'Revolution, well no ... but to have got independence for the country was no less a victory', Puri said by way of finding a placatory compromise for this group of drunks.
'Listen!' said Pandey, with hands on hips, as he struck a pose of great seriousness, 'We've got independence for our nation. All we need now is a revolution.'

– Yashpal, *This Is Not That Dawn*,
translated by Anand, 2010

In this epigraph taken from *Jhootha Sach* (1958, 1960), Yashpal's two-volume Partition novel in Hindi, we see an inebriated group of mostly upper-class, Sikh and Hindu men unself-consciously using the collective pronoun 'we' and referring to 'our nation' when debating whether the end of British rule in India signifies a 'revolution' or 'independence', whether the two are indeed one and the same thing, and whether the one should necessarily follow the other. This scene not only serves as a reminder of the limitations of the epithet 'postcolonial' when grappling with post-1947 realities and imaginaries in South Asia, but also highlights the contested nature of resistance and often-attendant notions of freedom, identity and nationhood. Throughout this book, I have sought as much to problematise the concept and praxis of resistance, whether this resistance is of a 'revolutionary' kind or not, as to (re)valorise it. Drawing on the works of queer and/or feminist scholars such as Ahmed, Butler, Cohen, Foucault, Puar and Sunder Rajan, the Introduction underscored how, for the purposes of this book, 'resistance' would be understood as a multi-layered and ambiguous concept, unsettling the public/private, but also the individual/collective, erotic/pragmatic and action/inaction dichotomies. By homing in on the contradictions that resistant impulses, sensibilities and acts are shown to accommodate and the anxieties that they generate in the literary texts under consideration, the chapters that followed foregrounded the refusal on the part of contemporary South Asian women writers to idealise resistance, whether feminist or otherwise, without negating or discounting its, often existential, significance.

This *de-idealisation* of resistance manifests itself in several ways. It is, of course, a striking feature of novels such as Freeman's *A Disobedient Girl* and Lahiri's *The Namesake*, which explicitly grapple with acts of what I refer to as troubled and troubling or distorted resistance. It is apparent also in how some of the novels examined in the preceding chapters grapple explicitly with nationalist resistance and/or chart the many other resistances unfolding and resistant subjectivities taking shape within national spaces. In texts as varied as *Broken Verses*, which focuses on the nonviolent resistance mounted by Pakistani citizens against the military dictatorship of General Zia-ul-Haq, and *The God of Small Things* and *The Lowland*, which are concerned with the Naxalite insurgency, we see how '[l]iving *in* the nation today' involves challenging the state and its policies while also necessarily 'living *with* the state' (Sunder Rajan, 2003: 1; emphasis in the original). In doing so, the texts collectively question the 'hegemony of the transnational in postcolonial criticism' and, by extension, the privileging of hybridity-driven modes of resistance in transcultural, diasporic settings (Boehmer, 2005: 190).

In *Stories of Women: Gender and Narrative in the Postcolonial Nation* which examines, amongst others, three of the novels also analysed in this study (*The God of Small Things*, *Difficult Daughters* and *A Married Woman*), Elleke Boehmer shows how the 'idealising tendencies' of nationalism, too, can be 'calibrated' by women writers 'with reference to the day-to-day contexts through which it is expressed in the world' and nationalism 'rethought in a feminising or more woman-centred direction' (2005: 207). Boehmer argues that Roy does this in *The God of Small Things* by demonstrating how '"small" familial and domestic realities impinge on the large questions of the nation-state', and Kapur in *A Married Woman* by identifying 'the narrative of erotic (specifically and subversively of homoerotic) self-awakening ... with the increasingly embattled narrative of secular nationalism' (2002: 208–11). In particular, in showing how Astha's fierce opposition to right-wing Hindu nationalist views and practices does not culminate in the rejection of the nation as an ideological and pragmatic category, but instead compels her to turn to 'brush and canvas to make her contribution to the country', *A Married Woman* provides a vocabulary for a distinctly inclusive nationalist sentiment (Kapur, 2002: 297). It brings to the fore the pernicious as well as progressive values that nationalist resistance can inhabit, reinforcing Dilip Simeon's assertion that '[d]epending on the social forces and processes which articulate it', nationalism 'can be defensive or imperialist, tolerant or chauvinist, universalist/humanist or racist' (1987: 67). Similarly, if, in Anam's first novel *A Golden Age*, Bengali nationalism is celebrated and presented as a necessary political project to counter the ethnocentric violence exercised by the West Pakistani government, her second novel *The Good Muslim* is a powerful indictment of religious and military nationalism in the newly independent state of Bangladesh. Despite its diasporic setting, Peres da Costa's *Homework* is another text which underscores the protean nature of nationalist resistance: if Mina's father's absurd Goan nationalism, rather than a virulent force, is a source of comic relief in the text, this nationalist struggle, as ridiculous as it is, is inseparable from his identity as a resistant, political figure, as evident in his preoccupation with the deeply unjust and inhumane ways in which the Australian nation was established and the exclusionary terms in which it continues to constitute itself.

Representations of violent militancy in Lahiri's *The Lowland* and Roy's *The Ministry of Utmost Happiness*, albeit in dramatically different ways, draw our attention to the psychological and physical damage wrought by armed resistance, while also recognising, to varying extents, that the struggle is against a patently unjust status quo and that nonviolent means may fail to bring about a shift in the prevailing power imbalances and a discernible improvement in the lives of the 'deliberately silenced, or the preferably unheard' (Roy,

2006: 330). But even when the acts of resistance do not entail the use of physical force or are not 'distorted' in the way that I have chosen to understand the term in Chapter 5, the texts considered in this study invite us to see how fraught resistance often is with affective and practical challenges, especially for women, making its wholesale celebration rather difficult, if not impossible. Consider, for example, how in *Broken Verses* Samina's time-consuming activism and her activist romance with the Poet, with the two becoming increasingly conflated with each other, make her an often absentee mother to Aasmaani, causing her daughter considerable suffering which continues long after Samina's disappearance. In Fernando's 'Of bread and power', despite successfully resisting parental pressure and leaving the familial home to forge a new life for herself in Colombo, Seela's resistant sensibility is hemmed in by her emotional need to be a good daughter. By the time the short story draws to a close, Seela is painfully aware of the conditional nature of her parents' love but is unable to cut off ties with them, and her practice of resistance refuses to be detached entirely from certain conventional expectations. Similarly, while Virmati's pursuit of higher education and her refusal to submit to her family's demands that she marry a man of their choice make her a wilful subject, her feminist wilfulness is tarnished by her inability to reject her lover's patriarchal demands, showing how difficult it may be for some women to shake off the multi-layered, pernicious yoke of patriarchal discourse. Relatedly, my examination of Nuggo's relationship with Raagni in 'A day for Nuggo' and of Maya's relationship with Nazia in *The Good Muslim* shows how the ability to resist societal injustice can itself be a marker of privilege, with this privilege being bound up with economic, educational and cultural capital as well as with the availability of time. While recognising both the specificity of 'female' and 'feminist' acts of resistance, these texts also confound attempts to interpret such acts in utopian and triumphalist terms, which contrasts sharply with how, as discussed in the Introduction, resistance has often been conceptualised in (masculine) anticolonial discourse.

Furthermore, the preceding chapters have shed light on how, in South Asian women's fiction, resistant figures, who are admirable in many respects, can behave in remarkably unappealing ways, with Aruna brazenly blackmailing her employers in 'Almost Valentine's Day'; Ammu in *The God of Small Things* threatening to love her children less if they fail to follow her dictates, which leaves her young daughter Rahel in a state of emotional limbo; the Poet in *Broken Verses* crassly objectifying Samina and attempting to reduce her to a national allegory in his anti-establishment poetry; and Anamika in *Babyji* conveniently downplaying the importance of state-led affirmative action aimed at redressing age-old caste inequities. In some cases, as my readings indicate, it is the textual silences marking the narratives of resistance which ambiguate our understanding and perception of the figures of defiance. In neither Roy's *The God of Small Things* nor *The Ministry of Utmost Happiness*, for example, is it unequivocally revealed to the reader whether Velutha and Musa resorted to violence as part of their participation in the Naxalite movement and the Kashmiri nationalist insurgency respectively. In Lahiri's 'The treatment of Bibi Haldar', the elliptical recounting of the circumstances leading up to Bibi's pregnancy provides no clear assurance to us that it was a consensual sexual encounter, even if the outcome was a much longed-for one for the protagonist, making the tenor of Bibi Haldar's defiance difficult to define.

Finally, resistance is de-romanticised and de-idealised by the ways in which contemporary South Asian women writers lend nuance to our understanding of writing itself as a contestatory practice. They do so, as we saw in my examination of Kandasamy's *The Gypsy Goddess* and Anam's novels in Chapter 6, by revealing the resistant potentialities as well as inadequacies of the written word. They also temper the risk of presenting writing as the only *artistic* resistant practice by valorising other forms of creative expression, whether it is painting for Astha in *A Married Woman*, batik dyeing for Seela in 'Of bread and power' or clothing and make-up for Anjum in *The Ministry of Utmost Happiness*. Moreover, in engaging with different forms of writing – articles, news reports, legal documents, employment contracts, petitions, interviews, letters and even seemingly random notes – alongside literary works, such as the Poet's dissident verses and the dramatic script focusing on the Babri Mosque that Astha pens, the fiction examined in this study resists being read as an unambiguous, self-congratulatory celebration of its own subversive power.

References

Abu-Lughod, L. (1990) 'The romance of resistance: tracing transformations of power through bedouin women', *American Ethnologist*, 17:1, 41–55. https://doi.org.10.1525/ae.1990.17.1.02a00030

Adiga, A. (2008) *The White Tiger*. New York: Free Press.

Aguiar, A. and J. Lahiri. (1999) 'Interview with Jhumpa Lahiri', *Pif*, September. Available at: www.pifmagazine.com/1999/09/interview-with-jhumpa-lahiri/ (Accessed: 17 March 2022).

Ahmad, A. (2007 [1997]) 'Reading Arundhati Roy *politically*', in A. Tickell (ed.), *Arundhati Roy's The God of Small Things*. London; New York: Routledge, pp. 110–19.

Ahmad, R. (2014) *The Gatekeeper's Wife and Other Stories*. Lahore: ILQA Publishers.

Ahmed, S. (1996) 'Beyond humanism and postmodernism: theorizing a feminist practice', *Hypatia*, 11:2, 71–93. https://doi.org.10.1111/j.1527-2001.1996.tb00665.x

Ahmed, S. (2010) *The Promise of Happiness*. Durham, NC: Duke University Press.

Ahmed, S. (2014 [2004]) *The Cultural Politics of Emotion*. 2nd edn. Edinburgh: Edinburgh University Press.

Ahmed, S. (2014) *Willful Subjects*. Durham, NC: Duke University Press.

Ahmed, S. (2016) *Living a Feminist Life*. New York: Duke University Press.

Ahuja, P. and R. Ganguly. (2007) 'The fire within: Naxalite insurgency violence in India', *Small Wars & Insurgencies*, 18:2, 249–74. https://doi.org.10.1080/09592310701400861

Alagappa, M. (2004) *Civil Society and Political Change in Asia: Expanding and Contracting Democratic Space*. Stanford, CA: Stanford University Press.

Ali, A. S. (1995) 'The rebel's silhouette: translating Faiz Ahmed Faiz', in A. Dingwaney and C. Maier (eds), *Between Languages and Cultures*

Translation and Cross-Cultural Texts. Pittsburgh, PA: University of Pittsburgh Press, pp. 75–90.
Ali, M. (2003) *Brick Lane*. London: Doubleday.
Ali, S. (2004) *Madras on Rainy Days*. New York: Picador.
Anam, T. (2012 [2007]) *A Golden Age*. Edinburgh: Canongate Books.
Anam, T. (2012 [2011]) *The Good Muslim*. Edinburgh: Canongate Books.
Anam, T. (2017 [2016]) *The Bones of Grace*. Edinburgh: Canongate Books.
Anderson, B. (1998) *The Spectre of Comparisons: Nationalism, Southeast Asia and the World*. London: Verso.
Anjaria, U. (2012) *Realism in the Twentieth-Century Indian Novel: Colonial Difference and Literary Form*. New York: Cambridge University Press.
Anjaria, U. (2015) 'Realist hieroglyphics: Aravind Adiga and the new social novel', *Modern Fiction Studies*, 61:1, 114–37. https://doi.org.10.1353/mfs.2015.0005
Arya, S. and A. S. Rathore. (2020) 'Introduction: theorising Dalit feminism', in S. Arya and A. S. Rathore (eds), *Dalit Feminist Theory: A Reader*. Abingdon; New York: Routledge, pp. 1–21.
Ashcroft, B., G. Griffiths and H. Tiffin (eds). (1989) *The Empire Writes Back: Theory and Practice in Post-Colonial Literatures*. London: Routledge.
Bajpai, R. (2010) 'Rhetoric as argument: social justice and affirmative action in India, 1990', *Modern Asian Studies*, 44:4, 675–708. https://doi.org.10.1017/S0026749X09990035
Baldwin, S. S. (1999) *What the Body Remembers*. London: Doubleday.
Bande, U. (2006) *Writing Resistance: A Comparative Study of the Selected Novels by Women Writers*. Shimla: Indian Institute Advanced Studies.
Banerjee, D. (2020) 'From cheap labor to overlooked citizens: looking for British Muslim identities in Kamila Shamsie's *Home Fire*', *South Asian Review*, 41:3–4, 288–302. https://doi.org.10.1080/02759527.2020.1835141
Banerjee, S. (2010) 'Mediating between violence and non-violence in the discourse of protest', *Economic and Political Weekly*, 45:11, 35–40.
Banerjee, S. (2017) *Activism and Agency in India: Nurturing Resistance in the Tea Plantations*. London; New York: Routledge.
Barker, C. (2000) *Cultural Studies: Theory and Practice*. Thousand Oaks, CA; New Delhi: SAGE Publications.
Barsamian, D. and A. Roy. (2004) *The Checkbook and the Cruise Missile: Conversations with Arundhati Roy*. Cambridge: South End Press.
Batra, K. (2008) 'Emergent sexual identities in Indian women's writing', *South Asian Review*, 29:1, 251–68. https://doi.org.10.1080/02759527.2008.11932588
Baxter, L. A. and C. Akkoor (2008) 'Aesthetic love and romantic love in close relationships: a case study in East Indian arranged marriages', in

R. C. Arnett and K. G. Roberts (eds), *Communication Ethics: Between Cosmopolitanism and Provinciality*. New York: Peter Lang, pp. 23–46.

Beauvoir, S. de (2009) *The Second Sex*, trans. C. Borde and S. Malovany-Chevallier. London: Vintage Digital, 2014.

Behere, P. K., S. T. S. Rao and K. Verma. (2011) 'Effect of marriage on preexisting psychoses', *Indian Journal of Psychiatry*, 53:4, 287–8. https://doi.org.10.4103/0019-5545.91900

Bell, M. (1998) 'The journalism of attachment', in M. Kieran (ed.), *Media Ethics*. London; New York: Routledge, pp. 15–22.

Berger, B. (2009) 'Political theory, political science and the end of civic engagement', *Perspectives on Politics*, 7:2, 335–50. https://doi.org.10.1017/S153759270909080X

Berger, J. (2007) *Hold Everything Dear: Dispatches on Survival and Resistance*. London: Verso.

Bhabha, H. K. (1985) 'Signs taken for wonders: questions of ambivalence and authority under a tree outside Delhi, May 1817', *Critical Inquiry*, 12:1, 144–65.

Bhabha, H. K. (1990) 'Introduction: narrating a nation', in H. K. Bhabha (ed.), *Nation and Narration*. London; New York: Routledge, pp. 1–7.

Bhalla, T. (2016) *Reading Together, Reading Apart: Identity, Belonging, and South Asian American Community*. Urbana, IL: University of Illinois Press.

Bhushan, K. and G. Katyal. (2002) *Lal Krishna Advani: Deputy Prime Minister*. New Delhi: APH Pub.

Bhutto, F. (2020) *The Runaways*. London: Penguin.

Boal, A. (2000 [1974]) *Theatre of the Oppressed*, trans. C. A. McBride, M.-O. L. McBride and E. Fryer. London: Pluto Press.

Boddy, K. and A. Smith. (2010) 'All there is: an interview about the short story', *Critical Quarterly*, 52:2, 66–82.

Boehmer, E. (2005) *Stories of Women: Gender and Narrative in the Postcolonial Nation*. Manchester: Manchester University Press.

Boehmer, E. (2013) 'Revisiting resistance: postcolonial practice and the antecedents of theory', in G. Huggan (ed.), *The Oxford Handbook of Postcolonial Studies*. Oxford: Oxford University Press, pp. 307–23.

Boehmer, E. and B. Moore-Gilbert. (2002) 'Introduction to special issue: postcolonial studies and transnational resistance', *Interventions*, 4:1, 7–21. https://doi.org.10.1080/13698010120117361

Bourdieu, P. (1990) *The Logic of Practice*, trans. R. Nice. Stanford, CA: Stanford University Press.

Bourdieu, P. (2001) *Masculine Domination*, trans. R. Nice. Cambridge: Polity Press.

Bose, B. (2007 [1998]) 'In desire and in death: eroticism as politics in Arundhati Roy's *The God of Small Things*', in A. Tickell (ed.), *Arundhati Roy's The God of Small Things*. London; New York: Routledge, pp. 120–31.

Brada-Williams, N. (2004) 'Reading Jhumpa Lahiri's *Interpreter of Maladies* as a short story cycle', *MELUS*, 29:3–4, 451–64. https://doi.org.10.2307/4141867

Brah, A. (1996) *Cartographies of Diaspora: Contesting Identities*. London; New York: Routledge.

Burki, S. J. (1991) *Pakistan: The Continuing Search for Nationhood*. Boulder, CO: Westview Press.

Butler, J. (1988) 'Performative acts and gender constitution: an essay in phenomenology and feminist theory', *Theatre Journal*, 40, 519–31. https://doi.org.10.2307/3207893

Butler, J. (1994) 'Against proper objects: introduction', *Differences: A Journal of Feminist Cultural Studies*, 6:2–3, 1–26.

Butler, J., Z. Gambetti and L. Sabsay (eds). (2016) *Vulnerability in Resistance*. Durham, NC: Duke University Press.

Butler, J. (2020) *The Force of Non-Violence: An Ethico-Political Bind*. London; Brooklyn, NY: Verso.

Cambridge Dictionary [Online]. (2022). Available at: https://dictionary.cambridge.org/ (Accessed: 21 March 2022).

Cardozo, K. M. (2012), 'Mediating the particular and the general: ethnicity and intertextuality in Jhumpa Lahiri's oeuvre', in L. Dhingra and F. Cheung (eds), *Naming Jhumpa Lahiri: Canons and Controversies*. Lanham, MD; Plymouth: Lexington Books, pp. 3–26.

Careless, S. (2000) 'Advocacy Journalism', *Interim*, 15 May. Available at: https://theinterim.com/issues/society-culture/advocacy-journalism/ (Accessed: 26 March 2022).

Chambers, C. (2011) *British Muslim Fictions: Interviews with Contemporary Writers*. Basingstoke; New York: Palgrave Macmillan.

Chambers, C. (2015) 'Tahmima Anam's *The Good Muslim*: Bangladeshi Islam, secularism, and the Tablighi Jamaat', in C. Chambers and C. Herbert (eds), *Imagining Muslims in South Asia and the Diaspora: Secularism, Religion, Representations*. Abingdon: Routledge, pp. 142–53.

Chambers, C. (2018) 'Sound and fury: Kamila Shamsie's *Home Fire*', *The Massachusetts Review*, 59:2, 202–19. https://doi.org.10.1353/mar.2018.0029

Chambers, C. and S. Watkins. (2015) '50th anniversary editorial', *The Journal of Commonwealth Literature*, 50:3, 259–66. https://doi.org.10.1177/0021989415599855

Chandra, U. (2015) 'Rethinking subaltern resistance', *Journal of Contemporary Asia*, 45:4, 563–73. https://doi.org.10.1080/00472336.2015.1048415

Charry, B. (2001) *The Hottest Day of the Year*. London: Black Swan, 2003.

Cohen, C. J. (2004) 'Deviance as resistance: a new research agenda for the study of Black politics', *Du Bois Review: Social Science Research on Race*, 1:1, 27–45. https://doi.org.10.1017/S1742058X04040044

Cohen, L. (2002) 'What Mrs Besahara saw: reflections on the gay goonda', in R. Vanita (ed.), *Queering India: Same-Sex Love and Eroticism in Indian Culture and Society*. New York; Abingdon: Routledge, pp. 149–60.

Connell, R. W. (2005) *Masculinities*. 2nd edn. Cambridge: Polity Press.

Currie, M. (2007) *About Time: Narrative, Fiction and the Philosophy of Time*. Edinburgh: Edinburgh University Press.

Dabundo, L. (2012) 'Domestic realism', in F. Burwick, N. M. Goslee and D. L. Hoeveler (eds), *The Encyclopedia of Romantic Literature*. Oxford: Wiley-Blackwell, pp. 370–6.

Danius, S., S. Jonsson and G. C. Spivak. (1993) 'An interview with Gayatri Chakravorty Spivak', *boundary 2*, 20:2, 24–50. https://doi.org.10.2307/303357

Das, K. (2014) *Selected Poems*, ed. D. Kohli. Delhi: Penguin India.

Dasgupta, R. (2005) 'Trivial pursuits', *Guardian*, 16 April. Available at: www.theguardian.com/books/2005/apr/16/featuresreviews.guardianreview8 (Accessed: 22 February 2022).

Davis, R. (1996) 'The iconography of Rama's chariot', in D. Ludden (ed.), *Contesting the Nation: Religion, Community, and the Politics of Democracy in India*. Philadelphia, PA: University of Pennsylvania Press, pp. 27–54.

Dawesar, A. (2005) *Babyji*. New York: Anchor Books.

Dé, S. (1992) *Strange Obsession*. New Delhi: Penguin Books.

DeLuca, T. (1995) *The Two Faces of Political Apathy*. Philadelphia, PA: Temple University Press.

Democracy Now! (2017) 'Full extended interview: Arundhati Roy on Democracy Now!', 20 June. Available at: www.democracynow.org/2017/6/20/full_extended_interview_arundhati_roy_on (Accessed: 16 March 2022).

Desai, A. (1963) *Cry, the Peacock*. London: Peter Owen.

Desai, A. (1977) *Fire on the Mountain*. London: Heinemann.

Desai, A. (1980) *Clear Light of Day*. London: Heinemann.

Desai, K. (2006) *The Inheritance of Loss*. London: Hamish Hamilton.

Deshpande, R. (2003) 'Social movements in crisis?', in R. Vora and S. Palshikar (eds), *Indian Democracy: Meanings and Practices*. New Delhi: Sage Publications, pp. 379–409.

Deshpande, S. (1990 [1980]) *The Dark Holds No Terrors*. New Delhi: Penguin Books.

Deshpande, S. (1992) *The Binding Vine*. London: Virago.

Devkota, H. R., M. Kett and N. Groce. (2019) 'Societal attitude and behaviours towards women with disabilities in rural Nepal: pregnancy, childbirth and motherhood', *BMC Pregnancy and Childbirth*, 19:1, 20. https://doi.org.10.1186/s12884-019-2171-4

Dickey, S. (2000) 'Permeable homes: domestic service, household space, and vulnerability of class boundaries in urban India', *American Ethnologist*, 27:2, 462–89. https://doi.org.10.1525/ae.2000.27.2.462

Dirlik, A. (1994) 'The postcolonial aura: Third World criticism in the age of global capitalism', *Critical Inquiry*, 20:2, 328–56.

Dutt, Y. (2019) *Coming out as Dalit*. New Delhi: Aleph.

Eckersley, R. (2016) 'Responsibility for climate change as a structural injustice', in T. Gabrielson et al. (eds), *The Oxford Handbook of Environmental Political Theory*. Oxford: Oxford University Press, pp. 346–61.

Ehrenreich, B. (2003) 'Maid to order', in B. Ehrenreich and A. R. Hochschild (eds), *Global Woman: Nannies, Maids and Sex Workers in the New Economy*. London: Granta Books, pp. 85–103.

Eliasoph, N. (1998) *Avoiding Politics: How Americans Produce Apathy in Everyday Life*. Cambridge: Cambridge University Press.

Epilepsy Society. (2018) 'Living with a long-term condition', September. Available at: https://epilepsysociety.org.uk/about-epilepsy/wellbeing/living-long-term-condition (Accessed: 21 March 2022).

Faiz, F. A. (1996) 'The Dawn of Freedom (August 1947)', trans. A. S. Ali, *Annual of Urdu Studies*, 11, 87.

Farag, J. R. (2016) *Politics and Palestinian Literature in Exile: Gender, Aesthetics and Resistance in the Short Story*. London: I.B. Tauris.

Felski, R. (1989) *Beyond Feminist Aesthetics: Feminist Literature and Social Change*. Cambridge, MA: Harvard University Press.

Ferguson, A. (2017) 'Love as a political force: romantic love, love-politics and solidarity', in R. Grossi and D. West (eds), *The Radicalism of Romantic Love: Critical Perspectives*. London; New York: Routledge, pp. 9–29.

Fernandes S. (2009) 'A pocket full of stories', in B. Bennet and S. K. Sareen (eds), *Of Sadhus and Spinners: Australian Encounters with India*. New Delhi: HarperCollins Publishing India, pp. 187–91.

Fernández-Menicucci, A. (2012) 'The art of the self: identity and performance in Sunetra Gupta's *So Good in Black* and Kamila Shamsie's *Broken Verses*', *Alicante Journal of English Studies*, 25, 73–87. Available at: https://rua.ua.es/dspace/bitstream/10045/36328/1/RAEI_26_06.pdf (Accessed: 21 March 2022).

Fernando, C. (1994) *Women There and Here: Progressions in Six Stories*. Sydney: Wordlink.

Field, R. E. (2004) 'Writing the second generation: negotiating cultural borderlands in Jhumpa Lahiri's *Interpreter of Maladies* and *The*

Namesake', *South Asian Review*, 25:2, 165–77. https://doi.org.10.108 0/02759527.2004.11932352

Fitz, B. E. (2005) 'Bibi's babel: treating Jhumpa Lahiri's "The Treatment of Bibi Haldar" as the malady of interpreters', *South Asian Review*, 26:2, 116–31. https://doi.org.10.1080/02759527.2005.11932404

Flynn, E. (2001) 'Strategic, counter-strategic, and reactive resistance in the feminist classroom', in A. Greenbaum (ed.), *Insurrections: Approaches to Resistance in Composition Studies*. Albany, NY: State University of New York, pp. 17–34.

Fortier, A.-M. (2003) 'Making home: queer migration and motions of attachment', in S. Ahmed et al. (eds), *Uprootings/Regroundings: Questions of Home and Migration*. Oxford; New York: Berg, pp. 115–35.

Foucault, M. (1996) 'The end of the monarchy of sex', in S. Lotringer (ed.), *Foucault Live (Interviews 1961–1984)*, trans. L. Hochroth and J. Johnston. New York: Semiotext(e), pp. 214–25.

Foucault, M. (1998 [1978]) *The History of Sexuality. Vol 1: The Will to Knowledge*, trans. R. Hurley. London: Penguin.

Fraser, N. (1997) *Justice Interruptus: Critical Reflections on the 'Postsocialist' Condition*. New York; London: Routledge.

Fraser, N. (2013) *Fortunes of Feminism: From State-Managed Capitalism to Neoliberal Crisis*. London: Verso Books.

Freeman, R. (2009) *A Disobedient Girl*. London: Viking, 2011.

Freitag, S. B. (1989) 'Introduction: Identity Constructions of Community in Banaras', in S. B. Freitag (ed.), *Culture and Power in Banaras: Community, Performance, and Environment, 1800–1980*. Berkeley, CA: University of California Press, 1992.

Gajarawala, T. J. (2020) 'The postman and the tramp: cynicism, commitment, and the aesthetics of subaltern futurity', *Cultural Critique*, 108, 40–68. https://doi.org.10.1353/cul.2020.0021

Gamson, J. (1995) 'Must identity movements self-destruct? A queer dilemma', *Social Problems*, 42:3, 390–407. https://doi.org.10.2307/3096854

Ghosh, N. (2018) 'Experiencing the body: femininity, sexuality and disabled women in India', in A. Ghai (ed.), *Disability in South Asia: Knowledge and Experience*. New Delhi: SAGE Publications, Inc.

Gidla, S. (2017) *Ants Among Elephants: An Untouchable Family and the Making of Modern India*. New York: Farrar, Straus and Giroux.

Goodison, L. (1983) 'Really being in love means wanting to live in a different world', in S. Cartledge and J. Ryan (eds), *Sex and Love: New Thoughts on Old Contradictions*. London: Women's Press, pp. 48–66.

Gooneratne, Y. (2002) *Masterpiece and Other Stories*. New Delhi: Indialog Publications.

Gopal, P. (2009) *The Indian English Novel: Nation, History, and Narration*. Oxford; New York: Oxford University Press.

Gopal, P. (2019) *Insurgent Empire: Anticolonial Resistance and British Dissent*. London; New York: Verso.

Gopinath, G. (2005) *Impossible Desires: Queer Diasporas and South Asian Public Cultures*. Durham, NC: Duke University Press.

Gowrinathan, N. (2021) *Radicalizing Her: Why Women Choose Violence*. Boston, MA: Beacon Press.

Green, G. (1991) *Changing the Story: Feminist Fiction and the Tradition*. Bloomington, IN: Indiana University Press.

Guha, R. (2007) *India after Gandhi*. Basingstoke; Oxford: Macmillan.

Guha, R. (ed.). (1982) *Subaltern Studies: Writings on South Asian History and Society*. Delhi; New York: Oxford University Press.

Gupta, P. (2011) 'Gandhi and the Goa question', *Public Culture*, 23:2, 321–30. https://doi.org.10.1215/08992363-1162057

Gupta, S. (2009) *So Good in Black*. New Delhi: Women Unlimited.

Hackett, R. A. and Zhao, Y. (1998) *Sustaining Democracy? Journalism and the Politics of Objectivity*. Toronto, ON: Garamond Press.

Hale, J. (2009) 'Suggested rules for non-transsexuals writing about transsexuals, transsexuality, transsexualism, or trans ____', 18 November. Available at: https://sandystone.com/hale.rules.html (Accessed: 23 March 2022).

Hariharan, G. (1992) *The Thousand Faces of Night*. New Delhi; New York: Penguin Books.

Harlow, B. (1987) *Resistance Literature*. New York: Methuen.

Harlow, B. (1998) 'On Literature and Resistance', *Against the Current*, May–June. Available at: https://againstthecurrent.org/atc074/p1835/ (Accessed: 18 February 2022).

Haskins, V. K. and C. Lowrie. (2015) 'Introduction: decolonizing domestic service: introducing a new agenda', in V. K. Haskins and C. Lowrie (eds), *Colonization and Domestic Service: Historical and Contemporary Perspectives*. New York; Abingdon: Routledge, pp. 1–18.

Heidemann, B. (2019) 'The symbolic survival of the "living dead": narrating the LTTE female fighter in post-war Sri Lankan women's writing', *The Journal of Commonwealth Literature*, 54:3, 384–98. https://doi.org.10.1177/0021989417723414 [First published in 2017 as an Online First article.]

Helff, S. (2013) *Unreliable Truths: Transcultural Homeworlds in Indian Women's Fiction of the Diaspora*. Amsterdam: Rodopi.

Herrero, D. (2019) 'Postmodernism and politics in Meena Kandasamy's *The Gypsy Goddess*', *The Journal of Commonwealth Literature*, 54:1, 70–83. https://doi.org.10.1177/0021989417719118 [First published in 2017 as an Online First article.]

hooks, b. (2000) *Feminism Is for Everybody: Passionate Politics*. London: Pluto Press.

Hosain, A. (1961) *Sunlight on a Broken Column: A Novel*. London: Chatto & Windus.

Huggan, G. (2001) *The Postcolonial Exotic: Marketing the Margins*. London; New York: Routledge.

Human Rights Watch. (2001) 'Hidden in the home: abuse of domestic workers with special visas in the United States', 1 June. Available at: www.hrw.org/report/2001/06/01/hidden-home/abuse-domestic-workers-special-visas-united-states (Accessed: 23 March 2022).

Human Rights Watch. (2006) 'Pakistan: proposed reforms to Hudood laws fall short', 6 September. Available at: www.hrw.org/news/2006/09/06/pakistan-proposed-reforms-hudood-laws-fall-short (Accessed: 22 February 2022).

Ibrahim, N. (1994–9) *Ami Birangona Bolchi*. Dhaka: Jagriti.

Imam, J. (1986) *Ekattorer Dingulee*. Dhaka: Sandhani Prakashani.

Jackson, E. (2014) 'Gendered diasporic identities in Jhumpa Lahiri's *The Namesake* and Monica Ali's *Brick Lane*', in S. R. Mehta (ed.), *Exploring Gender in the Literature of the Indian Diaspora*. Newcastle-upon-Tyne: Cambridge Scholars Publishing, pp. 104–18.

Jain, J. (2007) 'A phoenix called resistance', *Journal of Postcolonial Writing*, 43:2, 172–82. https://doi.org.10.1080/17449850701430523

Janowitz, M. (1978) *The Last Half-Century: Societal Change and Politics in America*. Chicago, IL; London: University of Chicago Press.

Javed, U. (2021) 'Domestic Exploitation', *Dawn*, 8 February. Available at: www.dawn.com/news/1606152/domestic-exploitation (Accessed: 30 March 2022).

Jeffrey, P. (1998) 'Agency, activism and agendas', in P. Jeffrey and A. Basu (eds), *Appropriating Gender: Women's Activism and Politicized Religion in South Asia*. New York; London: Routledge, pp. 221–44.

Kabir, A. (2001) 'Abuses of authority: English literature, colonial pedagogy, and Shakespeare in Manju Kapur's *Difficult Daughters*', *The Upstart Crow*, 21, 127–38. Available at: www.clemson.edu/centers-institutes/cedp/about/upstart-crow/content-files/vol-21.pdf (Accessed: 21 March 2022).

Kandasamy, M. (2014a) *The Gypsy Goddess*. London: Atlantic Books.

Kandasamy, M. (2014b) Meena Kandasamy. [Facebook] 15 September. Available at: www.facebook.com/notes/10159055395717009 (Accessed: 17 March 2022).

Kapur, M. (1998) *Difficult Daughters*. London: Faber & Faber.

Kapur, M. (2002) *A Married Woman*. New Delhi: IndiaInk.

Katrak, K. H. (1996) 'Post-colonial women writers and feminisms', in B. King (ed.), *New National and Post-Colonial Literatures: An Introduction*. Oxford: Clarendon Press, pp. 230–44.

Khair, T. (2001) *Babu Fictions: Alienation in Contemporary Indian English Novels*. New Delhi: Oxford University Press.

Khan, N. A. (2010 [2009]) *Islam, Women and Violence in Kashmir: Between India and Pakistan*. New York: Palgrave Macmillan.

Khanna, R. (2008) 'Communal violence in Gujarat, India: impact of sexual violence and responsibilities of the health care system', *Reproductive Health Matters*, 16:31, 142–52. https://doi.org.10.1016/s0968-8080(08)31357-3

Kidd, J. (2014) 'Meena Kandasamy Interview: "I don't know if I'm idiotic – or courageous"', *Independent*, 7 April. Available at: www.independent.co.uk/arts-entertainment/books/features/meena-kandasamy-interview-i-don-t-know-if-i-m-idiotic-or-courageous-9238644.html (Accessed: 17 March 2022).

King, H. (1993) 'Once upon a text: hysteria from Hippocrates', in S. L. Gilman (ed.), *Hysteria Beyond Freud*. Berkeley, CA; Los Angeles, CA; London: University of California Press, pp. 3–90.

Koepping, E. (2011) 'India, Pakistan, Bangladesh, Burma/Myanmar', in P. C. Phan (ed.), *Christianities in Asia*. Malden, MA: Wiley-Blackwell, pp. 9–44.

Koshy, M. (2014) 'Almost Valentine's Day', in S. Rundle and M. Bharat (eds), *Only Connect: Short Fiction about Technology and Us from Australia and the Indian Subcontinent*. Sandy Bay: Brass Monkey Books, pp. 25–46.

Král, F. (2009) *Critical Identities in Contemporary Anglophone Diasporic Literature*. Basingstoke; New York: Palgrave Macmillan.

Lahiri, J. (1999) *The Interpreter of Maladies*. London: Flamingo, 2000.

Lahiri, J. (2003) *The Namesake*. London: Flamingo.

Lahiri, J. (2013) *The Lowland: A Novel*. New York: Alfred A. Knopf.

Lahiri-Roy, R. and S. Peres da Costa. (2021) 'An infinity of traces: Suneeta Peres da Costa in conversation with Reshmi Lahiri-Roy', in C. Lokugé and C. Ringrose (eds), *Creative Lives: Interviews with Contemporary South Asian Diaspora Writers*. Stuttgart: Ibidem Verlag, pp. 92–104.

Lal, M. (1995) *The Law of the Threshold: Women Writers in Indian English*. Shimla: Indian Institute of Advanced Study.

Lal, S. (2019) 'Silence and the ethics of partial empathy in Tahmima Anam's *The Good Muslim*', *The Journal of Commonwealth Literature*, 57:3, 574–591. https://doi.org.10.1177/0021989419890658

Lane, R. J. (2006) *The Postcolonial Novel*. Cambridge; Malden, MA: Polity Press.

Lau, L. and Mendes, A. C. (2022) 'Romancing the other: Arundhati Roy's *The Ministry of Utmost Happiness*', *The Journal of Commonwealth Literature*, 57:1, 102–17. https://doi.org.10.1177/0021989418820701 [First published in 2019 as an Online First article.]

Lazarus, N. (1990) *Resistance in Postcolonial African Fiction*. New Haven, CT: Yale University Press.

Lokugé, C. (2000) *If the Moon Smiled*. New Delhi: Penguin Books.

London School of Economics. (2014) 'Interview: five minutes with Meena Kandasamy: "I think propaganda can be very beautiful based on what you are doing it for"', 16 March. Available at: https://blogs.lse.ac.uk/lsereviewofbooks/2014/03/16/20302/ (Accessed: 17 March 2022).

Loomba, A. (1991) 'Overworlding the "Third World"', *Oxford Literary Review*, 13:1–2, 164–91. https://doi.org.10.3366/olr.1991.008

Lorde, A. (2007 [1978]) 'The uses of the erotic: the erotic as power', in K. E. Lovaas and M. M. Jenkins (eds), *Sexualities and Communication in Everyday Life: A Reader*. Thousand Oaks, CA; London; New Delhi: SAGE Publications, pp. 87–92.

Lorde, A. (2019 [1984]) *Sister Outsider*. London: Penguin.

Malreddy, P. K. (2016) 'Solidarity, suffering and "divine violence": fictions of the Naxalite insurgency', in A. Tickell (ed.), *South-Asian Fiction in English: Contemporary Transformations*. London: Palgrave Macmillan, pp. 217–34.

Manorama, R. (2006) 'Background information on Dalit women in India', *Women's UN Report Network*, 11 December. Available at: https://wunrn.com/2006/12/india-dalit-women-in-india/ (Accessed: 26 March 2022).

Marcuse, H. (1969) *An Essay on Liberation*. London: Allen Lane.

Markandaya, K. (1954) *Nectar in a Sieve: A Novel*. New York: The John Day Co.

Martin B. and C. T. Mohanty. (1986) 'Feminist politics: what's home got to do with it?', in T. de Lauretis (ed.), *Feminist Studies/Critical Studies*. Bloomington, IN: Indiana University Press, pp. 191–212.

McClintock, A. (1992) 'The angel of progress: pitfalls of the term "postcolonialism"', *Social Text*, 31–2, 84–98. https://doi.org.10.2307/466219

McDowell, L. (1999) *Gender Identity and Place: Understanding Feminist Geographies*. Cambridge: Polity Press.

McLeod, J. (2000) *Beginning Postcolonialism*. Manchester; New York: Manchester University Press.

Medina, J. (2013) *The Epistemology of Resistance: Gender and Racial Oppression, Epistemic Injustice, and Resistant Imaginations*. New York: Oxford University Press.

Meegaswatta, T. N. K. (2019) 'Violence as a site of women's agency in war: the representation of female militants in Sri Lanka's post-war literature', *Journal of International Women's Studies*, 20:3, 28–43. Available at: https://vc.bridgew.edu/jiws/vol20/iss3/4/ (Accessed: 30 March 2022).

Mehta, R. (1977) *Inside the Haveli*. New Delhi: Mayfair Paperbacks.

Menozzi, F. (2020) *World Literature, Non-Synchronism, and the Politics of Time*. Cham: Palgrave Macmillan.

Merchant, H. (2010) 'Introduction', in H. Merchant (ed.), *Yaraana: Gay Writing from South Asia*. New Delhi: Penguin Books India, pp. xi–xxvi.

Midgley, J. (2011) 'Issues in international social work', in V. E. Cree (ed.), *Social Work: A Reader*. 1st edn. London; New York: Routledge, pp. 22–8.

Mirza, M. (2016) *Intimate Class Acts: Friendship and Desire in Indian and Pakistani Women's Fiction*. New Delhi: Oxford University Press.

Mirza, M. (2019) 'Serving in the Indian diaspora: the transnational domestic servant in contemporary women's fiction', *Journal of Postcolonial Writing*, 55:1, 108–20. https://doi.org.10.1080/17449855.2018.1424646

Mirza, M. and M. Koshy. (2021) 'Reading, writing and the contours of power: Mridula Koshy in conversation with Maryam Mirza', in C. Lokugé and C. Ringrose (eds), *Creative Lives: Interviews with Contemporary South Asian Diaspora Writers*. Stuttgart: Ibidem Verlag, pp. 171–9.

Mishra, P. (2011) 'Introduction', in T. Ali et al. (eds), *Kashmir: The Case for Freedom*. London; New York: Verso.

Mishra, P. (2012) 'The Gujarat Massacre: New India's Blood Rite', *Guardian*, 14 March. Available at: www.theguardian.com/commentisfree/2012/mar/14/new-india-gujarat-massacre (Accessed: 18 March 2022).

Misra, J. (2000) *Ancient Promises*. London: Penguin.

Mody, P. (2008) *The Intimate State: Love-Marriages and the Law in Delhi*. New Delhi: Routledge.

Mohsin, M. (2006) *The End of Innocence*. London: Penguin Fig Tree.

Mondal, M. (2017) 'On translating the stories yet unwritten: a Dalit perspective from India', *Words Without Borders*, 17 November. Available at: www.wordswithoutborders.org/dispatches/article/on-translating-the-stories-yet-unwritten-a-dalit-perspective-from-india (Accessed: 18 February 2022).

Mookherjee, N. (2015a) *The Spectral Wound: Sexual Violence, Public Memories, and the Bangladesh War of 1971*. Durham, NC: Duke University Press.

Mookherjee, N. (2015b) 'History and the Birangona: the ethics of representing narratives of sexual violence of the 1971 Bangladesh War', *Himal South Asian*, 9 November. Available at: www.himalmag.com/history-and-the-birangona-bangladesh/ (Accessed: 26 March 2022).

Morland, I. (2009) 'What can queer theory do for intersex?', *GLQ*, 15:2, 285–312. https://doi.org.10.1215/10642684-2008-139

Moss, L. (2000) '"The plague of normality": reconfiguring realism in postcolonial theory', *Jouvert: A Journal of Postcolonial Studies*, 5:1.

Moynihan, S. M. (2012) 'Affect, history, and the ironies of community and solidarity in Jhumpa Lahiri's *Interpreter of Maladies*', in L. Dhingra and F. Cheung (eds), *Naming Jhumpa Lahiri: Canons and Controversies*. Lanham, MD; Plymouth: Lexington Books, pp. 97–116.

Mukherjee, B. (1975) *Wife*. Boston, MA: Houghton Mifflin.

Mukherjee, B. (1989) *Jasmine*. New York: Grove Weidenfeld.
Mukherjee, N. (2014) *The Lives of Others*. London: Chatto & Windus.
Mukhopadhyay, S. and S. Chugh. (2012) 'Combating child labour through education', in S. Kak and B. Pati (eds), *Enslaved Innocence: Child Labour in South Asia*. New Delhi: Primus Books, pp. 251–74.
Mumtaz, K. and M. Yameena. (1996) *Pakistan: Tradition and Change*. Oxford: Oxfam.
Munaweera, N. (2013 [2012]) *Island of a Thousand Mirrors*. Gurgaon: Hachette India.
Munos, D. (2017) 'Of kaleidoscopic mothers and diasporic twists: the mother/daughter plot in the works of Jhumpa Lahiri', in R. S. Hedge and A. K. Sahoo (eds), *Routledge Handbook of the Indian Diaspora*. Abingdon; New York: Routledge, pp. 355–65.
My Friend Amy. (2009) 'An interview with author Ru Freeman', 3 September. Available at: www.myfriendamysblog.com/2009/09/interview-with-author-ru-freeman.html (Accessed: 23 March 2022).
Nadiminti, K. (2018) '"A betrayal of everything": the law of the family in Jhumpa Lahiri's *The Lowland*', *Journal of Asian American Studies*, 21:2, 239–62. https://doi.org.10.1353/jaas.2018.0014
Namboodiripad, E. M. S. (1994) *The Communist Party in Kerala: Six Decades of Struggle and Advance*. New Delhi: National Book Centre.
Namjoshi, S. (2000) *Goja: An Autobiographical Myth*. North Melborne: Spinifex.
Nandy, A. (1983) *The Intimate Enemy: Loss and Recovery of Self under Colonialism*. Delhi; Oxford: Oxford University Press.
Narrain, A. and G. Bhan. (2005) *Because I Have a Voice: Queer Politics in India*. New Delhi: Yoda Press.
Nast, H. J. (2002) 'Queer patriarchies, queer racisms, international', *Antipode*, 34:5, 874–909. https://doi.org.10.1111/1467-8330.00281
Natanel, K. (2016) *Sustaining Conflict: Apathy and Domination in Israel-Palestine*. Berkeley, CA: University of California Press.
Needham, A. D. (2005) '"The small voice of history" in Arundhati Roy's *The God of Small Things*', *Interventions*, 7:3, 369–91. https://doi.org.10.1080/13698010500268072
Newport, S. E. (2018) 'Writing otherness: uses of history and mythology in constructing literary representations of India's Hijras' (PhD dissertation, University of Manchester). Available at: www.research.manchester.ac.uk/portal/files/75066695/FULL_TEXT.PDF (Accessed: 30 March 2022).
O'Connor, F. (1963) *The Lonely Voice: A Study of the Short Story*. Cleveland, OH: World Pub. Co.
Omvedt, G. (2004) 'Untouchables in the world of IT', *Panos*, 2 January. Available at: http://panoslondon.panosnetwork.org/features/untouchables-in-the-world-of-it/ (Accessed: 23 March 2022).

Orleck, Annalise. (1997) 'Introduction: tradition unbound: radical mothers in international perspective', in A. Jetter, A. Orleck and D. Taylor (eds), *The Politics of Motherhood: Activist Voices from Left to Right*. Hanover, NH: University Press of New England, pp. 3–22.

Oxford English Dictionary [Online]. (2022) Available at: www.oed.com/ (Accessed: 21 March 2022).

Pan, A. (2021) *Mapping Dalit Feminism: Towards an Intersectional Standpoint*. New Delhi; Thousand Oaks, CA: SAGE Publications.

Pande, R. (2018) 'Being eunuch, the violence faced by Hijra's involved in sex work – a case study', in A. Bhattacharyya and S. Basu (eds), *Marginalities in India: Themes and Perspectives*. Singapore: Springer, pp. 207–28.

Parry, B. (1994) 'Resistance theory/theorising resistance, or two cheers for nativism', in F. Barker, P. Hulme and M. Iverson (eds), *Colonial Discourse/Postcolonial Theory*. Manchester: Manchester University Press, pp. 172–96.

Patea, V. (2012) 'The short story: an overview of the history and evolution of the genre', in V. Patea (ed.), *Short Story Theories: A Twenty-First-Century Perspective*. Amsterdam; New York: Rodopi, pp. 1–24.

Patil, A. (2008) *Kari*. New Delhi: HarperCollins.

Pawar, U. (2008) *The Weave of My Life*, trans. M. Pandit. New York: Columbia University Press, 2009.

Peres da Costa, S. (1999) *Homework*. New York: Bloomsbury.

Petty, L. (2006) *Romancing the Vote: Feminist Activism in American Fiction, 1870–1920*. Athens, GA: University of Georgia Press.

Phadke, S., S. Khan and S. Ranade. (2011) *Why Loiter? Women and Risk on Mumbai Streets*. New Delhi: Penguin Books.

Pinto, S. (2016) '"The tools of your chants and spells": stories of madwomen and Indian practical healing', *Medical Anthropology*, 35:3, 263–77. https://doi.org.10.1080/01459740.2015.1081902

Podgórniak, A. (2002) 'Magical realism, Indian style or, the case of multiple submission: *The God of Small Things* by Arundhati Roy', in G. Stilz (ed.), *Missions of Interdependence: A Literary Directory*. Amsterdam: Rodopi, pp. 255–63.

Prakash, G. (1999) *Another Reason: Science and the Imagination of Modern India*. Princeton, NJ: Princeton University Press, 2020.

Prashad, V. (2001) *Karma of Brown Folk*. Minneapolis, MN: University of Minnesota Press.

Pravinchandra, S. (2018) 'Short story and peripheral production', in B. Etherington and J. Zimbler (eds), *The Cambridge Companion to World Literature*. Cambridge: Cambridge University Press, pp. 197–210.

Puar, J. K. (2005) 'Queer times, queer assemblages', *Social Text*, 23:3–4, 121–39. https://doi.org.10.1215/01642472-23-3-4_84-85-121

Puwar, N. (2003) 'Melodramatic postures and constructions', in N. Puwar and P. Raghuram (eds), *South Asian Women in the Diaspora*. Oxford: Berg, pp. 21–42.

Rai, H. and K. M. Prasad. (1972) 'Naxalism: a challenge to the proposition of peaceful transition to socialism', *The Indian Journal of Political Science*, 33:4, 455–80.

Rajagopal, A. (2001) *Politics after Television: Religious Nationalism and the Reshaping of the Indian Public*. Cambridge: Cambridge University Press.

Rajan, V. G. J. (2011) *Women Suicide Bombers: Narratives of Violence*. London: Routledge.

Rajendran, A. (2015) *(Un)familiar Femininities: Studies in Contemporary Lesbian South Asian Texts*. New Delhi: Oxford University Press.

Ranasinha, R. (2016) *Contemporary Diasporic South Asian Women's Fiction: Gender, Narration and Globalisation*. London: Palgrave Macmillan.

Rank, M. R., L. M. Eppard and H. E. Bullock. (2021) *Poorly Understood: What America Gets Wrong about Poverty*. New York: Oxford University Press.

Rao, A. (2009) *The Caste Question: Dalits and the Politics of Modern India*. Berkeley, CA; Los Angeles, CA; London: University of California Press.

Ray, R. (1999) *Fields of Protest: Women's Movements in India*. Minneapolis, MN: University of Minnesota Press.

Ray, R. and S. Qayum. (2009) *Cultures of Servitude: Modernity, Domesticity, and Class in India*. Stanford, CA: Stanford University Press.

Reddy, G. (2005) *With Respect to Sex*. Chicago, IL: University of Chicago Press.

Reep, D. (1982) *The Rescue and Romance: Popular Novels before World War I*. Bowling Green, OH: Bowling Green State University Popular Press.

Romero, M. (2013) 'Nanny diaries and other stories: immigrant women's labor in the social reproduction of American families', *Revista de Estudios Sociales*, 45, 186–97. Available at: https://journals.openedition.org/revestudsoc/7694 (Accessed: 15 March 2023).

Romero, M. (2016) *Maid in the U.S.A.: Tenth Anniversary Edition*. Abingdon; New York: Routledge.

Romero, M., V. Preston and W. Giles. (2016) 'Care work in a globalizing world', in M. Romero, V. Preston and W. Giles (eds), *When Care Work Goes Global: Locating the Social Relations of Domestic Work*. Abingdon; New York: Routledge, pp. 1–26.

Rose, S. (1985) 'Is romance dysfunctional?', *International Journal of Women's Studies*, 8:3, 250–65.

Ross, O. (2016) *Same-Sex Desire in Indian Culture: Representations in Literature and Film, 1970–2015*. New York: Palgrave Macmillan.

Rouse, S. (1998) 'The outsider(s) within: sovereignty and citizenship in Pakistan', in P. Jeffrey and A. Basu (eds), *Appropriating Gender: Women's Activism and Politicized Religion in South Asia*. New York; London: Routledge, pp. 53–70.

Roy, A. (1997) *The God of Small Things*. New York: IndiaInk.

Roy, A. (2006) *An Ordinary Person's Guide to Empire*. New Delhi: Penguin.

Roy, A. (2008a) *The Shape of the Beast*. New Delhi: Viking.

Roy, A. (2008b) 'Azadi: it's the only thing Kashmiris want. Denial is delusion', *Outlook*, 1 September, 14–24.

Roy, A. (2010) 'Gandhi but with guns', *Guardian*, 27 March. Available at: www.theguardian.com/books/2010/mar/27/arundhati-roy-india-tribal-maoists-4 (Accessed: 18 March 2022).

Roy, A. (2017) *The Ministry of Utmost Happiness*. London: Hamish Hamilton.

Roy, A. (2019) 'India: intimations of an ending. The rise of Modi and the far right', *Nation*, 22 November. Available at: www.thenation.com/article/world/arundhati-roy-assam-modi/ (Accessed: 16 March 2022).

Russo, A. and L. Torres (2002) 'Lesbian porn stories: rebellion and/or resistance?', in A. Russo, *Taking Back Our Lives: A Call to Action for the Feminist Movement*. New York; London: Routledge, pp. 101–18.

Saeed, J. I. (2009) *Semantics*. 3rd edn. Oxford: Wiley-Blackwell.

Said, E. W. (1993) *Culture and Imperialism*. London: Chatto & Windus.

Salam, K. (2019) 'If you think Kashmir was turbulent in 2019, wait for next year', *Foreign Policy*, 19 December. Available at: https://foreignpolicy.com/2019/12/19/kashmir-autonomy-article-370-india-pakistan/ (Accessed: 16 March 2022).

Samuel, L. R. (2012) *The American Dream: A Cultural History*. New York: Syracuse University Press.

Saran, R. (2015) *Navigating Model Minority Stereotypes: Asian Indian Youth in South Asian Diaspora*. New York: Routledge.

Sathyanathan, C. (2021) 'Claiming the English Language as a Dalit Poet', *Indian Express*, 18 February. Available at: https://indianexpress.com/article/opinion/columns/claiming-the-english-language-as-a-dalit-poet-7277032/ (Accessed: 18 February 2022).

Sawhney, H. (2014) '*The Gypsy Goddess* by Meena Kandasamy review – horrifying events told with exquisite language', *Guardian*, 31 May. Available at: www.theguardian.com/books/2014/may/31/gypsy-goddess-meena-kandasamy-review (Accessed: 26 March 2022).

Scott, J. C. (1985) *Weapons of the Weak: Everyday Forms of Peasant Resistance*. New Haven, CT: Yale University Press.

Seagal, F. (2010) 'A Disobedient Girl by Ru Freeman', *Guardian*, 10 January. Available at: www.theguardian.com/books/2010/jan/10/a-disobedient-girl-ru-freeman (Accessed: 26 March 2022).

Seed, I. (2016) 'Foreword', in I. Seed (ed.), *Patches of Light: Short Stories from the Cheshire Prize for Literature 2015*. Chester: University of Chester Press, pp. xv–xviii.

Sehgal, P. (2017) 'Arundhati Roy's fascinating mess: being an activist and an artist is trickier than it sounds', *Atlantic*, July–August. Available at: www.theatlantic.com/magazine/archive/2017/07/arundhati-roys-fascinating-mess/528684/ (Accessed: 16 March 2022).

Sellars, K. (2016) 'Treasonable conspiracies at Paris, Moscow and Delhi: the legal hinterland of the Tokyo Tribunal', in K. Sellars (ed.), *Trials for International Crimes in Asia*. Cambridge: Cambridge University Press, pp. 1–24.

Selvadurai, S. (1994) *Funny Boy*. Toronto, ON: McClelland & Stewart.

Sengupta, A. (2014) 'Introduction: setting the stage', in A. Sengupta (ed.), *Mapping South Asia through Contemporary Theatre: Essays on the Theatres of India, Pakistan, Bangladesh, Nepal and Sri Lanka*. Basingstoke; New York: Palgrave Macmillan, pp. 1–63.

Shamsie, K. (2000) *Salt and Saffron*. Karachi: Oxford University Press.

Shamsie, K. (2005) *Broken Verses*. London: Bloomsbury.

Shamsie, K. (2017) *Home Fire*. London: Bloomsbury Circus.

Sharrad, P. (2015) 'The postcolonial historical novel: realism, allegory, and the representation of contested pasts', *Journal of Postcolonial Writing*, 51:5, 624–6. https://doi.org.10.1080/17449855.2015.1032477

Shaw, I. S. (2012) *Human Rights Journalism: Advances in Reporting Distant Humanitarian Interventions*. Basingstoke; New York: Palgrave Macmillan.

Shepherd, K. I. (2020) 'Macaulay is very relevant today and helps Dalits, OBCs join the global economy', *Wire*, 31 July. Available at: https://thewire.in/education/macaulay-english-medium-new-education-policy (Accessed: 26 March 2022).

Sidhwa, B. (1983) *The Bride*. London: Jonathan Cape.

Sidhwa, B. (1989 [1988]) *Ice-Candy-Man*. New Delhi: Penguin India.

Simeon, D. (1987) 'Communalism in modern India: a theoretical examination', *Social Science Probings*, 4:1, 47–71.

Siqueira, A. (2002) 'Postcolonial Portugal, postcolonial Goa: a note on Portuguese identity and its resonance in Goa and India', *Lusotopie*, 9:2, 211–3. Available at: www.persee.fr/doc/luso_1257–0273_2002_num_9_2_1527 (Accessed: 24 March 2022).

Slemon, S. (1995 [1988]) 'Magic realism as post-colonial discourse', in L. P. Zamora and W. B. Faris (eds), *Magical Realism: Theory, History, Community*. Durham, NC: Duke University Press, pp. 407–26.

Smith-Rosenberg, C. (1972) 'The hysterical woman: sex roles and role conflict in 19th-century America', *Social Research*, 39:4, 652–78.

Sökefeld, M. (2012) 'Secularism and the Kashmir dispute', in N. Bubandt and M. van Beek (eds), *Varieties of Secularism in Asia: Anthropological Explorations of Religion, Politics and the Spiritual*. Abingdon; New York: Routledge, pp. 101–20.

Song, M. H. (2013) *The Children of 1965: On Writing, and Not Writing, as an Asian American*. Durham, NC; London: Duke University Press.

Spivak, G. C. (1985) 'Subaltern studies: deconstructing historiography', in R. Guha (ed.), *Subaltern Studies IV: Writings on South Asian History and Society*. New Delhi: Oxford University Press, pp. 330–63.

Spivak, G. C. (1988) 'Can the subaltern speak?', in C. Nelson and L. Grossberg (eds), *Marxism and the Interpretation of Culture*. Basingstoke: Macmillan Education, pp. 271–313.

Spivak, G. C., D. Landry, and G. M. MacLean. (1996) *The Spivak Reader: Selected Works of Gayatri Chakravorty Spivak*. London: Routledge.

Srivastava, N. (2016) 'Minor literature and the South Asian short story', in A. Tickell (ed.), *South Asian Fiction in English: Contemporary Transformations*. London: Palgrave Macmillan, pp. 253–71.

Srivastava, N. (2018) *Italian Colonialism and Resistances to Empire, 1930–1970*. London: Palgrave Macmillan.

Stancati, M. (2011) 'A female Dalit poet fights back in verse', *Wall Street Journal*, 23 January. Available at www.wsj.com/articles/BL-IRTB-9747 (Accessed: 17 March 2022).

Straub, J. (2009) *A Victorian Muse: The Afterlife of Dante's Beatrice in Nineteenth-Century Literature*. London: Continuum.

Sukthankar, A. (ed.). (1999) *Facing the Mirror: Lesbian Writing from India*. New Delhi; New York: Penguin Books.

Sunder Rajan, R. (1993a) 'The feminist plot and the nationalist allegory: home and world in two Indian women's novels in English', *Modern Fiction Studies*, 39:1, 71–92. https://doi.org.10.1353/mfs.0.1045

Sunder Rajan, R. (1993b) *Real and Imagined Women: Gender, Culture, and Postcolonialism*. London: Routledge, 2003.

Sunder Rajan, R. (2000) 'Introduction: feminism and the politics of resistance', *Indian Journal of Gender Studies*, 7:2, 153–65. https://doi.org.10.1177/097152150000700201

Sunder Rajan, R. (2003) *The Scandal of the State: Women, Law, Citizenship in Postcolonial India*. Durham, NC: Duke University Press.

Tabassum, W. (2013) 'Cast-offs', in U. Butalia (ed.), *Katha: Short Stories by Indian Women*. London: Saqi.

Taylor, D. (2018) 'Interview with Meena Kandasamy', 9 November. Available at: www.debbietaylor.co/interview-with-meena-kandasamy/ (Accessed: 17 March 2022).

Thakore, B. K. (2016) *South Asians on the U.S. Screen: Just Like Everyone Else?* Lanham, MD: Lexington Books.

Thapar, S. (1993) 'Women as activists; women as symbols: a study of the Indian nationalist movement', *Feminist Review*, 44:1, 81–96. https://doi.org.10.2307/1395197

Tharu, S. J. and K. Lalitha. (1991–3) *Women Writing in India: 600 B.C. to the Present. Vol. 1: 600 B.C. to the Early 20th Century.* New York: Feminist Press.

Thompson, E. P. (1963) *The Making of the English Working Class.* London: Gollancz.

Tickell, A. (2007) *Arundhati Roy's* The God of Small Things. London; New York: Routledge.

Tickell, A. (2015) 'Driving Pinky Madam (and murdering Mr Ashok): social justice and domestic service in Aravind Adiga's *The White Tiger*', in P. K. Malreddy et al. (eds), *Reworking Postcolonialism: Globalisation, Labour and Rights.* Basingstoke: Palgrave Macmillan, pp. 150–64.

Tickell, A. (2018) 'Writing in the necropolis: Arundhati Roy's *The Ministry of Utmost Happiness'*, *Moving Worlds: A Journal of Transcultural Studies*, 18:1, 100–12.

Tilly, C. and S. G. Tarrow. (2006) *Contentious Politics.* Boulder, CO: Paradigm Publishers.

Tomlinson, B. (1996) 'The politics of textual vehemence, or go to your room until you learn how to act', *Signs*, 22:1, 86–114. https://doi.org.10.1086/495137

Twist, J., B. Vincent, M.-J. Barker and K. Gupta. (2020) 'Introduction', in J. Twist et al. (eds), *Non-Binary Lives: An Anthology of Intersecting Identities.* London: Jessica Kingsley Publishers, pp. 14–27.

United Nations High Commissioner for Refugees. (2000) *The State of the World's Refugees 2000: Fifty Years of Humanitarian Action.* New York: Oxford University Press.

Ur-Rehman, Z. and M. Abi-Habib. (2020) 'Sewer cleaners wanted in Pakistan: only Christians need apply', *New York Times*, 4 May. Available at: www.nytimes.com/2020/05/04/world/asia/pakistan-christians-sweepers.html (Accessed: 21 March 2022).

Vanita, R. (2005) *Gandhi's Tiger and Sita's Smile: Essays on Gender, Sexuality and Culture.* New Delhi: Yoda Press.

Vanita, R. and S. Kidwai. (2001 [2000]) 'Introduction: modern Indian materials', in R. Vanita and S. Kidwai (eds), *Same-Sex Love in India: Readings in Indian Literature.* Basingstoke: Palgrave Macmillan, pp. 191–217.

Vargas, J. H. (2011) 'Critical realisms in the global South: narrative transculturation in Senapati's *Six Acres and a Third* and García

Márquez's *One Hundred Years of Solitude*', in S. P. Mohanty (ed.), *Colonialism, Modernity, and Literature: A View from India*. New York: Palgrave Macmillan, pp. 22–54.

Verba, S. and N. H. Nie. (1987 [1972]) *Participation in America: Political Democracy and Social Equality*. Chicago, IL: The University of Chicago Press.

Virdi, J. (2003) *The Cinematic ImagiNation: Indian Popular Films as Social History*. New Brunswick, NJ: Rutgers University Press.

Viswanathan, G. (1987) 'The beginnings of English literary study in British India', *Oxford Literary Review*, 9:1, 2–26. https://doi.org.10.3366/olr.1987.001

Waiker, P. (2018) 'Reading Islamophobia in Hindutva: an analysis of Narendra Modi's political discourse', *Islamophobia Studies Journal*, 4:2, 161–80. https://doi.org.10.13169/islastudj.4.2.0161

Wajid, S. (2006) 'No retreat', *Guardian*, 15 December. Available at: www.theguardian.com/books/2006/dec/15/gender.world (Accessed: 26 March 2022).

Walonen, M. K. (2019) 'Histories of resistance, political violence, and revolutionary possibility in the neoliberal-era Naxalite novel', *The Journal of Commonwealth Literature*, 57:2, 276–90. https://doi.org.10.1177/0021989419849243

Wiemann, D. (2017) 'Indian writing in English and the discrepant zones of world literature', *Anglia*, 135:1, 122–39. https://doi.org.10.1515/ang-2017-0008

Williams, P. (2013) '"Writing the poetry of Troy": Mahmoud Darwish and the lyrical epic as postcolonial resistance', in W. Goebel and S. Schabio (eds), *Locating Postcolonial Narrative Genres*. New York: Routledge, pp. 61–75.

Wilson, E. (1993) 'Is transgression transgressive?', in J. Bristow and A. R. Wilson (eds), *Activating Theory: Lesbian, Gay, Bisexual Politics*. London: Lawrence & Wishart, pp. 107–17.

Wilson, J. and D. Tunca. (2015) 'Postcolonial thresholds: gateways and borders', *Journal of Postcolonial Writing*, 51:1, 1–6. https://doi.org.10.1080/17449855.2014.988434

Wire. (2019) 'Arundhati Roy on freedom and resistance', 21 July. Available at: www.youtube.com/watch?v=BOoRjBzGoUE (Accessed: 23 February 2022).

Wisker, G. (2010) 'Teaching *The Color Purple*', in G. Wisker (ed.), *Teaching African American Women's Writing*. Basingstoke; New York: Palgrave Macmillan, pp. 21–41.

Yashpal. (2010) *This Is Not That Dawn*, trans. Anand. New Delhi: Penguin Books.

Young, E. (2018) *Contemporary Feminism and Women's Short Stories*. Edinburgh: Edinburgh University Press.

Young, I. M. (2003) 'Political responsibility and structural injustice', *The Lindley Lecture*, University of Kansas, 5 May.

Zakaria, A. (2019) 'Remembering the War of 1971 in East Pakistan', *Al Jazeera*, 16 December. Available at: www.aljazeera.com/opinions/2019/12/16/remembering-the-war-of-1971-in-east-pakistan (Accessed: 26 March 2022).

Zamora, L. P. (1995) 'Magical romance/magical realism: ghosts in U.S. and Latin American fiction', in W. B. Faris and L. P. Zamora (eds), *Magical Realism: Theory, History, Community*. Durham, NC: Duke University Press, pp. 497–550.

Žižek, S. (1996) *The Indivisible Remainder: An Essay on Schelling and Related Matters*. London; New York: Verso.

Index

Notes: 'n' after a page reference indicates a note on that page. Works of literature are listed under their authors' names.

Abi-Habib, M. 104
abortion 72–3, 183
Abu-Lughod, Lila 65
abusive language 191–2
activism 8, 155–6
   and motherhood 68, 72–3
Adiga, Aravind 111
advocacy journalism 184
affective ties, negotiation of 87
age hierarchy 124
agency 9, 10, 88, 90, 100, 109, 163, 175
aggressive nonviolence 182
Ahmad, Aijaz 52, 76
Ahmad, R., 'A day for Nuggo' 88, 89, 104–9, 111, 208
Ahmed, Sara 9, 59, 74, 92, 119, 148, 188, 206
Ahuja, Pratul 83
Anam, Tahmima
   Bones of Grace, The 204n8
   Golden Age, A 20, 180–2, 191, 196, 203, 207
   Good Muslim, The 180, 182–91, 196, 203, 207
Anderson, Benedict 153–4
anger 192–203
Anjaria, U. 22n10, 99
anti-colonial resistance 2, 21n2

anti-Muslim riots, Gujarat 19, 118, 138–9, 141–2
(anti-)normativity 160–8
anti-politics 31
apathy 23–31
arranged marriage 24–5, 44n1, 47, 89–95, 130
Arya, Sunaina 196
Arya Samaj 25
Ashcroft, Bill 2
assemblage 7
Australia 154, 157, 207

Babri Masjid-Ram Janam Bhoomi controversy 130
Babri Mosque demolition 19, 118, 129–34, 148n3
Bande, Usha 5
Barker, C. 9
beauty 62–3
Bell, Martin 184, 185
Berger, Benjamin 24
Berger, John 135
Bhabha, Homi K. 2
Bhan, Gautam 119
Bharatya Janata Party 129
birangona 183, 188–9, 191
Boal, Augusto 14
Boddy, K. 116

Index

bodily resistance 124, 168–77
body, the
  gender positioning 129–34
  and motherhood 67
Boehmer, Elleke 2, 38, 206
Bollywood 47
Bose, Brinda 52
Bose, Subhas Chandra 45–6n13
boundary transgression 5
Bourdieu, Pierre 63, 113
Brada-Williams, Noella 22n9
Brah, Avtar 158
Buddhism 116n1
Butler, Judith 10, 75, 84, 136, 151, 181–2, 198, 206
bystanders' journalism 185–6

Cardozo, Karen M. 166
Careless, S. 184
caste and the caste system 52–5, 98, 104–9, 111, 119–28
casteist sexual violence 192–203
Chambers, Claire 17, 56, 180, 186, 204n5
Chandra, Uday 150
Chatterjee, Bankimchandra 16
Christians 104
Chugh, Sunita 170
class bias 103
class exploitation 104–9
class identity 168–77
Cohen, Cathy J. 10, 89, 206
collectivist action 118
collectivist struggles 18
colonial domination 2
colonialism 4
communalism 3
Connell, R. W. 53
contestation 150
counter-hegemonic work 11
critical realism 15
cross-dressing 141, 142
cultural continuity 162
cultural displacement 165–6

Dabundo, L. 15
Dalit massacre (1968) 180, 191–203

Dalit women 191–203
Dalit writings 12–14, 193, 196
Darwish, Mahmoud 1–2
Das, Kamala 97
Dasgupta, Rana 41
Davis, Richard 130
Dawesar, Abha, *Babyji* 19, 119–28, 143–7, 209
Dé, Shobha 129
de Beauvoir, Simone 98
defiance 8, 9
DeLuca, Thomas 24, 35
Desai, Anita 5, 16
desire 37, 120–8, 145, 158, 164
Devadasi system 204n13
Dirlik, Arif 3
disability 96–104, 116n5
disengagement 24, 31–8
disobedience 8
distorted resistance 150–1
domestic relations, problematics of 89
domestic servants 104–9, 168–77
  transnational 109–16
domestic violence 196–7
Donoghue, Emma 87
Draft Hindu Bill 33, 38
dramatic traditions, vernacular 12
duplicitous defiance 109–16
Dutt, Yashica 13

education 26, 37, 90, 170, 178n10, 208
Ehrenreich, B. 107
Eliasoph, Nina 31
embodied nonviolence 182
emotional vulnerabilities 87
engagement 24
English language 12–14, 193–4
English literature 27
Epilepsy Society (UK) 96
erotic love 54–5
erotic resistance 168–77

failure of resistance 150
failure to resist 150
familial economics 89–95
Fanon, Frantz 3

Farag, J. R. 17
female autonomy 26
female modesty 55
female solidarity 101–2
Ferguson, Ann 56
Fernández-Menicucci, Amaya 39
Fernando, C., 'Of bread and power' 88–96, 208
Field, Robin E. 166
first-person plural narrative 15
Fitz, Brewster E. 15, 99, 116n6
Flynn, Elizabeth 150, 171, 175
Fortier, Anne-Marie 158
Foucault, Michel 8–9, 123, 206
Francophilia 160–8
Fraser, Nancy 11, 36
freedom 118, 135
Freeman, Ru, *A Disobedient Girl* 151, 168–77, 178n9–12, 206

Gajarawala, Toral Jatin 201
Gamson, Joshua 80–1
Gandhi, Mahatma 32–3, 45n10, 182
Ganguly, Rajat 83
gender, and social relations 188
genres 17–18
Ghosh, Nandini 96, 101
Gidla, Sujatha 13–14
Goa 152–60
Gono Adalat, the 190–1
Gooneratne, Yasmine 179
Greene, Gayle 4
Guha, Ramachandra 129–34
Guha, Ranajit 10–11
Gujarat, anti-Muslim riots 19, 118, 138–9, 141–2
Gupta, Pamila 153

Hale, Jacob 119
happiness scripts 92, 161–2
Harlow, Barbara 2, 6
Helff, Sissy 160
heteropatriarchy 119
heterosexual desire 164
Hijras 136, 138–40, 143–4, 148n8, 148n10
Hindu Marriage Act 44n3
Hindutva ideology 129

home and homeland 152–60
homing desire 158
homosexuality 19, 126, 148n6
 see also same-sex relationships
hooks, bell 21n4
hopelessness 152
Hudood Ordinances 28, 40–1, 44–5n6, 57–8, 77, 85n7
Huggan, Graham 3–4, 6
human rights journalism 184
Human Rights Watch 41, 110
hysteria 97–8, 116n3

Ibrahim, Nilima 204n9
identity 34, 41–2, 60, 80–1, 163, 168, 193
 caste 194–6
 class 168–77
 gender 52–65, 129–34
 identity markers 2–3, 7
ideology 53
Imam, Jahanara 204n7
immigration 160–8, 177n6
Immigration and Nationality Act (US) 70
imperialism 155
Indian National Army 38, 45–6n13
Indian Penal Code 148n6
injustice 6, 51–2, 61, 62
intersexuality 19, 118, 134–42
irrelevant resistance 152–60

Jain, Jasbir 151
James, Henry 38
Jeffrey, Patricia 68
Joshi, Murli Manohar 146
journalism 184–6, 201–2, 203n3
judicial failure 202

Kabir, Ananya 26
Kandasamy, Meena, *The Gypsy Goddess* 14–15, 20, 180, 191–203, 209
Kapur, Manju
 A Married Woman 19, 119, 129–34, 143–7, 207, 209
 Difficult Daughters 18, 23–4, 44, 63, 96

Index

Harish's role 31, 33–9, 44n5, 45n13
maternal legacies 39
Swarna Lata's role 31–5, 38, 39
Virmati's failures of will 24–8
Virmati's political disengagement 31–40
Kashmir 80–1, 85n2, 86n10, 86n11, 144, 146, 209
Katrak, Ketu 6
Khair, Tabish 16
Khan, Nyla Ali 81
Khouri, Elias 12
Kilvenmani Dalit massacre 20, 180, 192–203
King, H. 98
Koepping, Elizabeth 104
Koshy, M., 'Almost Valentine's Day' 88, 89, 109–16, 172, 208
Král, Françoise 167

labour, sexual division of 105
labour rights 104–9
Lahiri, Jhumpa
    Lowland, The 18, 51–2, 206–8
      ambiguity 60–1
      and death 82–4
      Gauri and Udayan's relationship 62–5, 84
      indictment of Naxalism 65
      linguistic choices 61–2
      and motherhood 69–72
      and romantic love 47, 60–5, 85
      Udayan's humanitarian instincts 62, 63, 65
    Namesake, The 20, 151, 160–8, 206
    'Treatment of Bibi Haldar, The' 15, 88, 96–104, 209
Lahiri-Roy, R. 152
Lal, Malashri 5, 45n10, 89
Lal, Saumya 180, 189
Lalitha, K. 5
Lane, Richard J. 15
language 12–14, 16, 31, 32, 121, 191–4
Lazarus, Neil 3

lesbian grief 74
life-writing 14, 193
long-distance nationalism 153–4
Loomba, Ania 3
Lorde, Audre 174–5, 200–1

McClintock, Anne 21n1
magic realism 15–17, 152–60, 177n2
male dominance 7, 34, 56, 21n4
male honour 183
male privilege 127
Malreddy, P. K. 83
Mandal Commission protests 19, 118, 120, 125–7
Manorama, Ruth 197, 204n13
Markandaya, Kamala 21n3
marriage 18–19, 24–5, 36, 121, 161–2, 165–6
Martin, Biddy 80
masculinity 53
maternal legacies 39–44
Medina, José 9, 91–2, 119
Menozzi, Filippo 192
mental health 152, 158
minority literature 17–18
Mirza, M. 47, 111, 112
Mistry, Rohinton 16
model minority stereotype 177n6
Modi, Narinder 86n11
Mody, Perveez 24–5
Mohanty, Chandra 80
Mondal, Mimi 12–14
Mookherjee, Nayanika 183, 188, 191, 204n9
Morland, Iain 118
Moss, Laura 16–17
motherhood 19, 65–73
Moynihan, Susan Muchshima 102
Mukherjee, Bharati 110, 111
Mukherjee, Neel 61
Mukhopadhyay, Sudesh 170

Nadiminti, Kalyan 70
Namjoshi, Suniti 169
Nandy, Ashis 79
Narrain, Aravind 119
narration and narrative voice 99, 101, 191–203

Nast, Heidi 126
Natanel, K. 31
nationalism 152–60, 206, 207
nation-building 2
Naxalite movement 48–9, 51–3, 60–2, 64–5, 70–3, 75, 83–4, 85n4, 86n8, 206, 209
Needham, Anuradha Dingwaney 67
needs politics 36
negative agency 109
Nehru, Jawaharlal 153
new social realism 22n10
Newport, S. E. 140
non-violent resistance 43, 48–9, 151, 182, 206
novel, the, hegemony of 17

O'Connor, Frank 17, 18
Omvedt, Gail 125–6
Operation Searchlight 203n1
optimism 80
ordinary defiances 19, 87–116
   disability 96–104
   duplicitous 109–16
   familial economics 89–95
   labour rights 104–9
   transnational domestic servitude 109–16
Orleck, Annalise 65, 68

parental authority 89–95
Parry, B. 11
Patil, Amruta 122
patriarchal control 60, 130
patriarchal norms 122
patriarchal oppression 4, 6, 21n4, 35, 89, 91, 186
patriarchy 29, 34, 39
Pawar, Urmila 197–8
Peres da Costa, Suneeta, *Homework* 14–15, 20, 151–60, 177n2, 207
personal, the 6–7
Petty, Leslie 38
physical confrontation 113–14
Pinto, Sarah 116n3
poetry 12, 47, 193

political will, lack of 107
positivist essentialism 80
postcolonial, usage 21n1
postcolonial studies 1, 2
postcolonialism 3
Prasad, K. M. 61
private/public divide 9–10, 75
Progressive Writers' Association 16
Protection of Women Act 41, 46n14
protest politics 18, 32
psychological warfare 79
Puar, Jasbir K. 7, 119, 206
publishing industry 6
Puwar, N. 10

queer writers 14
queerness and queer resistance 19, 118–48
   definition 118, 119
   and intersexuality 134–42
   invisibility 132–3
   and religion 134–42
   religious fundamentalism and 129–34
   and social privilege 120–8
   and space 142–8
   transgressive power 127

Rai, Haridwar 61
Rajagopal, Arvind 120
Rajendran, Aneeta 119–20
Ranasinha, Ruvani 40–1, 100
Rao, Anupama 127
rape 45n6, 72, 127, 138–9, 183
Rathore, Aakash Singh 196
Ray, Raka 10, 33, 34, 110, 112
reactive resistance 171, 175
realism 15–16, 22n10
Reddy, Gayatri 139, 148n8, 148n10
Reep, Diana 56
refugees 156–8, 203n2
religion, and queer resistance 129–42
religious fundamentalism 129–34, 180, 183, 189, 204n5

Index

resistance 1–11
  conceptualisation 8–11, 206, 208
  criticism of 3
  de-idealisation 206–7, 209
  idealisation 205–9
  problematic practice of 151
  range of 6
  to resistance 1–8
resistance studies 7
romantic love 47–85
  and death 73–85
  gendered identities and 52–65
  heterosexual 52–65
  motherhood and 65–73
  and resistance 18–19
  as resistance trope 54
Romanticism 27
Romero, Mary 110
Rose, Suzanna 62
Ross, Oliver 146
Rouse, Shahnaz 45n6
Roy, Arundhati
  God of Small Things, The 15, 18, 48–9, 60, 123, 206–9
    and death 73, 75–7
    and erotic love 54–5
    and gendered politics 52–5
    and motherhood 66–7
    and romantic love 47, 52–5, 85
  Ministry of Utmost Happiness, The 18, 19, 47, 50–1, 119, 207–9
    Anjum's intersexuality 134–42
    and death 77–82
    and motherhood 72–3
    Musa's death 77–8, 81–2
    and romantic love 58–60
    Tilo's activism 81
    Tilo's archive 59
  Shape of the Beast, The 49
Rushdie, Salman 16
Russo, Ann 124, 127

Said, E. W. 3
same-sex desire 120–8, 145
same-sex relationships 120–34, 146
Sangeeta–Khobragade case 110
Saran, Rupam 177n6
Sathyanathan, Chandramohan 12–13, 193
Satthianadhan, Krupabai 16
satyagraha 182
Scott, J. C. 19, 87, 107
Seagal, Francesca 171
secularism 180
Sehgal, Parul 79
self-assertion 32
self-expression 32
self-identity 24, 29, 35–6, 80
Selvadurai, Shyam 137
Sengupta, Ashis 12
Seth, Vikram 16
sex 36
sexual exploitation 53
sexual violence 192–203, 204n9
sexualisation 201
sexuality 123, 168–77, 183
  denial of 98, 101
Shamsie, Kamila
  Broken Verses 18, 23, 24, 48, 206, 208, 209
    Aasmaani's political disengagement 28–31, 36, 39–44
    and death 73–4, 77
    maternal legacies 39–44
    and motherhood 67–9
    and romantic love 47, 55–8
    Samina's activism 42–4, 57
  Salt and Saffron 145
Sharrad, Paul 16
Shaw, Ibrahim Seaga 184
Shepherd, Kancha Illiah 194
Sher-Gil, Amrita 134
short story form 17–18, 87–9
Sidhwa, Bapsi 16
Simeon, Dilip 207
sitting, politics of 112–13
Slemon, Stephen 157
Smith, Ali 116
Smith-Rosenberg, Carroll 97
social privilege, and queer resistance 120–8
social realism 16, 22n10
social relations, and gender 188

South Asian Americans 160–8
space, and queer resistance 142–8
Spivak, Gayatri Chakravorty 11, 80, 86n13, 100
Sri Lanka 168–77
Srivastava, N. 17–18, 21n2
state violence 73–6
strategic resistance 175
structural inequalities 116
structural injustices 9
structural oppression 61–2, 77
subaltern, the 10–11, 100, 111–12, 115–16, 168–77, 184–5, 187–8, 190–1, 194, 200–2
subversion 8
suicide 74, 178n9
suicide attempt 28, 165
Sunder Rajan, Rajeswari 5, 7, 9–10, 109, 179, 206

Tabassum, Wajida 172–3
Taylor, D. 201
temple prostitution 204n13
temporal fluidity 9
textual silences 209
textual vehemence 199
Thapar, Suruchi 32
Tharu, Susie 5
Thompson, E. P. 108
Tickell, Alex 15, 111, 141, 143
Tomlinson, Barbara 199
Torres, Lourdes 124, 127
transgressive behaviour 160–8
transgressive decisions, empowering potential of 176–7
transnational approach 20
transnational domestic servitude 109–16
transnationality 160–8
troubled resistance 150–2, 206
Twist, J. 142

United States of America 70–2, 109–16, 128, 143–7, 160–8, 201

upper-caste privilege 127
Ur-Rehman, Z. 104

Vanita, Ruth 129, 148n7
Vargas, J. H. 15
victimhood 10
violent resistance 50–1, 151, 207–8
Virdi, J. 47
Viswanathan, Gauri 27
vulnerability 10, 198–9

Walker, Alice 168–9
Walonen, M. K. 61
whiteness 166
wilfulness 9, 25, 32, 53, 101, 104, 119, 169, 208
Williams, Patrick 1–2
Wilson, Elizabeth 156, 157
women
  clothing 60
  constraints 87–8
  Dalit 191–203
  erotic power 168–77
  life trajectory 97
  mother/sexual being dichotomy 68–9
  sexualisation 201
Women's Action Forum 57–8, 85n7
women's writing 20, 179–203
  anger 191–203
  dissenting 180–91
  feminist readings 179
  importance as resistant practice 190–1
  interpretation of 4–8
  narration 191–203
  subversive power of 203, 209

Yashpal 205
Young, Emma 88
Young, Iris Marion 9
Young, Robert 2

Zamora, Lois Parkinson 15
Zia-ul-Haq 30–1, 40, 45n8, 206

EU authorised representative for GPSR:
Easy Access System Europe, Mustamäe tee 50,
10621 Tallinn, Estonia
gpsr.requests@easproject.com

www.ingramcontent.com/pod-product-compliance
Lightning Source LLC
Chambersburg PA
CBHW051610230426
43668CB00013B/2054